本书为湖南省哲学社科基金项目“世界主要语言推广机构的比较研究”（15YBA400）的部分成果

外语写作中的母语语言文化研究

叶洪◎著

How to Enhance Native Language and Culture through Foreign Language Writing

中国政法大学出版社

图书在版编目（CIP）数据

外语写作中的母语语言文化研究/叶洪著. —北京:中国政法大学出版社，2019.7
ISBN 978-7-5620-9112-7

Ⅰ.①外… Ⅱ.①叶… Ⅲ.①第二语言—写作—教学研究 Ⅳ.①H09

中国版本图书馆CIP数据核字(2019)第158253号

书　名　外语写作中的母语语言文化研究
WAIYU XIEZUO ZHONG DE MUYU YUYAN WENHUA YANJIU
出版者　中国政法大学出版社
地　址　北京市海淀区西土城路25号
邮　箱　fadapress@163.com
网　址　http://www.cuplpress.com（网络实名：中国政法大学出版社）
电　话　010-58908466(第七编辑部) 010-58908334(邮购部)
承　印　北京鑫海金澳胶印有限公司
开　本　720mm×960mm　1/16
印　张　14.25
字　数　220千字
版　次　2019年7月第1版
印　次　2019年7月第1次印刷
定　价　56.00元

目　录

摘 要

本书结合社会学、教育学、语言学及语言哲学等理论，以及笔者博士、博士后研究和近年来的教学科研成果，探讨外语写作中母语语言文化的教育问题。笔者以中国外语写作学习者为研究对象，从语言与文化密不可分的联系入手，创造性地推导出跨文化批判写作教学法的理论框架和实现途径，为我国外语学科建设及教学改革提供理论支撑和实证素材。

本书作者是一位跨越中西文化的英语教师、学者，她通过自身学习和教授英语写作的经历，探索如何通过外语写作来提升母语和目的语的语言文化水平。笔者首先审视自己如何从一个“怵写”的中国学生、教师，在国外留学期间成长为一名热爱英文写作的学者；然后对二语写作的研究文献、发展历史和研究方法进行了梳理，在此基础上结合广东外语外贸大学“以学促学”写作教改经验，推导出既能提升目的语水平，又能提升母语语言文化水平的跨文化批判写作教学理论；最后举例论述该理论在对外文化传播和英语写作课堂中的应用方法。

在澳大利亚留学期间（2005-2010 年），笔者从一个腼腆机械的英语学习者、写作者，成长为一个充满激情和自信的英语作者，提高了对自己跨文化身份的认识。这种转变与笔者和其博士生导师之间不间断的邮件交流息息相关。笔者将电子邮件文本视为“跨文化交流的载体”，笔者（外语写作者）和博士生导师（母语作家）在中英两种语言文化之间建立创造性的对话，激发写作动机，提高写作技巧和跨文化敏感性。通过创造真实的学习环境和互动关系，笔者摆脱了对外语写作的恐惧，形成了富有创意、个性和活力的写作风格。同时，笔者也增强了对母语文化的认识和认同感，形成了跨越中西文化的复合人格。

除了笔者的个人经历，本书还跟踪考察了广东外语外贸大学的写作教学案例。广东外语外贸大学王初明教授首创的“写长法”（后演变为“以写促学”教学法）是21世纪初中国最具创新性与进步性的写作教学法，其一系列大胆的教学和课程改革满足了学生的个人情感需要，打破了原有的写作语境，将学生的写作与现实生活中的兴趣联系起来，引导学生进行文化探索。笔者在对该教学法多年跟踪研究的基础上，结合西方后现代社会文化理论和写作语境研究成果，从新的角度对该教学法的理念与操作进行了诠释。笔者认为“以写促学”的基本思想可概括为在后现代批判理论指导下，通过创造性地选择和建构语境因素，以达到改革写作教学和提升整体外语水平的目的。

笔者针对目前我国外语教育中存在的“重外语、轻母语”的现状，提出了跨文化批判写作教学原则。这种教学法的目的是使学生跨越母语和目的语的界限，寻找跨文化“第三空间”，提高母语和目的语的使用能力，以同时满足社会和个人的需求。该教学法从学习者的母语文化和身份出发，通过各种交互和互动，鼓励学生进行跨文化主题的创造性写作，并在双语使用中采用多种表达方式和语言形式，从而在跨文化交流中建造一个“复合作者身份”。为此，要求写作教育者以及学习者重新审视外语教学的性质、目的和内容，并通过开发创造性的写作教学法，让学习者能够在“生产性双语教育”中获得认知和情感的发展，增强母语和目的语的语言文化水平。

本书以傅莹、戈鲲化和贝淡宁三个跨文化传播典例和笔者在中南大学进行的教改实验为例，阐述了跨文化批判教学法的应用方法。首先，笔者通过三个案例，剖析了成功的跨文化传播者如何构建复合文化身份，如何采用第三种视角和寻找文化交集等交际策略。笔者博士毕业后（2010-2013年），在曾任教的中南大学进行了跨文化批判写作教改试验，旨在赋予外语教师和学生社会责任，让英语学习者超越自身的历史和文化束缚，释放写作潜能，主要方法包括重塑写作理念、重构写作语境和重建师生关系。

跨文化批判写作法为中国英语写作教学开辟了新的可能性。多种语境因素的利用以及写作中的跨文化交流不仅为写作提供了源源不断的资源，也提高了学生的创造力和跨文化交际能力。这种新的外语写作教学法赋予外语教师和学生社会责任，让他们能够在全球化的环境中扮演文化外交官的角色，成为中华文化的传承者、传播者和创新者，增强社会凝聚力。

第一章

我的写作之路

《清明上河图》是一部耐人寻味的作品。凝视着这幅画卷，我再次陷入沉思。据说近几个世纪以来这幅作品的真迹命运多舛，许多收藏家冒着生命危险才将其保护下来并上交给了国家。我手中的复制品来源于一段邂逅的友谊。2001 年我在欧洲旅游时，遇到了一位来自中国河南的游客，她办理入住手续时全部行李被小偷盗走，于是我便将自己的旅费拿出一部分帮她渡过难关，她回国后就将这幅心爱的画寄给了我。五年后，我将这幅卷轴转赠给了我的博士导师 Trevor Hay（海雷）。我刚到澳大利亚攻读博士学位时，是他帮我度过了最迷茫无助的时光。对我来说，这幅《清明上河图》意味着祖国的文化、跨文化旅行者的无助和赋能。人们总说爱和善都是循环往复的，这幅卷轴，以一种意想不到的方式，贯穿于我的所有文字，成为此书内容和结构的灵魂。

首先，《清明上河图》中，一座横跨于江的虹桥是这幅画的核心。河中一艘船的船身倾斜，眼看即将撞到桥上，在人群中引起巨大骚动。人们对着小船指手画脚，大呼小叫，桥顶附近的人将一根绳子垂到下面船员伸出的手臂上，来营救他们。船上的人拼命地划着船，试图调整角度避免沉船。我国的外语写作教育正如这艘即将触桥沉没的船，面临重重危机，需要及时调整方向或实施救援。

其次，本书的主要研究方法是民族志（包括自我民族志）、叙述学、批判教育学和文化研究。民族志研究是对特定人群（如一所中国大学）的写作实践进行全面描述，强调研究对象内部之间及其与社会政治背景之间的互动关系。就像《清明上河图》是画家对其社会生活进行的“真实自然”的描述。

最后，本书采用“多层次叙述”的表现形式，将研究者的写作经历和写作文本、外语写作教育历史、研究文献与方法、新教学法的推导和应用典例等，交织成一幅中国外语写作教育画卷，正如《清明上河图》卷轴中的主体画面、画家手记和各位收藏者的评论、印章交相辉映，和谐地构成了这幅传世名作。

1.1 我的写作之路

所有的民族志研究都始于一个处于灵魂深处的重要的故事。

——Gregory〔1〕

1.1.1 作家梦的破灭

其实，我对写作研究的兴趣来源于我对写作的恐惧。

我是中国教育的典型产物。

我从小就一直梦想着能够成为一名作家，但随着我所受的教育越来越多，这个梦想却变得越来越渺茫。

小时候的我是个求知若渴的书迷，我坚信自己能像那些大作家一样成为一名大文豪。在幼小的我的眼中，这些大作家的文字非常贴近生活，笔下描述的也只不过是一些人人都耳熟能详的事情。但是我的长辈们“好心”地打消了我的梦想，他们说写作很特别，只有有天赋的人才能“写作”，而我所学的写作不过是学写些短文、信件、报告等模式化的文章来应付考试。于是，我开始放弃当作家的“愚蠢野心”，耐心等待老师教我写作。

遗憾的是，我发现自己满心期待的写作课并非作家的“孵化器”，而是作家梦想的“终结者”。我们主要通过背诵来模仿措辞造句和段落格式，不断重复着烦琐无趣的写作练习。就这样，我心中的作家梦渐渐枯萎，但有时，小小的梦想之火突然燃起，我在写作中会产生灵感，找到绝妙的写作话题，运用疯狂的比喻或者叛逆的论点，但是，往往会被老师忽视或遭到批评。就这

〔1〕 Gregory, E., Tracing the steps. In J. Conteh, E. Gregory, C. Kearney & A. Mor - Sommerfeld (Eds.), *On writing educational ethnographies: The art of collusion* (pp. ix-xxiv), Stoke on Trent, UK; Sterling, VA: Trentham Books, 2005b.

样，我的作家天性完全消失，慢慢沦为一个没有丝毫写作野心的虔诚读者。

糟糕的是，每当有写作任务来临时，我都会感到非常焦虑。经过漫长而痛苦地查阅资料、模板和字典的过程，才能憋出一篇干巴巴的文章。这更令我相信自己没有写作天赋，根本不可能成为作家！

但我还不是写得最糟的，在18年的学习生活中甚至还算表现出色。取得硕士学位后，我成为中国一所重点大学的英语教师。在接下来的十多年里，我看到一届又一届的学生们不断重复着从抓住梦想到梦想幻灭的循环——尽管我秉性温柔，但不觉间却成为终止学生梦想的帮凶。虽然我努力激发学生们的写作热情，并使之保持活力，但我感到自己正与一股强大的洪流作斗争，这股洪流正吞噬着我和学生们成为作家的梦想。

我急切地想重拾自己的作家之梦，也迫切想帮助我的学生找回他们的梦想。为此，我要找出这种恐惧的原因，探寻能够消除这种恐惧的方法。这促使我离开祖国，远隔亲人，从北到南穿越地球，从东到西跨越文化的海洋，开始了我的学术之旅。

1.1.2　英语写作之路

我第一次接触书面英语是在20世纪70年代后期，当时我就读于中国湖南省长沙市的一所小学，中国的伟大领袖毛主席的大部分早期教育也是在长沙完成的。有一天我看到一本有趣的书，红色的封面上写满了标语，年长我三岁的姐姐骄傲地告诉我那些歪歪扭扭的文字是英语，意思是："毛主席万岁！"我惊愕于英语的神奇和强大，它甚至可以歌颂我们的伟大领袖毛主席！

1984年上初中后我开始学习英语。依稀记得当时的英语课上并没有教授毛主席的作品，取而代之的是拼写和语法，口语和写作也未过多涉及。初二的英语课令我印象深刻，当时年轻漂亮的女老师在英语课上开展了一个别开生面的讲故事环节，要求学生们自己编写或复述一个英语小故事，在课堂上讲给大家听。最初几周，我们乐此不疲，但很快兴趣就开始慢慢消退，因为同学们的故事有的枯燥无味，有的含糊晦涩。这些"外国"故事中的情景、逻辑甚至是词汇对于我们来说既陌生又难以理解，我怀疑连复述者本人都对故事提不起兴趣。所以当轮到我时，我决定做出一点创新。

我打算讲一个妇孺皆知的中国民间故事，虽短但流传久远。当孩子们不依不饶地吵着要听故事时，大人们便会用这个故事来打发他们。这个故事家喻户晓，在理解层面上毫无问题，我相信同学们听到他们儿时的故事用英文说出来，一定会有意想不到的滑稽效果。复述前夜，我将故事翻译成英语，上课时我走到讲台上，煞有其事地开始讲故事：

"Once upon a time there was a big mountain; and in the mountain there stood a temple; and in the temple there lived an old monk and a young monk. The younger monk begged the older monk to tell him a story, and this was the story he was told: Once upon a time there was a big mountain; and in the mountain there stood a temple; and in the temple there lived an old monk and a young monk. The younger monk begged the older monk to tell him a story, and this was the story he was told…"

头几秒钟，全班鸦雀无声，当同学们反应过来后全班便爆发出了热烈的欢呼声和笑声。对我来说，这是一次很有启发性的经历，因为我此前从未意识到可以用英语来讲述"我们自己"的故事。我们可以将英语变成自己的语言，为己所用，而不只是用它来描述远方的异国生活。此外，当我们缺乏口语练习或英语写作的点子时，可以在博大精深的中华文化中寻找灵感，这是多么有趣好玩的事！

我的第二任英语老师谢老师是一位和蔼可亲的绅士，1988 年高一期末，他要求我们在暑假期间写英文日记，这是我第一次完整意义上的英文写作，也是我第一次尝试用英语表达自己的想法，所以对我来说这是一次伟大的探索。首先，我可以用另一种语言来展现自己的日常生活，比如写我养的金鱼和假期看的书，这给我带来了很大的成就感和乐趣！其次，我发现自己可以不受约束，"自由自在"地驾驭语言。

当时中国正努力向着"四个现代化"的目标前进，改革的思想为大家所拥护。我们在语文课上能够自由地尝试新形式和新思想，这种自由感自然而然地扩展到了我对英语写作的感知当中。日记没有课上写作的条条框框，去除了很多限制条件，我将自己的想象力尽情地挥洒在笔尖。我用一种既非英语又非汉语，而是只属于自己的混合语言书写着自己的想法。我仍记得我在读书笔记的结尾段这样写道："In order to read far and wide, I cost my eyes." 意思是："为了博览群书，我牺牲了视力。"

当时我并没有意识到自己写作的"无法无天"，但那种创作自由带来的满足感和自豪感至今仍记忆犹新。老师规定写3篇日记，而我却主动写了8篇，而且还不辞劳苦，用父亲办公室的打字机将所有日记一字不差地打了出来(20世纪80年代末的中国还是前电脑时代)。

然而在看到老师的反馈上满是红色的更正后，我的写作热情迅速降温。我沮丧地意识到英语写作也有必须遵循的模式和规则，这些我当时都不会。但如果不尊重写作规范，写作的内容可能就没有意义。这种认知在我的脑海中蒙上了一层阴影。作为一个年轻的学生，规则和限制带给我的更多的是恐惧，而非启迪。

但在作文底部谢老师的评语又令我重新振作起来，他这样写道："真棒！你的努力和激情将助你在未来取得成功！我相信你会为英语学习做出更多的贡献。"我实在想不通谢老师如何能够预测到我在十年后会从事英语教学和研究工作。感谢谢老师，是他布置的暑假英文日记的作业和他热情洋溢的鼓励，最终促使我走上了探索英语写作学习和教育的道路。

我对英语写作的热情因语言形式的限制而有所减退，在后来写作时就开始变得小心翼翼。高二高三年级的学习对我的英语写作帮助不大，直到毕业我对英语写作都几乎没有提起太大兴趣。毕竟除了几次考试之外，英语写作的练习少得可怜。英文写作只在高一年级的暑假与我短暂结缘后便又远离了，只留下我独自在黑暗中摸索出路。

1990年我考入一所师范学院，主修英语教育。当时的课程安排注重英语的听说，其次是语法和文学，英语写作的练习依旧是最少的，对我们来说也是最"没用"的。写作课上老师从词汇开始讲起，然后是语法、句法、段落和文体风格，课堂大部分时间都在学习写作教科书，分析定义和学习课本中给出的范例，好像写作本身似乎不如"写作知识"那么重要。当我们还没有学完"文体风格"部分时，一学期就结束了，我们也几乎没有写下任何东西。

总之，我不记得大学写作课老师究竟是否教过如何写作，因此写作在我心中变得更加神秘。学习英语写作对我来说完全是一个"自学"和"摸索"的过程。由于缺少恰当的指导和写作练习机会，我开始对写作产生恐惧。即使是最简单的写作，如用英语写一则学校舞会通知，对我来说也是一个挑战。

然而我在同学中还不是最差的，在获得学士学位后，我被一所重点大学录取为研究生，主修英语语言和文学。研究生阶段，写作实践变得频繁，许多课程都要求撰写学期论文，但写作仍然是靠自己的摸索。

研究生阶段开设了一门写作课，授课老师是一位美国女教师，她要求我们上交几篇文章。但不知什么原因，这位教师学期还没结束就被学生罢免，或许是因为大家不喜欢她随心所欲的授课方式和态度，我始终不得而知。20世纪90年代，外教在中国已不再像“晨星”那样罕见，学生们也不再像以前那样对他们怀有强烈的信仰和敬意。反而当外教在价值观、思想观念、教学方法等方面与学生发生冲突时，会成为众矢之的，被“群起而攻之”。

在学会写作之前，我就毕业了，成为中国南方一所重点大学的英语教师。在英语系，只有具有良好的口语能力和英语水平（或是最具个人魅力）的优秀教师才有资格教授“综合英语”这门课并担任班级导师。这门课程囊括英语的听、说、读、写四种技能，所占学分也最多（每学期6学分）。我有幸成为其中一名教师。

“综合英语”每周有六节课，一般一周完成一个单元。每个单元大部分的教学活动都是围绕一篇英文的经典文学作品进行。其中3–4个小时用于对新词、语法点和课文的理解，课后的理解练习时间为1–2小时。另外，课堂中还会就课文的主题或人物性格进行讨论，听读一些与课文相关的材料。有些老师会要求学生们写一篇文章摘要。但实际上，考试之前分给写作的练习时间是所有技能中最少的。

国家高等教育委员会分别在本科第二年和第四年对英语专业学生的语言能力进行测试。这两个考试都包含写作模块，分值占15%–20%。对老师来说，这个模块既麻烦又可贵。麻烦在于似乎大多数学生根本不知道如何写作。天知道他们写作课上到底在做什么！因此，帮助他们应付考试中的写作任务就落在了我们综合英语老师的肩上。写作模块的可贵在于如果练习得当，能够有效地提高学生的整体成绩。

全国考试前十周，我们会进行两年一次的“填鸭式”培训。在所有快速提高学生写作分数的策略中，“10–12句作文法”的写作宝典受到了老师和学生的一致欢迎。因为这个公式没有过多的“空泛”的讲述和练习，只需按照模板进行填充练习即可：

模板包括三个部分：第一段落用 2–3 句阐明主题；中间部分为 2 或 3 段共 6–8 句，举 2–3 个理由支持上述观点；结尾段落用 2–3 句重复观点进行首尾呼应；其中每段都要包括主题句、解释句和举例句。

在此模块的基础上，学生们会按作文各个部分背诵相应例句。由于这些例句适用于任何文章和主题，因此也被称为“万能句”。如此一来，写作就变得非常容易，以至于一些老师把这样的策略当作写作的万能法宝。

经过几周训练，学生们便能以较好的成绩通过考试。但是，他们真的学会写作了吗？我对此表示怀疑，并深感内疚。世纪之交，中国开始高度重视和积极推广“素质教育”和“创新能力”，我们到底对学生做了什么？我们究竟是在教他们写作，还是在教他们害怕写作？我个人的英语写作史令自己陷入一片黑暗之中；接下来，我又在黑暗的隧道中引导学生们摸索前进的道路。不过在隧道的另一端，我依稀看到了亮光，但是要怎样才能够到达那里呢？

我自身的写作史充满了迷茫和奋争。我对发现新的文化资源感到惊喜，对获得自由表达的机会感到兴奋，对写作惯例的束缚感到沮丧，对教育环境中相互冲突的利益感到困惑。在这个过程中，我从一个年轻的学生成长为一名英语教师，然后成为一名研究人员，但这种无助感始终困扰着我：我该如何重新燃起英文写作的热情？我能帮助我的学生成为自信的英文写作者吗？

1.2　赋能之路

我的赋能之路始于 2003 年到广东外语外贸大学参加的一次写作会议。广东外语外贸大学作为世界上最开放、推行改革最激进的大学之一，在过去的二十年里一直在研究英语写作教学，并尝试了一系列创新型课程，其中的一些项目对中国其他大学产生了广泛的影响。例如，广东外语外贸大学的王初明教授在 1999 年开创的“写长法”。这个教改试验通过满足学生的情感需求，将学生从过分强调文字长度和语法准确性等语言限制中解放出来，有效地提高了学生的英语学习信心和能力，为今后的一系列教学和课程改革奠定了基础。

中国其他大学的许多师生也都参与了该项目并取得了丰硕成果。2003 年，该项目作为会议主题在第一届全国英语写作教学与研究学术研讨会中被隆重推介。

自此，我开始对英语写作理论和教学研究产生浓厚兴趣，积极参加相关会议和项目，在自己的写作研究中更加注重写作教学的创造性和批判性。2004 年，我与同事在共同编写的一本专著《新编英语写作》中，提倡将英语写作作为一种学习方法，而不仅仅是一种语言工具，并向教科书使用者介绍了一些创造性的写作策略。

多年应试性的学习环境，使我的写作水平非常有限。因此，当 2005 年我离开祖国来到澳大利亚攻读博士学位时，一种无助感更加剧了我对于写作的恐惧。我在努力融入异国生活时，发现自己辛辛苦苦学来的交际能力在语言和文化上都不断受到挑战和嘲弄。我第一次发现，我虽然会讲英语却不知道何时该打招呼何时该拥抱；我能讲出许多食物的名称却不懂得餐桌礼仪；我会写作却不确定给邻居的邀请函上要囊括哪些信息。我学了十多年的英语，也教了十多年的英语，却不知道该怎样告诉外国人我的名字，是汉语拼音还是英文名抑或是其他的变体？一言以蔽之，我虽然会说点外语，但是我仍通过自己的母语去理解世界。[1]

在博士学习的最初阶段，这种迷茫感和无助感一直伴随着我，但后来，我对于写作的恐惧开始慢慢消退，虽然我当时浑然不觉。在博士毕业前夕，当我翻看和整理与博士生导师 Trevor 和 Julie 的邮件通信，以及我博士期间所写的 20 万字的英文研究手记时，我才突然发现自己已成长为一个优秀的英语写作者。这些文字见证了我在博士学习过程中所经历的探索、困惑和顿悟时刻，充满了那些成功和低迷日子的回忆。我发现，自己内心的恐惧和焦虑已经被写作的激情和自信所取代，这种转变在我与导师 Trevor 的往来邮件中尤为明显。我们在 200 多封电子邮件中畅所欲言，各自表达自己对生活、文化和研究的理解。以英语和汉语的语言和文化差异、相似之处为谈话和写作话题令我感到非常有趣和放松。渐渐地，可怕的写作任务（尤其是用英文邮件同导师交流）变成了一种令人兴奋的自我表达，使我欲罢不能！

---

〔1〕 Kramsch, C. J., *Context and culture in language teaching*, Oxford: Oxford University Press, 1993.

当我对写作的恐惧正慢慢转变成对写作的热情时，另一种转变也在悄然发生：我的跨文化敏感性和交际能力也在写作中得到了提高。此外，我在英语语言和文化方面的知识也得到了丰富，同时对自己母语文化的理解和欣赏也得到了深化。最重要的是，视野的拓宽使我能够探索和协商出中西方文化之间的舒适地带——第三空间。

1.3　作者归来

2005-2010 年博士学习期间，我与我的导师 Trevor 进行了一系列作为一种“真正的语言学习”形式的电子邮件通信。在某种程度上，这些电子邮件起到了“跨文化对话”的作用，通过这种对话，双方都可以改变自己的文化身份，并利用英语和汉语的语言文化来培养写作技巧和跨文化意识。为了让它更适合学术语篇，并与叙事方法保持一致，我们各自给自己分配了一个角色名称：“小叶”和“海雷”。

来自中国的博士生小叶在一个陌生的国家面临着适应异国语言和文化的双重挑战。作为一名害怕英语学习和写作的学生，在学习的开始阶段，她感到自己没有能力适应新的文化身份和环境，在与他人交流的过程中经常被文化差异和冲突所困扰。然而，随着她与海雷跨文化交流的深入，变化悄然发生了。

海雷，母语为英语的澳大利亚作家、学者，资深的语言教育家、研究者，是中国文学和文化方面的专家，曾出版多部关于中国的小说和专著。目睹小叶在英语写作和跨文化交际中的困境，他用电子邮件作为一种“跨文化的对话”，来激发小叶的自信心，巧妙地让每一次文化接触都成为“创造性对话”的来源，[1]开启了一场写作和跨文化探索的冒险之旅。

展示这些电子邮件的另一个目的是，它生动地实现了 Laurel Richardson's[2]所说的“写作是一种研究方法”。本书旨在探索通过创造性写作教学法增强学

---

〔1〕 Fisher, R., *Creative dialogue: Talk for thinking in the classroom*, London: Routledge, 2009.

〔2〕 Richardson, L. W., & Pierre, E. A. S., Writing: A method of inquiry. In N. K. Denzin & Y. S. Lincoln (Eds.), *The SAGE handbook of qualitative research* (3rd ed.), Thousand Oaks, CA: Sage Publications, 2005, p959-978.

生写作能力的可能性。那么，如何通过撰写这些电子邮件来探讨这一问题呢？对话者是如何通过电子邮件往来被赋能的呢？如何在电子邮件中找到作者“身份”和个性的“声音”？在创造性写作中，文化和语言的灵感来源是什么？叙事学和民族志的方法在写作实践中是如何被运用的呢？

接下来，我将通过展示和评论这些电子邮件的形式来回答这些问题，目的是表现一个动态的交流过程。在这个过程中，教学问题在写作中得到生动的体现——“写作已经成为一种研究的方法”。

1.3.1 电子邮件通信

(1) 第一封信

12/12/2005

Dear Dr Hai Lei,

This is Xiao Ye. Thank you very much for helping with my PhD application. I am very happy to be your student. Please accept my hearty gratitude. I have a Chinese painting ‘Qingming Shanghe tu’ (Along the River During the Qingming Festival). It was a gift from a Chinese woman whom I met and helped in the Netherlands when she lost all her belongings to a theft. I am sending it to you as a token of gratitude for your generous help with my PhD application. Please accept[1] it.

Yours sincerely,

Xiao Ye

Dear Xiao Ye,

Thank you very much for the painting. It is an amazing piece of artwork, isn’t it? I wish your future thesis would be something like this, a narrative of your inquiry in English writing, with multi-layers of narratives like the painting. Welcome to our team.

Hai Lei

[1] 互动话语的形式体现了学习者的文化特征。

(2) Luck (Yuanfen /缘分)[1]

27/1/07

Dear Hai Lei,

Thank you and Catherine for the coffee and company yesterday. My problem doesn't seem so intolerable when it is shared. Hopefully your understanding and support, as well as the tactics you taught me, will help to tide me over the difficulties.

As I have realized, everyone (including spouse, parents, and children) comes to our life for a reason. Of the billions of people in the world, we just encounter some, stay with a few and live with only one or two for a lifetime. So it is sheer luck, or fate (Yuanfen/缘分) that brings us together. These relations are by no means stable or everlasting, and soon we will have to part and go our separate ways. So maybe I shouldn't have asked too much; instead I should rejoice at what I have possessed, and cultivate it with love and affection.

Similarly all things happen for a reason. If we try hard but still lose it, that means it is beyond our control. So we should accept whatever comes our way, and have peace of mind, knowing that it is meant to be like that.

This Chinese wisdom of Zen Buddhism (Chanzong/禅宗)[2] does help to calm me down a bit. Since we are not able to tie anyone or anything to ourselves permanently, we shall learn to cherish what we have and rid the lure of greed. In this way, we could be a lot happier and more content, instead of feeling bitter about the losses.

Talking of *Yuanfen*, I can't help wondering how amazing it is that we have met. That day I was almost giving up my hope when Lyn Yates shook her head, saying, 'Sorry, but I don't think we have anyone to supervise you on the project.' But then suddenly her face lit up, 'Hang on! There might be one. He is just at the corner of the corridor. Let me see if he is in today.' And there you were, in your office, waiting for me.

---

〔1〕 自我民族志如果不是自我反省的话又能是什么呢？哪一个作家不审视自我呢？

〔2〕 禅宗是佛教的一个流派，它强调直接的、经验性的知识和通过冥想获得启迪。

Every time I think of that day, I just feel lucky and blessed. Had you not been in the office on the day, or hadn't have time to talk to me, or hadn't have helped me with my application, what would I have been now?

It is *Yuanfen* that has brought me across the ocean into your office, and through you, to Julie. What else could I ask for except my heartfelt joy and gratitude?

And further more, because of you, many other people entered my life, like lovely Catherine. We wouldn't have met had you not introduced us to each other in your office. And there are a lot more…

This chain effect was triggered, in the very beginning, by an invisible *Yuanfen* between us. Who knows in the previous lives, we may have met somewhere and known each other already! That is perhaps why I feel so at home with you.

Well, thank you for being my supervisor in so many ways.

See you next week!

Xiao Ye

Dear Xiao Ye,

Thank you so much for your lovely thoughts; it also cheers me and lifts me when I am down, to think of this wonderful 'luck' or, whatever it is that makes some things happen just as they should, even though the chances seem so slight. It's strange, but when I was a kid I really believed in re-incarnation, then I became much too sophisticated to think such things, and now as a 'lao touzi' I am almost back to my youthful, naive sort of faith, and I think I was stupid to spoil my own dream of past places and past lives with too much thinking (yue xiang yue hu tu) and not enough dreaming. We should never lose our capacity to dream. Look forward to seeing you next week before you go.

Hai Lei

(3) Naughty baggage[1] (Tiaopi de xingli/调皮的行李)

Thursday, 13 December 2007

Dear Hai Lei,

How are you?

It has been a week since I left Melbourne, and finally my computer has been set up and connected to the internet.

Thank God we had a safe trip back home, after being stranded in Guangzhou for one day because the connected plane was cancelled that night.

But unfortunately our baggage didn't make it. Both of our suitcases got lost. In the past week we have been contacting Melbourne and Guangzhou airports, but so far no trace has been found of our precious baggage. I wonder where they have wandered? And I fear I would never be able to see them again.

What have I lost? Well, virtually everything except my passport, air tickets, my son, and laptop body (all accessories lost). It took me a few days to accept the cruel fact that I have to live without all the important things, my mobiles, my favorite clothes, all important documents, research materials and more.

Most sadly I have lost three library books I borrowed and brought with me from the University of Melbourne. This would be a big intellectual loss to me on top of the financial losses.

Well I still hope my suitcases would turn up after some adventures. Meanwhile I have to prepare for the worst.

Please wish me good luck!

Xiao Ye

Hi Xiao Ye. What a bugger! I am using my magic powers to command your bags to return to you. Did you put your name and address on them? Keep me posted...Surely they will turn up sooner or later...Hai Lei

[1] 创造力并不是一个纯粹的智力过程。它因其他能力而更加丰富，特别是有趣的想象力。

Dear Hai Lei,

I feel my bags are heading toward me under your magic power, but I didn't put my name and address on them since we had never lost anything in the past. So please help them to find their way home.

Many thanks,

Xiao Ye

Dear Hai Lei,

How amazing! Your magic powers indeed worked!

Just now I was informed that two suitcases were left in Melbourne airport; both baggage tags were missing, but with small white tapes (the mark I made). Only two days ago they told me they searched the airport and found nothing there. How they came to be found will remain a mystery to others.

I am so relieved. A lesson to learn is we should always put contact information on the bags, because modern technology is not so reliable. Or you should be lucky enough to have an almighty supervisor like mine.

Thanks and cheers!

Xiao Ye

Wonderful news Xiao Ye-and great for me-found bags mean power also not lost. [1]

Dear Hai Lei,

Merry Christmas and happy New Year!

In China we are having a cold and wet Christmas. Except the business promotions, there is a very few other implications of the festival in our city.

---

[1] 这位土生土长的英语作家现在正在修改英语语法以模仿汉语语法来达到创造性的目的。

I am recovering from all the fuss of claiming my lost baggage in the past two weeks. So far I have reunited with one of the suitcases. It finally reached me after lingering on Melbourne for one week, then visited Sidney and Hong Kong, and stranded in Guangzhou for another week. However, the other one, which contains all my research documents, is still at large.

The latest report showed it had been missing until yesterday, when it was arrested in Melbourne airport, shoved onto the plane and sent to China via Singapore. Who knows whether the cunning thing will run away again or not? If it could come to me on time, it would be a good Christmas present for me indeed.

Thank you for your love and care, help and support in the past year, which has been a constant rejuvenation of my mind and spirit. Wish both of my supervisors a marvelous 2008!

Xiao Ye

Hi Xiao Ye: I am on the (suit) case. Merry Xmas. HL

(4) Husbandry: The industry of rearing husband[1]

Wed 13-Feb-08

Dear Hai Lei,

Glad to hear you are enjoying yourself at the beach. I have just returned from my beach tour, back from the paradise to earth.

Sanya (三亚) is a beautiful seaside city in Hainan, somewhat like Melbourne. However, I found hotel and seafood doesn't go with creative thinking. So together with a stuffed stomach, I return home with an empty mind.

Moreover, I wasn't able to shake off the baggage of boys. They made me a cook, an alarm clock and a washerwoman. The fact is the longer I stay at home, the more I

[1] 声音不仅仅是一种非沉默，而是一种斗争的场所，是作家文化定位、局限性和可能性的体现。

lose my PhD halo effect, and regain my housewife essence.

Well, it won't be long before I travel to Beijing and Guangzhou for data collection. Until then I will be preparing for that.

Xin Chun Kuai Le, Gong Xi Fa Cai![1]

Xiao Ye

Dear Xiao Ye: I think it is time for you to reclaim your identity as Creative Superwoman - change into your magic costume with white leather boots and scarlet cape and throw away clock, washing, cooking and boys! Hai Lei

(5) Bloody tricky English[2]

Sun 08-Jun-08 2:10 AM

Hai Lei, thank you for reading my stories. You are my only audience though, since I haven't found anyone else who could or would like to roam with me in the crazy world. However I would have to pause for a while because I am starting my trip back home today, the long flight from Indianapolis to Chicago to Shanghai to Changsha.

By the way, my husband has got everything ready for your visit to Changsha, and he is proud of having a chance to hospitalize you in his realm.

Thanks again, and see you soon,

Xiao Ye

Dear XiaoYe: I sincerely hope you mean Howard is going to be hospiable to me rather than hospitalise me. Hai Lei

---

Sorry Hai Lei, for the shocking error I have made. I suspect that it is not the

〔1〕 新春快乐，恭喜发财！

〔2〕 跨文化学习者需要寻找能够将文化障碍转化为文化桥梁的文化接口。

first time that I have used this word erroneously, and realize why I have mysteriously lost some friendship. Please forgive me and enjoy Howard's hopitability since he likes you as much as I do. By the way I have landed safely in Changsha, yet may still need time to recover.

Thank you again for correcting a fatal error for me.

Look forward to seeing you and Catherine soon.

Xiao Ye

Subject: hoping, hopping and hospitality

Dear Xiao Ye: even I made an error in my last email ('hospiable' instead of hospitable). And it is hospitality not 'hopitability' as in your last email, which may have something to do with the movement of kangaroos.

Hai lei[1]

Dear Hai Lei, I swear I am driven crazy by the word 'hospitality'. Does it have a verb form at all? By the way please don't be annoyed if I use some other words offensively in the time to come, and please rescue me from the 'bloody tricky English!'

(6) Lantern Festival

21/02/08

Dear Hai Lei,

Happy Lantern Festival!

Today is the 15th of the lunar year, the second major festival of the Chinese New Year, and officially the end of the festive season. In the old times, young people

---

[1] 写作被看作是一个积累和改变的过程，是对突出的思想、技术、文字和图像的储存和重组，直到它们结合在一起形成一个新的创造性作品。

went out and met each other today while appreciating the lanterns hung on the streets. Here is a poem depicting this tradition, a bit sentimental though.

Shengchazi (生查子)[1]

Qunian Yuanye shi, huashi deng ru zhou; (去年元夜时，花市灯如昼;)

Yue shang liushao tou, ren yue huanghun hou. (月上柳梢头，人约黄昏后。)

Jinnian Yuanye shi, yue yu deng yijiu; (今年元夜时，月与灯依旧;)

Bujian qunian ren, lei shi chunshan xiu. (不见去年人，泪湿春衫袖。)

Lantern Festival
Last year at the Lantern Festival,
The flower markets were bright as day.
When the moon mounted to the top of the willow,
Young lovers met after yellow dusk.

This year at the Lantern Festival,
The flowers and the lights are the same.
Only I see not my love of yesteryear,
Tears drenched my spring gown.

All the best,[2]

Xiao Ye

Hi there Xiao Ye; I think I have read this beautiful poem before; it has that exquisite ‘lapidary’ quality of Chinese poetry. Thank you... long live this kind of ’sentimentality’. These beautiful, perfect, round, bright,

[1] 使用目标语言作为传递本国文化的手段，使作者在一个本来无助的没有话语权的语言系统中拥有一种会话的能力和技巧。

[2] 包括翻译在内的各种文学资源可成为跨文化写作的丰富源泉。

moon-like words help me remember more and more of the things I once loved, by the light of a Chinese lantern gently stirring in the spring breeze... I remember nights like this in Nanjing... like my 'love of yesteryear'. Thanks Xiao Ye, for your wonderful intuition. Hai Lei

(7) Baby historian[1]

Sent: Wed 27-March-09 8: 48 PM

Dear Hai Lei,

How are you this week?

I am working on chapter 2-A historical overview of English writing education in Chinese universities-the backdrop against which Guangwai's innovation took place. I find it a bit challenging, since the notion of 'history', 'sociopolitical' and 'overview' seem too big and profound to be manageable. Anyway I am trying and writing, hoping to finish the chapter in a week.

How are things with you? How are your eyes? Do you feel better or have you consulted a doctor?

Probably I will come to uni next Monday, if you don't need to see me this week.

Best,

Xiao Ye

My eyes are ok, bit sore and blurry sometimes, like I am looking at things under water...but I see everything that is worth seeing-from the inside, like a fish. I will be around on Monday, drop in anytime. HL

Sent: Sat20-April-08 9: 53 AM

Dear Hai Lei,

How was your week?

Sorry I am still working on the chapter of the Chinese history of English educa-

[1] 学会从局内人和局外人两种视角来看待某一语言和文化是跨文化交际趋于成熟的标志。

tion. It has taken me much longer than I expected. The more I read, thought and wrote, the more I felt inadequate and helpless. You are right, we are all infants before the colossus of history.

In order to write this chapter, I have been giving myself a big dose of Chinese history these days. Choked a few times, I am progressing steadily. To my happy surprise I found I am rather fond of history now. The wars and the movements suddenly make more sense to me. Thanks to the thesis writing process, I think I am slowly being molded into a doctor of philosophy.

So far it has taken me longer to write this chapter. Hopefully I can finish the draft early next week. Don't expect too much. I am still a baby when babbling about history and tradition.

Have a good weekend.

Warm regards,

Xiao Ye (the little green fern)

We are all infants before the colossus of history. Keep going, you will be great. Maybe you can make some point in your intro about your own experience of history-the Children of Mao, etc. Interesting that I was experiencing my own 'infancy' of China about that time I am also burying myself in history-the history of literature in English about China. Really enjoying it.

the more I think about this the more I like it-it is exactly what I have always wanted you and Catherine to do - you should locate yourself (through your author/researcher voice and perspective) as an authority inside your own culture, and then work outwards to an audience that either does not know this culture as you do, or has forgotten its own roots. In looking at the interaction between Chinese language/literature/history and Western pedagogy you have a wonderful topic for intercultural education. Jia you[1], Dancing Fern. The fronds will grow rapidly up-

〔1〕 Jia you：加油。

wards from now on. HL

Yes Hai Lei, the more I read, think and write about it, the more I become aware of the interaction between Chinese history and Western pedagogy in English writing education. We do have a good topic at hand. It makes more sense if I talk from my own perspective. Well I will send you what I have written down next week to let you see if it will work.

So it seems my purpose in doing the research has to include the grand mission—to connect the broken connections between Chinese tradition and modernity through EFL writing education for a generation that has forgotten about their cultural origin.

Little frond

(8) Keening, keening the osprey calls[1]

18/11/08

Dear Hai Lei,

How are you doing?

When working on our joint presentation on AARE (Nov 30th), Julie suggested I give the audience some taste of Chinese literature by citing a poem. What a good idea! I am thinking of using the first few lines of *The Book of Songs* (《诗经》), and I have found a music version of the poem (but too large to be attached for you to hear). So I need to translate the poem into English. There are a lot of English versions, but it would be more fun if I use my own[2], wouldn't it? Do you have some ideas about it? Or can you help with the translation?

Thanks and have a good weekend.

Xiao Ye

---

[1] 翻译是跨文化教学的重要手段，可以帮助学习者深入了解语言文化的特殊性和共性。

[2] 学习一门外语的乐趣既来自于在不同文化之间创造意义的力量和过程，也来自于这些意义是“我们的”而不是“他们的”的感觉。

I would be delighted to help with translation. HL

Dear Hai Lei,

Thank you for agreeing to help. I wonder if you can read Chinese font on your mailbox, so I have a copy of the letter attached as well.

The first four lines of *The Book of Songs* are as follows:

关关雎鸠，在河之洲，窈窕淑女，君子好逑。《诗经》1000-500 B. C.

Guanguan jujiu, zaihe zhizhou, yaotiao shunv, junzi haoqiu. 《Shijing》

My interpretation of the lines is that it depicts the picture of a young farmer boy picking wild herbs by the riverside. He is missing or wooing an elegant young lady, who is at the other side of the river. The poem begins by mimicking the sound of ospreys, an analogy of the young man's inner crying for his mate. So I attempted to translate these lines as the following, very tasteless though.

Quack quack, cries the osprey, on the other side of the stream;

That elegant young belle, Is my mate in the dream.

Please help.

Thanks,

Xiao Ye

24/11/08

This is really good, but I suggest changing 'quack' which is associated with ducks-I would make this 'shrill cries the osprey, across the stream, like my call to a fair beauty, the mate of my dream'. The lines are a little tighter, now, more in keeping with Chinese style. What do you think? HL

Thanks Xiao Hai. Now the 'quack' sounds funny to me. Apart from 'shrill', do we have any other options? I want it to be more like a male's call and can be repeated as in the Chinese original. Also, the first, second and fourth lines are rhymed with 'iu' in the original. So more work?

Brain rackingly

Xiao Ye

My only other suggestion would be 'Keening, keening osprey…' (keening has both the sound and the meaning, like yearning, or longing…this is my best offer. So the new version might be:

Keening, keening osprey, Calls across the stream,
As I call to my fair beauty, my mate in every dream.

Keening is good! Xiao Ye

(9) Terrorist tourist[1]

Tuesday, 26 April 2008 10: 56 PM

Dear Hai Lei,

How are you? I have arrived home after being stranded in Shanghai for one day. Here is some little funny experience I had on my way back.

My plane from Australia landed safely in Shanghai, just in time to see my connecting plane to Changsha rose into the sky. Being one and a half hour late, I missed my plane home and was left in Shanghai for the night. Since I had to stay in the big busy city, I'd better make the most out of it. I decided to venture into the city to get a glimpse of Shanghai for myself.

Wearing my warm winter clothes, and carrying my two large bags, I staggered onto the platform of the maglev train（磁悬浮列车）, which carried me from Pudong airport to the city. The guard stopped me for a check. I was very pleased, for it seemed the security was tight. Just as what I was told, the train was fast as a lightening. It covered 30 km in 7 minutes.

From the maglev station, I transferred to City Subway line 2. It was from here

〔1〕如果想要作者的写作充满自信和意义，那么需要将作者的个性特征在写作中显露出来。

that things started to go wrong. Before I got into the train, I was stopped by security again. He checked my bags carefully and inspected my winter clothes. I realized now it was mid-summer and most people were in short sleeves. But as I didn't expect to be held up in Shanghai, I took no clothes with me. So I had to be either in warm sweater or underwear-unfortunately there is nothing between them. All right I didn't care how I looked since no body knew me here.

But it seemed some people did care. From the moment I stepped into the train, I sensed that others were gazing at me. Young or old, men or women, their eyes were instantly engaged on me and my bags when they got in the train. What? I began to feel annoyed. Were I looking so stupid? Or were they taking me as a terrorist, carrying two bags of explosives to bomb the train? The answer seemed obviously positive. One after another, they clung their eyes to my bags and then my face, my sweater, before anxiously looking away. I expected that someone would report me to security office or ring the emergency bell if there was one.

I felt a sense of guilt, for my presence had put so many innocent people in fear and anxiety. To avoid even more chaos, I didn't put down my heavy bags, instead I held them close to me and stood near the door. I did this out of two concerns: first if I were truly a terrorist I would have squeezed into the crowd rather than keeping a distance from them; second if I did want to kill with my explosives, I would have left the bags down in somewhere and got ready to escape.

My overture obviously worked. The atmosphere eased a bit, and one or two brave young men even dared to stand near me. One stubborn gazer lowed his weary eyes and began dozing off; another relaxed and started to text to his girlfriend (because he had a vague smile in face while keying). I was a bit relieved, too, and gradually realized why the man at the platform suddenly disappeared after I asked him for directions.

I started to get bored by the long ride. Looking around, people were minding their own business, no longer paying much attention to me. I was a bit disappointed. Being the center of attention seemed more satisfying. Shifting my weary feet, I questioned myself, 'Must a terrorist leave the explosives and slip away? Might some really heroic ones sacrifice their lives for their cause? Could I be one of those martyrs?'

I changed my posture, moved to a pole, and while still holding my two bags, I leaned on the pole and closed my eyes. This subtle movement caught the attention of quite a few. Through my closed eyes, I could feel they were stirred and examining me with new fear. I could almost hear them talking to themselves, 'Is this a desperate terrorist?' 'why is she wearing a red sweater, thick jeans with red logo, carrying one red bag and the other with red stripes? What does all the red symbolize?' 'Why does she have that disillusioned expression on her face?' Satisfied with regained attention, I added some more complex expressions to my face and waited for them to take effect.

Disappointingly, the effect wasn't taking as fast as the train moved. As we were coming to some majors city stops, many people just got off the train and went out of my influence zone. Surprisingly they weren't so panic as I expected, as most of them were walking out instead of running out of the train! Not many passengers were left in my spell, and they seemed quite confident now. I knew they must have thought since I hadn't acted in the most crowded moment of the train, I wasn't qualified to be a terrorist, at least not a skilled, threatening one. With my identity in crisis, I fumbled in my bags, got my big sun glasses and put them on my face. In this deep underground tunnel, who would put on sun glasses other than a terrorist?

This attempt must have achieved some effect, for the boy keeping sending love messages looked up from his mobile and stared at me. I beamed, enjoying the warmth of people's gazes on my face. But the boy got off at the next stop, and the very few passengers left behind bowed down their heads and kept dozing off. I sighed, trying desperately to regain my reputation. At that moment I felt an itch in my nose. I waited patiently for a few second for the energy to build up. Then with all my might, I gave a deafening sneeze. People all looked up, eyes moving from my mouth to my bags, then lazily sank back into their naps.

This was my last shot, for they must have thought, 'If this sneeze hasn't been able to detonate the explosive, then there isn't much to worry about after all'.[1]

Hi there Xiao Ye: thank heavens for the unlikely terror of the trains... I am feeling a bit black today and your story has cheered me, so I am adding it to the Ye Hong anthology in my email folders. Hope it doesn't explode. So, now you are unfolding the sub-plot of an under-narrative: underground, underwear and under suspicion. Kelian de, ke'ai de Xiao Ye[2], I know exactly how you feel. I too have been regarded with deep suspicion and apprehension when, in fact, I am incapable of organizing any sort of plot, except in a story. Hai Lei[3]

(10) A smelly hamburger[4]

Jun 6, 2008

Usually I don't like shopping for others on my overseas trips since I don't want to burden myself with the task of searching for the item or having to carry the purchase around with me on the trip, not to say all the correspondence, delivery, andquality guarantee issues. But this time when my sister begged me to bring back a Bose Headset for her boss from the States, I had to say yes. Anyway this is my sister's only request, and she even gave up her own beloved skin-care products in the US for an exchange.

This task proved to be no easy in the beginning. The very moment I boarded the plan to Chicago I started looking for information of the Headset. Good it was on the shopping magazine (I guess that's howmy sister and her boss found it), but unfortunately it wasn't sold on the Sky Mall. At least I found the contacts of the company and

---

〔1〕 作者个性化的声音推动写作前进，成为写作过程中的发电机。

〔2〕 Kelian de, ke'ai de Xiao Ye：可爱的小叶。

〔3〕 跨文化学习产生于跨文化旅行者所遇到的文化紧张和冲突。

〔4〕 是文化张力还是文化冲突？这些“跨文化旅行者”的故事解决了哪些冲突？如何在英语写作中找到自己？

carefully noted it down in my diary.

I made the phone call first thing I checked into my hotel. They answered and said they could send it to me by courier. I was delighted, though a bit puzzled. If the headset could be posted, why the boss of my sister wanted me to buy it for him in the States? Probably he wants to save the postage? Since I had promised to help, I may well do my very best. So I asked if there were any retail shops. The operator sounded hesitant. After a long while he gave me some addresses in some other cities which were all foreign to me. I guessed I might never be able to find the shops so I decided to use the postal service.

I took out the piece of paper with the product information, and read it to the operator. Good they had it! But the price was \$50 higher since we needed to pay tax and postage. I thought the boss might not have expected the extra cost and I'd better ask for permission before making the purchase. So I hung up the phone, and sent an email to my sister.

Three days later I got the reply; the answer was OK, though I sensed some disappointment for the extra cost of postage. I made another phone call to the Bose Company. This time the lady on the line was very fond of me and tried hard to help. She disclosed an important fact to me that the voltage in the US and China is different, so I may not be able to use the headphone in China at all. I was panicky. My sister's boss never mentioned this.

Hanging up the phone I sent another email to my sister asking for clarification. While waiting for her reply, I travelled from the west coast to the east coast, constantly checking the email and worrying for the headset.

She never replied.

Since there were not many days left I decided to try the Bose Company again. This time a young man took the call, and as to my concern on voltage difference, he suggested a simple solution—buy an adaptor. How silly I had been! I should have thought of it myself! Maybe that was why my sister and her boss didn't even bother to give me a reply.

Even greater news came from the young operator who told me that my call was just in time for a promotion. I could get either two batteries or one adapter and one battery free. I was overjoyed. We didn't have to increase budget again. But what would the boss prefer? Did he already have some accessories?

To make sure and save time, I made a phone call to my sister who said she knew nothing about it and asked me to call her boss directly. My phone card was running out of credit but I made the call to the Manager Zhang. He sounded kind and polite. When asked about the choice for free accessories. He said one adapter and one battery would be fine. Then he proceeded to ask if there was any other product in the States that would be more economical but just as good. I told him I had no idea about it. Then he started to tell me about the other products of Bose headset that he found on the internet, until my card ran out of minutes. So I was left to make the decision on my own.

I called the company one more time and asked about the other products, feeling guilty for being such a nuisance. Luckily every time I was attended by a different operator. Finally I decided that the best choice was still the product we wanted to buy in the first place.

I placed the order, paying a total of 400 US dollars, plus 3% international transaction fee from my Australian credit card. I will not ask for the 12-dollar surcharge from my sister's boss of course.

Since I was staying in Purdue University graduate residence building, the delivery address was hard to locate. I took out my house booking sheet and read the address to the operator. When it was finally done, I was immensely relieved.

Then began the waiting. The day for departure was drawing near. If I couldn't receive the headset before I left, all effort would end in vain. I regretted having left them with my address. Why didn't I give them the manager's address in Beijing so the headset could be sent directly to him? But again, this would cost him more for overseas shipping, and would make no difference from buying it in China by himself. At least I could earn his gratitude for taking it all the way back to China for him, I comforted myself.

One, two, three days had passed, I still didn't get my parcel. All the shifts of front desk had become familiar with me and I didn't have to open my mouth to ask before they shook they heads and said, 'No, still not.' In a rage, I called Bose Company, demanding for an answer. They checked their record and told me the post had been signed and received by a 'Rich' in my delivery address. I rushed downstairs to ask front desk 'who is Rich'. They all looked puzzled. The company must have got the wrong address, they suggested. I stormed back to my room to call the company. They checked the address. It was 100% accurate. In despair I took the house booking sheet down to front desk and showed them the address on it. Immediately they apologized that the address on it was not exactly theirs, but the conference center of the University. They called the center for me, but it was closed for the day.

At least there was hope. The next day I rang the conference center, asking for 'Rich'. The lady answering my phone said, 'That's me. The post is sitting on my desk. We could deliver it to your building if you don't mind waiting'. I did. I had to leave for China the next day!

So I took out the map and found the place. In scorching sun I walked for half an hour through the campus and found the center (first time I really tour the Uni since I came). At the doorway breathlessly I asked for 'Rich'. The cleaning lady said, 'There is no "Rich" here.' I nearly fainted. With dwindling hope I found the office. There I saw right away, my precious parcel was sitting on one of the desks! A smiling lady explained, 'Rich' is her last name.

Hugging the bigcarton I hurried back to my room. For a moment I didn't know where to keep it for the last day. I didn't trust my room and the key. They may not be safe enough for my dear headset! New concerns arose at packing time. How can I fit the big carton into my backpack? Certainly I won't check it in with my suitcase, but to keep it with my cabin luggage. So I had to open the cardboard case and fit its contents into my bag. Three smaller boxes were revealed, containing the headset, the adapter and the battery separately. Even the smallest one was the size of a hamburger pack! Carefully I put them into my bag next to my laptop. All other stuff in my bag had to be left behind in the States in order to save room for the boxes, including my cute umbrella, my slippers and pajamas, my washing kit, and all food.

The backpack was so heavy that I could barely lift it up to my back, but I made it. Long flight and time for transfer made me dizzy. I had no appetite for the hamburger distributed to passengers by the flight attendants, so I put it with the box in my backpack, in case I might need it before I got home.

When I staggered out of Changsha airport, it was 11 pm at night, 30 hours after I departed from Purdue Uni. Home at last! There would be no need for the hated hamburger any more. I fumbled into my bag, got the box and tossed it into the dustbin. Looking at the remaining boxes, I felt a great sense of achievement. The headset was safe in China. It still needed to be taken to Beijing from Changsha, I knew, but at least my part of the job had been done.

The next day (yesterday), when I was doing face massage in a beauty parlor, my mobile rang. My sister had arranged for someone to come and get the headphone to be taken to Beijing. I hurried back, found a bag, and put in the three boxes and solemnly handed it to the deliverer.

Early this morning, telephone rang. It was my sister. I was expecting a happy thankful tone, bu ther voice sounded different. My heart pounded. In a low voice of suppressed anger, my sister asked, 'We couldn't find the battery of the headset. Why did you send my boss a box of smelly hamburger?' [1]

Subject: Emergency care

Dear Xiao Ye: I am helpless with laughter; now I do need hospitalizing (no verbform) for a problem of incontinence caused by too much laughter. Hai Lei

[1] 第一人称叙述的“内在自我”可能会传达出最引人入胜的叙述，因为这让叙述者对自我表达感到很自在，而且在完成任何需要表现身份和创造力的任务时都能轻松自如。

(11) Losing/gaining me[1]

Jun 8, 2008

I am still in shock since I have previewed the deep sorrow of my family upon my death and realized how important my existence and safety is for all of them!

Since I left home[2] I have been keeping in touch with my husband and parents via email or telephone almost daily. However, when I started to travel with the tourist group, I lost the means of communication because the hotels we stayed in deprived us of the internet and telephone access since they had been deprived of a large part of the profit by our group booking.

I didn't take it so seriously in the beginning. From time to time I would try to find a place with internet connection and send a message home. Or I would use the pay phone to ring my family. But for some unknown reason, my prepaid phone cards had been running out of credits very quickly (now I know it was because I kept moving places so the local access numbers become long distance calls). When this became increasingly difficult in the past five days, I had to stop contacting my family all together, until today.

We parked in a restaurant for dinner just now, and there was a pay phone by the street. Seeing some of my fellow travelers making phone calls in the booth, I gathered my courage to borrow a card from them and made a call to my husband.

He answered, with a 'Wei?' (Hello) in a hoarse low voice. I sensed something wrong. Gently I said, 'LaoGong, ShiWo' (It's me, darling). Then all I heard was loud wailing.

He cried, breathless, murmuring something I couldn't understand. He cried, pauseless for a long minute, and then another. I was terrified. Something disastrous must have happened. His business crashed? Or his family member lost? Must be

---

〔1〕 对旅途经历的反思不仅会产生新的故事和知识，而且还会为作家的生活创造新的条件，使他们成为变革的推动者。

〔2〕 出国之后，我的身份究竟是什么？我能够真正自如地使用英语吗？

Kyle! I waited in silence for the worst to come.

He continued to cry, full of grievance. With big fear I asked, ‘What is wrong dear?’ He couldn't stop weeping, but managed to speak out ‘Why didn't you call earlier?!’

I was shocked. My negligence had brought him so much pain and grief! Then he murmured something, ‘Call your parents. They have cried their eyes out...’ He was still weeping in the phone, so I could only say ‘Sorry, please forgive me’, and hung up the phone.

It was my father who answered the phone. He just said one ‘Wei’ (Hello), then passed the phone to my brother. In the phone I could hear both my parents were crying loudly.

My brother told me that in the past three days they had tried all the contacts I left with them, even the police headquarters of New York. Since I was moving place every day, they weren't able to locate me. Their fear was intensified when news reported an accident in Great Canyon, killing four women, two being PhD students.

Nobody could talk to me on the line as they couldn't stop weeping. Only Kyle stayed calm. He said happily, ‘I thought you will be alright mum. They are making a big fuss over nothing!’

It was time for us to get on the coach and leave. I had no time to explain or comfort my family; all I could say was ‘Sorry. I am sorry. I am alright.’

Hanging off the phone, I went back to the bus. An old song kept echoing in my ears: ‘Your mother was crying, your father was crying, and I was crying too, because we were losing you…’

The genuine grief and sorrow that my family showed on my presumed tragedy deeply moved me. Before this I had thought we come to and leave the world all alone, without much impact on anybody. Now I realized that my life and wellbeing is much more important than I had weighed, and it is my obligation to live well and safely.

Subject: Gaining you

Dear Xiao Ye: You are 'important' to many people in this life, even Kyle who thinks you are indestructible. Now you must find a way to be important to yourself without underestimating what you mean to others. This is a beautiful, sad story that almost makes me feel guilty that I was not worried, that I knew you were safe and well while your husband and family did not. Try not to get lost again, Wonder Woman. I have added them to the YeHong anthology in my email folders. Keep the stories coming for your spellbound audiences. The writer is back! Hai Lei

1.3.2 跨文化对话作为赋能

展示上述电子邮件通信的目的如下：

第一，它是对 Laurel Richardson 的“写作是一种研究方法”论断的创造性延伸和体现。就我而言，写作是对“跨文化和内文化”探究的方法——一种真正的语言学习形式。正是通过对这些电子邮件的写作和分析，我体验了一种新的写作教学法——外语写作的跨文化教学法。

第二，电子邮件交流不仅是发现的工具，也是展示发现过程的一种手段。它展示了我是如何从一个刻板、胆怯、被动的“学生”逐渐转变成一个自信、充满激情的作者。随着我们电子邮件交流的推进，我的写作变得越来越生动，话题的选择越来越广泛，表达方式也越来越丰富。最终，我对写作的热爱和激情让我再也无法停止写作。

第三，除了写作能力的提高，我的文化身份也通过邮件交流得到了恢复。为了适应英语世界，我的母语文化身份一直受到压抑。重新获得的文化认同使我能够更加自信地与外国文化交流，这些邮件交流为我培养跨文化认同和跨文化意识提供了一个起点。

第四，自我民族志的故事是跨文化理论和教育学很好的例证。这些故事以一种直接而生动的方式，展示了文化话题如何成为创造性的谈话和写作的源泉；如何利用中英文之间的语言和文化差异来产生写作创意和跨文化知识；如何在不同的环境中转换声音和观点；如何在批判和鼓励的环境中发展创造力，以及这种跨文化和创造性的写作如何帮助消除写作中的恐惧和焦虑。

第五，电子邮件本身就是写作中一个“第三空间”的范例。以不同文化背景为基础的两种语言相互作用、和谐共存，形成一种独特的写作风格，并且通过这种风格，对话双方都能享受和发展跨文化的知识和技能。

第六，自我民族志的故事构成了本书的多层次叙述的一部分，与研究的论述者、被访者、教师的故事一起，为这次研究提供了多种视角。

小叶的外语写作仍然存在很多问题，例如，不够地道的表达，文化基础不足，以及相对简单和单一的语言结构和措辞。虽然要成为一个真正的作家还有很长的路要走，但值得庆祝的是，她在写作中找回了激情和信心，不再怯懦也不再把写作当作令人头痛的一件事了。此外，她在写作中找到了自己的声音，这使得她的写作相对来说更加轻松和富有创造性。最重要的是，通过写作，小叶增强了自己的文化意识，重新获得了文化身份，成功地与外部世界进行互动。她的中国文化身份和外国经历赋予了她一种新的混合文化身份，使得她能够在自己的文化世界中徜徉。

小叶与海雷之间往来的电子邮件无疑是这一转变的催化剂。那么，是什么魔力唤醒了小叶内心沉睡的作家梦呢？

据我所知，这个魔法药剂中至少有四种成份：

（1）文化是创造性写作的媒介。

“创造力是通过文化来驱动和表达的。”[1]其中最重要的是海雷一直在敦促小叶，要保留自己的中国文化身份，抓住一切机会来加强自己的文化知识。同时，他鼓励小叶在不同文化之间穿梭，为自己探索一个舒适的跨文化空间。随着身份的改变，小叶对跨文化写作的信心和技巧不断增强。

（2）敢于冒险。

跨文化探索在很大程度上与冒险的意愿有关，简单的小冒险有助于克服对拒绝的恐惧、对失败的恐惧和对变化的恐惧。在写作初期，小叶对如何写作和写什么有很多恐惧。当她第一次在给海雷的邮件中使用中国文化典故时，比如禅宗的说法，或者使用有趣的儿童式的比喻时，比如“调皮的行李”，她

〔1〕 Robinson, K., *Out of our minds: Learning to be creative*, Oxford: Capstone; John Wiley, 2001.

不确定海雷是否会喜欢又是否愿意去阅读。但他的移情反应消除了她的恐惧，激发了她冒险的勇气。渐渐地，小叶学会了大胆地、更为诙谐地写作，因为她相信自己不会被嘲笑或束缚。随着更多的思考和实践，她的作品逐渐延伸到了更有创意和更有趣的方向，比如《恐怖游客》（Terrorist tourist）和《臭汉堡》（The smelly hamburger）。

（3）批判和鼓励。

创造性写作和文化探索在鼓励和促进创新思维和冒险精神的氛围中才会蓬勃发展，否则，将会消亡或减弱。而小叶有着一个敏锐和充满批判性的读者，这一点在电子邮件交流中是显而易见的。

（4）文化探索是互动的、互惠的。

文化探索不是一个纯粹的个人过程。小叶的创作灵感来源于其他人的思想和激励，尤其是海雷。

海雷和小叶之间的互动也对她的写作产生了重要的影响。当其中任何一方产生有创意的想法时，往往会立即在回信中得到回应，继而灵感就像雪球一样越滚越大。例如，小叶将论文的草稿发给海雷时，并不确定会收到什么样的反馈，于是便在邮件标题上写下了一句“A glimpse of the ugly daughter-in-law：Unbound feet”[1]，读完草稿后，海雷这样回复道：

“亲爱的神奇的小叶：没有丑陋的儿媳妇，没有扭曲变形的小脚，没有又臭又长的裹脚布……我对你充满了钦佩。你在英语写作方面表现出天赋和后天习得的技巧，对所有跨文化旅行者都是一种鼓舞。我多么希望我能像你这样写中文啊！你不是作家梦的终结者，你是作家梦的圆梦人。我为你欢呼！”

---

〔1〕来自一个中国俗语“丑媳妇见公婆”。

第二章

中国语言教育的历史回顾

仅仅从一个时代或当时的时代条件来理解和解释一部作品，永远不能使我们深入其语义内涵。

——Bakhtin[1]

Bakhtin（巴赫金）说的没错，但是真的要研究中国语言教育的历史背景吗？这一问题困扰了我好久。作为一名中年女教师兼英语研究人员，我热爱教学并且非常愿意接受教学创新。我发现“创造力”“现代性”和“赋能”既令人兴奋又令人神往，而像“传统”“历史”和“社会政治”这样的词就显得非常吓人，我害怕自己永远无法掌握它们。读得越多，想得越多，写得越多，我就越感到历史的浩瀚和自己的力不从心。过去这些年里，为了完成博士、博士后研究，我恶补了一下中国历史。我逐渐意识到，在这之前自己不仅对历史知之甚少，而且那点有限的历史知识也扭曲偏颇。作为70年代的“毛主席的接班人”，我们以往受到的教育是要大胆批判传统，摒弃传统文化，例如，我对孔子始终存在着非常矛盾的心理。我认为语文课上学到的孔子的思想充满了大智慧，但令我困惑的是，这位古代的伟人过去却被认为腐朽不堪，其思想应被抛弃。

不追根溯源就无法真正了解一个事物。所以，为了更好地研究中国语境

---

〔1〕 Bakhtin, M. M., *Speech genres and other late essays* (V. W. McGee, Trans.), Austin: University of Texas Press, 1986.

下的写作实践，最好的办法就是“将其嵌入广泛的中国教育思想和时间的历史画卷中来分析”[1]。此外，历史背景对于教育研究至关重要。随着大背景（政策、社会、范式、文化等）的变化，研究的重点和方法也发生了变化。换言之，随着社会政治状况的变化，研究对象、研究问题、理论框架和研究方法都在发生变化。因此，教育研究人员不能将自己封闭起来，试图解决与社会发展无关的孤立问题。

2.1 中国语言教育简史

中国教育史一直是国内外学者研究的焦点。我研究的作品包括 Hayhoe 关于中华文明、教育和现代化的系列出版物[2]，De Bary 对中国传统渊源的追寻[3]，Elman 与 Woodside 的《中华帝国晚期的教育与社会》[4]，Biggerstaff 的《中国现代早期官办学校》[5]，Legge 对中国经典的研究[6]，Price 对近代中国教育与文化的研究[7]。

这些作品为我们提供了对于中国教育和知识传统详尽而全面的描述，为研究中国外语教育，特别是英语写作教育的发展提供了历史背景。尽管在编辑合集中包含了一些国内作者的声音，但上述大部分文献都是从西方的角度出发的。

---

[1] Peterson, G. , & Hayhoe, R. , Introduction. In R. Hayhoe, G. Peterson & Y. Lu (Eds.), *Education, culture, and identity in twentieth-century China*, Ann Arbor: University of Michigan Press, 2001, p1-21.

[2] Hayhoe, R. , *China's universities, 1895-1995: A century of cultural conflict*, New York: Garland Pub, 1996. Hayhoe, R. , *Portraits of influential Chinese educators*, Dordrecht, The Netherlands: Springer, 2007.

[3] De Bary, W. T. , The Confucian revival in the Song, In W. T. De Bary, W. -t. Chan, J. Adler, I. Bloom & R. Lufrano (Eds.), *Sources of Chinese tradition* (2nd ed.), New York: Columbia University Press, 1999, p587-666.

[4] Elman, B. A. , Changes in Confucian Civil Service Examinations from the Ming to the Ch'ing Dynasty. In B. A. Elman, A. Woodside & J. C. o. C. S. (U. S.) (Eds.), *Education and society in late imperial China, 1600-1900*, Berkeley: University of California Press, 1994, p111-149.

[5] Biggerstaff, K. , *The earliest modern government schools in China*, Port Washington, N. Y. : Kennikat Press, 1972.

[6] Legge, J. (Ed.), *The Chinese classics*, Hong Kong: Hong Kong University Press, 1960.

[7] Price, R. F. , *Education in modern China* (2 ed.), London; Boston: Routledge & K. Paul, 1979.

付克[1]从爱国教育家的角度出发，总结了1985年以前中国外语教学的历史。对比修辞和英语写作领域的华裔美国学者游晓晔以自己独特的视角，即“局内人”和“局外人”的视角，对英语写作史进行了精辟的论述。

这些作品令我受益匪浅，但在讲述语言教育的社会历史时，需要有自己的关注点，否则很容易在历史的巨人面前迷失。本研究的目的之一是阐明推动中国外语教育发展的内在动力，以及在此过程中人们是如何被剥夺和赋予权力的，所以，中国人所经历的态度和身份认同困境是进行研究的一个很好的起点。阅读已有的文献，加上自己的理解，使我看到了过去几个世纪里中国人对待本土和西方文化态度的明显倾向。假如我们把它想象成一个天平：左端是中国的修辞传统；右端是以英美修辞为代表的西方写作规范。纵观历史，天平一直在向一端倾斜。为什么呢？造成这些矛盾态度的社会政治力量非常值得研究。这也将是本章其余部分围绕的主题。[2]

2.1.1 1949年之前

中国的外语学习和交流可以追溯到秦汉时期（公元前200年左右），秦汉时期的陆上和海上“丝绸之路”促进了中国与世界其他地区的贸易、文化、技术和宗教交流。当时，中国是一个独立的、多民族的东方帝国，在政治、经济和文化发展方面处于领先地位。然而这种形象在20世纪西方帝国主义用鸦片和火药强行打开中国的大门后被彻底粉碎。面对这场前所未有的民族危机，中国人不得不痛苦地承认自己已经远远落后于西方列强，必须要学习敌人的语言和文化，并在科技上追赶他们。

19世纪，中国课堂上第一次出现英语后，便被一致认为比不上儒家经典。人们都认为英语是西方野蛮人的语言，称它为“魔鬼的语言”[3]。就连洋务运动的改革者也提出了“中学为体，西学为用”的口号，主张以中国伦常经

---

[1] 付克：《中国外语教育史》，上海外语教育出版社1986年版。

[2] 虽然文中已经明确指出，介绍中国教育史（尤其是英语写作教育）是非常必要的，但我认为不应以下面这段文字称为“历史”，反而可以称为“叙事”——关注“广泛主题和概念”的故事，作为一种“寻求解释性理解”，这种理解“往往会塑造我们对中国教育传统的看法和词汇”。

[3] You, X. *Writing in the Devil's Tongue*: *A history of English composition in China*; Southern Illinois University, 2010.

史之学为根本，以西方科技之术为应用。换言之，它是政治和文化保守主义与大胆的改革政策的矛盾结合（Yuan，2001），中国文化本质的核心仍被坚定地认为是儒学和理学，整个政治制度是建立在中国文化本质的基础之上的。

儒学

儒家经典通常指的是“五经”和“四书”。“五经”是由孔子自己编辑、传授和其弟子及再传弟子传承的历史知识体系，而“四书”主要是孔子追随者的著作，是孔子名言的记载和诠释或孔子儒家思想的发展。关于儒家思想的核心，存在不同观点，有学者将其概括为“仁”“忠”“孝”“中庸”等（Confucius & Lin，1938）。一般认为，西方古典教育以语法、逻辑和修辞学来发现真理，而中国古代教育则以求道为中心。孔子特别强调教育中的个人修养是社会秩序合理化的基础。

新儒学（理学）主要发展于宋朝（960-1279 年），是融合了儒家、道家和佛教思想因素的哲学。如今的儒家经典主要由朱熹（1130-1200 年）编纂，成了后来元、明、清三代儒家正统的基础，同时也是科举考试的核心，对社会各阶层的读写和学习的文化态度产生了深远影响。[1]

清朝时期，统治者仍坚持维护旧的政治结构和意识形态，力图通过以西方技术为生命线的自强运动来振兴中国。然而，这种思想在甲午中日战争（1894-1895 年）落败后受到了严重的挑战。改革迫在眉睫，不仅要改革其军事力量，而且要改革其政治、文化和意识形态。

文化、政治运动

随后进行了一系列运动和改革，如百日维新（1898 年）、辛亥革命（1911-1912 年）和新文化运动（1915-1921 年）等运动和革命不仅削弱和消除了延续了两千多年的中国封建制度，更重要的是，动摇了以儒学和理学为主要内容的中国传统文化的根基。

该时期运动的共同目标是改革中国的教育制度，包括废除科举制度，废

---

〔1〕 Peterson，G.，& Hayhoe，R.，Introduction. In R. Hayhoe，G. Peterson & Y. Lu（Eds.），*Education，culture，and identity in twentieth-century China*，Ann Arbor：University of Michigan Press，2001，p1-21.

除八股文，建立新式学校，派遣留学生。

1905 年，科举制被废除。在封建统治阶级统治的 1300 多年里，科举制要求学生“两耳不闻窗外事，一心只读圣贤书”。在这种教育下，传统的文人大多只懂得儒家经典，而对科学技术的实践技能和知识知之甚少。大多数人缺乏独立思考的能力、批判精神和创造力，尤其在“八股文”这种文体形式中可见一斑。

八股文

在多数中国人看来，八股文多以死板空洞著称，其文风过于强调机械形式，而忽视、制约了写作的创造性。这种体裁的起源可以追溯到宋代，当时考官主要考查考生的经学知识。

标准八股文由八个部分组成，每个部分称为“股”。“股”在古代汉语中是指平行结构。文中大部分内容为大量的排比，以及经典的典故和习语。其中每一节的句子数、整篇文章中的词数以及所使用的词、词组和参考文献都有严格的规定。明清时期，八股文在科举制度中得到了广泛应用。为确保考生顺利通过，往届考生的范文经政府官方许可后在商业印刷厂印刷出版。

八股文的拥护者认为，其方式在选拔人才和官员方面比诗歌和散文更为先进。主考人能够用统一的方式批改文章，有助于实现一定程度的全国标准化。他们还坚持认为，只有真正有能力的考生才能写出高质量的八股文。[1]

然而，八股文后来受到了强烈的批判，常被认为迂腐守旧，也有人将其归咎于明代古典诗文的衰落。还有观点称，实际上，许多通过考试的考生其自身能力根本无法满足政府职位的实际需要。19 世纪初，八股文与科举制度最终被一起废除。

洋务运动

为了经济增长而改变的知识模式与需要保持政治秩序的儒家传统之间开

---

〔1〕 Elman, B. A. , *Changes in Confucian Civil Service Examinations from the Ming to the Ch'ing Dynasty*. In B. A. Elman, A. Woodside & J. C. o. C. S. （U. S. ）(Eds.), *Education and society in late imperial China, 1600-1900*, Berkeley: University of California Press, 1994, p111-149.

始出现了根本性矛盾。19 世纪末和 20 世纪初的这种紧张局势给西方思想传入中国创造了良好的机会。进步学者呼吁在全球和西方标准的基础上创造一种新的中国文化。20 世纪之交，洋务运动通过派遣留学生，兴办教会学校，以及增设外语课程培养了一批有改革思想的士大夫。正是在这一时期，美国和英国对中国及其教育制度开始产生越来越大的影响。[1]

最成功的国际学习项目之一就是由美国提供的庚子赔款奖学金。该奖学金由支付给美国的义和团补偿金资助，提供给在美国留学的中国学生。这个项目的许多受益者成为中国政治和知识改革，特别是教育制度改革的中坚力量。

胡适是中国自由主义和语言改革的重要贡献者。他是五四运动和新文化运动时期的领导知识分子之一。胡适是当时文学革命的主要倡导者，他提倡用白话文取代文言文，倡导一种新的写作形式。他鼓励现代作家表达真实的情感，而并非模仿古人，以避免早期作家所追求的陈词滥调、空洞的典故和不必要的排比。[2]

林语堂是 20 世纪最有影响力的作家之一，他在海外攻读硕士学位和博士学位之前曾在中国的教会学校接受教育。林语堂在写作中倡导一种非正式的个人散文风格（性灵文学），当时这种风格在西方国家非常盛行，目的是把人们从古文规则或框架的禁锢中解放出来。他认为，作家应该避免空洞的陈词滥调来表达真情实感，文章不必遵循固定风格。

1903 年，中国主流学校开始引进英语课。通过学习英语书籍和英语写作，中国学生接触到英美修辞学，并在作文中混合应用中英两种修辞策略。其中，儒家修辞学强调逻辑思辨、类比、注释和历史典故，而西方修辞学则倾向于用证据证明。

回归到天平的比喻，中西修辞的融合表明了文化偏好的天平的倾斜。几千年来，中国人一直将文化重心置于左端的汉语，而面对自 19 世纪后半叶以来西方帝国主义的生死挑战，中国人的文化重心渐渐开始向右倾斜。

---

〔1〕 Dunch, R., Mission schools and modernity: The Anglo-Chinese college, Fuzhou. In R. Hayhoe, G. Peterson & Y. Lu (Eds.), *Education, culture, and identity in twentieth-century China*, Ann Arbor: University of Michigan Press, 2001, p109-136.

〔2〕 Hu, S., *Selected essays of Hu Shi: The New Cultural Movement*, Beijing: Xinhua Publishing House, 1993.

2.1.2 1950–1976 年

1949 年，中华人民共和国成立，中国进入了一个全新的时代。经过一个世纪以来西方列强的侵略和 20 多年的内战，[1]中国迎来了光明的未来。

新中国成立前期，教育制度在形式和内容上深受苏联影响。教育形式上主要涉及高等教育系统，内容上将道德政治教导视为国家的首要任务。[2]这一时期教育的另一显著特点是，中国学术传统从旧精英主义转向大众教育，50 年代的“扫盲运动”可以从某种程度上说明这一点。

新中国成立后的十年内开展的扫盲运动，是一项提高中国人民整体文化素质，特别是农村人口等低社会经济阶层人民文化素质的积极举措。除了具有快速集体化的政治功能外，扫盲运动的另一个主要特点是因材施教，灵活性教学。[3]例如，根据当地农民的迫切需要编写了一本供农民使用的教材。在教农民识字时，教师从教授农具、牲畜、农作物等与农民生活直接相关的事物名称开始，有效提高了学习者的学习效果，让他们在较短时间内获得基本的读写能力，能够自己记工记账。扫盲运动的教育理念——优先考虑实际生活用字，即注重“实用识读能力”，从而迅速给学习者带来满足感，是值得我们借鉴的。

2.1.3 1977–1989 年

文化大革命后，中国就像刚刚从水里捞出的溺水者一样，不断呼吸着新鲜的空气。随着邓小平对经济改革和对外开放的大胆呼吁，中国人意识到西方许多需要中国学习的东西。20 世纪 80 年代，中西学术交流蓬勃发展，对中

---

〔1〕 正如我在后面提出的，中国被西方剥削的“宏大叙事”是一个持续不断的故事，它反映了中国年轻爱国人士对西方的看法。

〔2〕 Price, R. F., Convergence or copying: China and the Soviet Union. In R. Hayhoe & M. Bastid (Eds.), *China's education and the industrialized world: Studies in cultural transfer*, Armonk, N. Y.: M. E. Sharpe, 1987, p158–183.

〔3〕 Hay, T., Satellites and ladders: The ancient game of Chinese literacy. In D. A. Myers & A. Patience (Eds.), *The politics of multiculturalism in the Asia/Pacific*, Darwin, N. T.: Northern Territory University Press, 1995, p85–95.

国的教育价值观发挥了不可忽视的作用。思想和新闻自由空前高涨，出现了不同的思想流派，要求进行更多的经济、政治和文化改革。

2.1.4　1990年至今

改革开放以来，中国以前所未有的速度发展。20世纪90年代，中国在全球化的背景下成长为一个经济和政治强国。21世纪，中国始终坚持教育在经济、政治、社会和文化生活中的重要地位。中国的教育工作者和政治家们尤其强调以提高创造力作为“振兴国家”的重要手段。

呼吁创造力

随着新千年的到来，包括中国在内的许多国家和地区对创造力的呼声都越来越高。英格兰的大量精力和资金被用于构思和发展创造力，这导致了创造性在教学和学习中的前景化和政治化。[1]美国的幼儿教育“一直以培养有创造力的孩子为核心”[2]。其他国家地区，如澳大利亚[3]、日本、新加坡[4]，也有类似举措。

作为一个有着五千年历史的国家，中国正在重塑其作为一个具有创造性的发展中国家的形象，以便在竞争日益激烈的全球市场中生存和繁荣发展。为了实现这一新的伟大目标，政府主张以科学发展观为指导思想，以建立和谐社会作为重点。[5]此外，中国各行各业都在呼吁培养具有创新精神的高素质劳动力，越来越多的雇主将创造力列为员工最重要的素质之一。

中国政府界定的创意产业，包括建筑、艺术、出版、计算机软件、数字

---

〔1〕 Burnard, P., Reflecting on the creativity agenda in education, *Cambridge Journal of Education*, 36 (3), 2006, p313-318.

〔2〕 Feldman, D. H., & Benjamin, A. C., Creativity and education: an American retrospective. *Cambridge Journal of Education*, 36 (3), 2006, p319-336.

〔3〕 White, J., Creativity in research: Courage, inclusion and governmentality. *Creative Approaches to Research*, 1 (2), 2008, p4-8.

〔4〕 Fryer, M., Creativity across the curriculum: A review and analysis of programs designed to develop creativity, from http://www.ncaction.org.uk/creativity/creativity_across_the_curriculum.doc, September 9, 2006

〔5〕 Li, X., China ranks first in science and technology human resources, from http://news.xinhuanet.com/politics/2009-09/17/content_12071287.htm, September 19, 2009.

娱乐、大众传媒和时装等部门，经政府积极推动，在国民经济中所占的比重越来越大。中国的创意行业为毕业生提供了越来越多的就业机会，其全球化的性质同样为语言专业学生提供了许多特殊机会。

针对这一需求，中国教育部发布了新的《高等学校英语专业英语教学大纲》，强调在英语学习和教学中培养创造力的重要性。新的要求明确指出：

在教学中应注重培养学生能力，包括学习和利用知识的能力、分析和解决问题的能力以及独立思考和创新的能力。其中，培养学生的创新精神应是重中之重。

国学、汉学复兴

近年来，中国兴起了一种复兴儒家经典的新趋势，即“国学”或“汉学”。与“西学”相反，“国学”包含了对中国古典语言和文学的研究，以及其中隐含的哲学方法。

2014 年，中共中央总书记、国家主席习近平在文艺工作座谈会上精辟地指出：

文化是民族生存和发展的重要力量。人类社会每一次跃进，人类文明每一次升华，无不伴随着文化的历史性进步……在几千年的历史流变中，中华民族从来不是一帆风顺的，遇到了无数艰难困苦，但我们都挺过来、走过来了……历史和现实都证明，中华民族有着强大的文化创造力。每到重大历史关头，文化都能感国运之变化、立时代之潮头、发时代之先声……中华文化既坚守本根又不断与时俱进，使中华民族保持了坚定的民族自信和强大的修复能力。

随着中国重新站在世界文明的前列，中国文化的价值开始得到中国和西方人民的重新评判和欣赏。一些研究者已经预见到中国文化在不久的将来会井喷式复兴。目前，作为语文课的补充，一些儿童开始学习和背诵古代经典；各种经学和诵经班出现；有关古代经典著作的出版物盛行起来；甚至有的企业家也会参加国学课来充实自己。

当代国学复兴趋势有着鲜明的特征，即将古代文化通俗化和大众化，以便更易于为公众所接受，如中国中央电视台的“百家讲坛”“中国诗词大会”“中国汉字听写大会”“中国成语大会”等节目。自2001年以来，来自世界各地的演讲者就中国的历史和文化发表了生动有趣的演讲，并获得了很高的评价。一位很受欢迎的讲师袁腾飞，因其特殊的讽刺和喜剧风格使观众对历史文化产生了浓厚的兴趣，被称为历史上最酷的历史老师和中国新“文化巨星”。

显然，近年来，中国对传统文化产生了强烈的需求，如何将文化转化为创意产业已写入许多中国城市的发展议程。[1]除了复兴古代经典和历史，参观和欣赏历史遗址和文物的人也在增加，其中大多数人都是在文化大革命期间被剥夺了接触中国传统文化的机会。

中国文化的复兴还促成了中外合作的500多所孔子学院的建立。针对某些外国媒体怀疑中国政府利用孔子学院作为“文化渗透”的手段，时任中国国家汉语国际推广领导小组办公室主任的许琳表示，传播自己的母语或本土文化是人类的本能，这对传播者和接受者都是有益的。人类的历史不仅是物质交流的历史，也是文化和精神交流的历史。正是通过这种物质和文化交流，人类实现了共同的理解、价值观和要求。许琳还表示，为了传播中国文化，我们应该努力提高文化的“四个能力”——竞争力、影响力、亲和力和可转化性。

个性化与多样化

人们在对待古代文化的态度开始改变的同时，也变得更加理性。他们渴望个性化，期待自己有做出选择的能力，并有所作为。

例如，近年来，在学校教科书中选取的范文更加多样化。中国革命作家鲁迅的杂文，曾经是中小学语文课堂教学的重点，现在增加了梁实秋、戴望舒、金庸等人的作品，并在教科书中增加人文内容。这种转变标志着文学经典的拓展，教学大纲中包含的文学不仅仅促进了价值灌输，在促进语言习得和

---

〔1〕 Keane, M., *Created in China*: *The great new leap forward*, London: Routledge, 2007.

文化意识方面也发挥了越来越重要的作用。[1]

中国人在重拾对自身文化的兴趣和信心的同时，也对外界产生了浓厚兴趣。随着全球化进程的加快和互联网的崛起，中国2001年加入世界贸易组织、2008年主办奥林匹克夏季运动会、2009年出席哥本哈根联合国气候大会上的等，都表明中国现已成为国际社会中不可或缺的一部分。现在中国人不仅对西方流行文化（如美食）情有独钟，而且对其精神食粮的态度也非常开放。

近十年来，中国人对英语语言和文化的态度无疑是积极的。尽管一些人表示担心接受英语教育会受到西方或美国价值观的影响，但更多人则表示能够接受这些价值观，且并不认为学习英语会对中国的语言和文化构成任何威胁。[2] Cahill认为，中国学生擅长英语写作，学得很快。她还注意到，西方和中国之间的修辞差异已经让位于两者之间的相似性和共性，很难说哪一种修辞风格更加优越或者主流。Fraiberg和游晓晔教授也重申了这一观点，他们指出，资本、文化、历史和意识形态的动态流动催生了混合身份和创新的写作方式。

近年来，网络写作中也出现了中西修辞风格融合的趋势。各种形式的网络写作，如博客、Facebook和Twitter已经成为时尚。MOMO[3]对互联网上新出现的不同的写作风格进行了有趣的描述。例如，“红楼体”“知音体”“梨花体”“纺锤体”“走进科学体”等。

这些不同的写作风格的作者们，努力表现自己的独特品位、地位或心态。以一种比较时尚的写作风格为例，这种风格的主要特点之一是混合使用英语和汉语，作者通常是西方生活方式的崇拜者，致力于在作品中加入英文名称，如品牌、制造商和产地。这类作者的特征是经常在星巴克喝咖啡，在肯德基吃快餐，读外国杂志，使用外国产品，等等。

中国在经济和政治上步入正轨，使得中国能够从各种渠道进行教育模式

---

〔1〕 Corbett, J., *An intercultural approach to English language teaching*, Clevedon, Buffalo, Toronto, Sydney: Multilingual Matters, 2003.

〔2〕 Cahill, D. I., *Contrastive rhetoric, orientalism, and the Chinese second language writer*, Ann Arbor, Mich.: University Microfilms International, 1999.

〔3〕 MoMo：“侃一侃这些网络文体”，载《博客天下》2009年第11期。

和思想的“平缓而又折中的选择”[1]。国外教育投入不再被视为“奴役形式”，而是被大力吸收和运用，以缩小我国与工业化国家之间的专业差距。这增强了跨文化交流和理解，为多语言和多元文化的“混合或融合”奠定了基础。

中国人现在正在试图重新平衡头脑中已经被打翻或倾斜的天平。这就对语言教育工作者提出了挑战：我们如何才能在教学中，特别是在英语写作课堂上，保持中西方文化的适当平衡？

2.1.5 小 结

从以上对中国教育传统的社会政治背景的简要叙述中，可以看出贯穿中国动荡历史的诸多线索。

首先，教育在中国的文明追求中一直扮演了重要角色。自孔夫子时代起（公元前551年至公元前479年），人们就把教育作为一种修身养性和为国家服务的手段而加以重视。“教育救国”是几代中国社会和政治改革家的呐喊。如今，教育在中国的现代化追求中受到前所未有的重视，习近平总书记多次强调优先发展教育，“教育强则国家强”。

尽管教育的价值在中国思想史上很少受到质疑，但对于应该提供什么样的教育却鲜有共识。从秦始皇焚书坑儒，到宋代理学的备受推崇；从20世纪初科举制的废除，到后人“教育救国”的努力；从“文革”时期的“革命”教育，到邓小平“教育要面向现代化、面向世界、面向未来”的呼吁，中国教育史上普遍存在着“深刻而持续的文化不确定性以及对此的质疑和争议”。

其次，中国的英语教育史始于半殖民化时期，一直面临着身份认同维护与变迁的困境。[2]这种历史的张力，可以用“体用二分法”来说明。在英语教育中，“体”（本质）和“用”（功用）分裂表现为对语言能力的强调和对

---

[1] Hayhoe, R., Past and present in China's Educational relations with the industrialized world In R. Hayhoe & M. Bastid (Eds.), *China's education and the industrialized world: Studies in cultural transfer*, Armonk, N. Y.: M. E. Sharpe, 1987, p271-290.

[2] Gao, Y., Sociocultural contexts and English in China: Retaining and reforming the cultural habitus. In J. Lo Bianco, J. Orton & Y. Gao (Eds.), *China and English: Globalization and the dilemmas of identity*, Bristol, Buffalo, Toronto: Multilingual Matters, 2009, p56-78.

语言文化和思想价值的忽视。对个别学习者来说，这种困境反映在对英语学习态度上持续的矛盾心理，即第二语言教育中始终面临保留母语文化的纯洁性和完整性与构建复合文化身份之间的冲突。[1]因此，外语学习的工具性动机得到了强有力的培养。但由于“认识异文化”不可避免地将认识者打上异文化的烙印，[2]母语和目的语文化之间一直存在着未解决的紧张关系。

当代计划经济向全球化市场经济的转变，为中国人开辟了身份建构的新的可能性，同时也加剧了“体用之争”紧张的局面。如何处理好不同文化传统之间的关系，[3]从而在不丧失本土文化认同的情况下从西学中获益，成为中国教育工作者和政策制定者迫切需要解决的问题。

最后，对于中国来说，20世纪是一个“民族化”和“国际化”并存的时代。在这个时代，中国不再被动地受到外部力量的驱动，而是根据外部挑战进行历史上第一次“重塑自我”。寻求恰当的文化身份和发展模式的过程与文化的借用和适应交织在一起，在这一过程中，来自欧洲、美国、日本和苏联的外来思想在改变中国的同时，自身也“被中国化”。通过对外来文化影响的批判性接受，中国在平衡国际影响与民族认同形成方面正变得越来越成熟。

上文中，我根据自己的经历、历史史料和我对英语写作教育的理解，对中国的英语写作教育及其背景作了简要描述。虽然我希望自己的叙述能公平地、客观地介绍各种观点，但不可避免地会被我的立场所影响。换句话说，无论我想要做到多彻底、多细致，我自己的经历和文化处境，以及目前的物质条件，充其量只能让我“接近现实”[4]。

历史的记载清楚地告诉我们，英语与中国现代化和全球化进程密切相关，

---

〔1〕 Li, X., Track (dis) connecting: Chinese high school and university writing in a time of change. In D. Foster & D. R. Russell (Eds.), *Writing and learning in cross-national perspective: Transitions from secondary to higher education*, Urbana, Ill.; Mahwah, N. J.: National Council of Teachers of English; L. Erlbaum, 2002, p49-87.

〔2〕 Lo Bianco, J., Introduction. In J. Lo Bianco, J. Orton & Y. Gao (Eds.), *China and English: Globalization and the dilemmas of identity*, Bristol, Buffalo, Toronto: Multilingual Matters, 2009, p1-20.

〔3〕 Bourdieu, P., *Sociology in question.* London; Thousand Oaks, Calif.: Sage, 1993.

〔4〕 Li, X., Composing culture in a fragmented world: The issue of representation in cross-cultural research. In T. J. Silva & P. K. Matsuda (Eds.), *Second language writing research: Perspectives on the process of knowledge construction*, Mahwah, N. J.: Lawrence Erlbaum Associates, 2005, p125.

并始终被认为是“一种充满威胁、欲望、毁灭和机会的语言”[1]。当代许多语言研究者的理论，即“文本的产生和接受与思想意识冲突的问题有着不可分割的联系”。因此，写作教学不能脱离思想意识和价值的考量，因为这种分离“传播了一种促进文化和学术同化或排斥的话语”[2]。中国外语教育史上的“体用之争”，以及当前英语写作教育中存在的问题，在很大程度上是对各种话语所倡导的意识形态价值不加批判地接受和反映的产物。

2.2 当前英语写作教育的现状及其问题

在叙述完中国语言教育的历史背景后，我们现在将注意力集中在英语写作教育的现状上：政府和教育机构提倡的教学目标是什么？在英语写作教学中有哪些普遍的做法？当前教学实践中存在哪些问题，又探索了哪些创新方法？本综述旨在厘清教育目标与当前现实之间的差距，为讨论新的写作教学方法进行铺垫。

2.2.1 教学目标与现实

中国英语教育的目标大致可以概括为三个方面：（1）提高学生的语言能力和交际能力；（2）提高学生的跨文化能力；（3）培养学生的创新精神和思维能力。由于本书有很多关于语言技能和交际能力的讨论，故而将本节重点放在另外两个目标上，观察在实际的英语写作教学和学习中是否已经达到了这两个目标。

2.2.2 英语写作的创造性

在当代中国，“创造性”和“创造力”已经成为非常重要的一项能力。特别是在教育方面，培养创造力的任务已被写入教学大纲，并给予高度优先

---

〔1〕 Pennycook, A., *Global Englishes and transcultural flows*, London; New York: Routledge/Taylor & Francis, 2007.

〔2〕 Hardin, J. M., *Opening spaces: Critical pedagogy and resistance theory in composition*, Albany: State University of New York Press, 2001, p7.

地位。例如，在高等教育的英语写作要求中反复强调创造性的重要性。《大学英语课程要求（试行）》中明确规定："学生应能就一般议题发表个人意见。"这种对写作中个人表达的强调，符合中国改革后的教育方针，即"以学生的创新精神和个人主义发展为中心"。

尽管在英语教学中倡导要努力培养学生的创造性，但在中国，这是一个相对较新的尝试。因此，还有许多工作要做。特别是英语写作，在过去的几十年里，由于听说教学法的主导地位，英语写作一直被忽视，在创造性学习和教学实践中，英语写作仍几乎是一张"白纸"。到目前为止，中国的外语写作仍被普遍认为是一种提高语言准确性以满足标准化评估的手段。中国大多数学校仍然遵循传统的教学方法，机械的训练抑制了学生的创造力和写作乐趣。

这种状况引起了教育工作者、研究者和政策制定者的重视，因此，中国的英语写作教育受到了越来越多的关注。许多人要求改革写作教育，一些学校和大学开始尝试创新教学法，以提高学生对英语写作的兴趣和创造力。

2.2.3 文化教育

语言教育的另一个主要目标是提高学生的跨文化交际能力。在过去的数十年中，全球化对英语教育的影响为外语文化的教与学提出了更高的要求。人们普遍认为，外语教育正处于一个重要的转折点——从以语言交际为目的的外语教学，到以跨文化交际为目的的外语教学。同时这也是一种支持跨文化意识和能力发展的途径。〔1〕

针对这一趋势，教育部修订了语言教学政策。在《高中课程标准》中，提高学生的文化意识和跨文化能力被列为英语课程的主要目标之一。如上所述，跨文化能力，包括文化知识、文化理解和跨文化交际意识和能力，已经成为英语学习中除听、说、读、写外的第五大关键技能。

---

〔1〕 曹洁："高中英语教材中文化内容设计的问题及改进建议"，载《英语教师》2009年第8期。Crozet, C., & Liddicoat, A., The challenge of intercultural language teaching: Engaging with culture in the classroom. In J. Lo Bianco, A. Liddicoat & C. Crozet (Eds.), *Striving for the third place: Intercultural competence through language education*, Melbourne: Language Australia, 1999, p113 - 125. Lo Bianco, J., Culture: Visible, invisible and multiple. In J. Lo Bianco & C. Crozet (Eds.), *Teaching invisible culture: Classroom practice and theory*, Melbourne: Language Australia, 2003, p11-38.

文化教育的地位在中国似乎已经通过开创性研究和倡议得到了广泛认可，但在中国的大多数语言教育中，文化仍然是一个相对次要和补充性的组成部分，对于哪些内容需要教授以及如何教授的问题，没有给予足够的指导。因此，教师和学生都倾向于忽视文化和语言之间的内在联系，把文化看作是文本中微不足道的背景信息，只有在时间允许的情况下才会涉及。这导致了语言教学的"残缺"——中国英语学习者的语言能力较强，而跨文化交际能力较弱。换句话说，虽然学生可能在能力测试中取得高分，但他们却无法成功地与外国人交流，因为不了解国外的习俗、传统、价值体系、宗教或规范。这些问题在全球化背景下的当代中国变得尤其尖锐和复杂。

2.2.4 当前教学法存在的问题

许多研究者认为 EFL（English as a Foreign Language）写作教学法存在诸多问题。与英语学习的其他技能（听力、口语、阅读）相比，写作相对来说是不被重视的，因此，写作成了英语学习的最大困难。造成这种后果的还有一个重要原因是学生缺乏写作自信，从而导致英语写作的焦虑和恐惧。[1]

中国教育，尤其是语言教育，主要缺点之一就是忽视对学生的创造力的培养。大约 80%的语言专业毕业生承认自身缺乏独立思考、解决问题和其他重要的基本素质。文秋芳是中国一位颇有影响力的英语教育家和研究者，她指出，中国英语专业的学生由于受到大学里的训练方式的影响，在批判和逻辑思维能力方面比较薄弱。这种不足既是由写作造成的，也能通过写作反映出来。[2]

另一种常见问题是写作内容和想法的匮乏，一部分原因是过于强调写作的语法层面，另一部分原因是在国家英语考试中，写作部分给学生提供固定的主题句，这使学生在思想延伸和语言方面的创造性受到严重限制。

缺乏跨文化意识是目前语言教育的另一个缺陷。[3]通过对 200 名奥运志

---

〔1〕 Cheng, Y. S., "A measure of second language writing anxiety: Scale development and preliminary validation": *Journal of Second Language Writing*, 13 (4), 2004, p313-335.

〔2〕 文秋芳等："构建我国外语类大学生思辨能力量具的理论框架"，载《外语界》2009 年第 1 期。

〔3〕 高一虹、林梦茜："大学生奥运志愿者对世界英语的态度——奥运会前的一项主观投射测试研究"，载《新疆师范大学学报（哲学社会科学版）》2008 年第 4 期。

愿者的研究，作者发现中国大学生对世界英语的变体知之甚少却存在明显偏见。因此，如何提高学生的多语言意识和多元文化意识，为奥运会等世界事务做好准备，成为语言教育工作者面临的一个挑战。曹洁[1]在文章中表达的观点与高一虹、林梦茜的观点产生了共鸣，她在文章中强调，通过在语言教材中引入更多的文化成分来培养学生的世界观，可以加深他们对自身文化的理解，提高跨文化交际能力。

中国的 EFL（English as a Foreign Language）写作教育正受到越来越多的关注。中国教育部英语高教督导委员会成员李力教授表示，中国的毕业生在实践技能、创造力、自尊心、自信心和解决问题能力等方面远远落后于西方学生，因此英语教育改革是非常必要的。解决办法在于重新界定英语教学的概念——将英语教学作为一种提高学生整体发展和幸福感的手段，而不是作为一种语言工具的习得。[2]2003 年以来，中国英语写作教学与研究国际研讨会每年都会在中国举行（2009 年除外）。尽管英文写作中的创造性和跨文化能力的具体问题没有得到很好的解决，但会议的召开确实表明了当今中国对提高英语写作能力的日益重视和为此付出的努力。

针对目前我国外语学习中存在的问题，教育界提出了创新和改革的要求。例如，中国外语界著名学者王立非鼓励语言教师在二语习得和二语教学中借鉴国际理论，创新中国的英语教学。文秋芳呼吁改革现行英语专业课程和教学方法，更加注重语言学习的"输出驱动"能力。此外，重视文化创意教育的教材也越来越多，如《跨文化交际：实用教材》[3]《跨文化交际外语教学》[4]等。其中《大学英语创意写作丛书》[5]在致力于提高学生的综合英语语言能

---

〔1〕 曹洁："高中英语教材中文化内容设计的问题及改进建议"，载《英语教师》2009 年第 8 期。

〔2〕 祁寿华：《西方写作理论、教学与实践》，上海外语教育出版社 2000 年版。

〔3〕 Hu, C., *Intercultural communication: A practical coursebook*. Beijing, Foreign Language Teaching and Research Press, 2006.

〔4〕 王振亚：《以跨文化交往为目的的外语教学——系统功能语法与外语教学》，北京语言大学出版社 2005 年版。

〔5〕 Smallwood, I., Lung, L., & Green, C., *College English creative writing*, Shanghai: Shanghai Foreign Language Education Press, 2005-2006.

力的同时，也提供了一些创造性的尝试。[1]

总之，尽管教育的目标是培养学生的英语写作能力、创造力和跨文化交际能力，但中国英语写作教学大多仍是僵化的机械训练。作者认为，上述传统的英语写作教学法有如下的弊端：

（1）教学过度强调语法等语言技术问题，采用的模式化写作控制以及总结性评估方式压制了学生写作的乐趣和个性化表达，甚至会引发对写作的恐惧和焦虑；

（2）教学以机械模仿和填空式训练为主，容易滋生抄袭、剽窃等不良倾向，造成“高分低能”的现象，导致学生写作范围狭窄、内容空泛、写作内容单一等问题，不利于创造力和批判思维能力的培养；

（3）更严重的是，由于写作教学脱离学生生活实际，使学生缺乏写作动机和兴趣，长此以往会影响他们的整体学习动机和学习能力；

（4）忽视写作教育中的文化因素，限制学生自由，减少了他们在母语和非母语文化环境下对写作资源的选择，也影响了学生的写作能力。这可能会扼杀他们的创造力，剥夺他们运用写作来培养跨文化意识和能力的机会。

但到目前为止，却很少有人试图去解决中国英语学习的关键问题，尤其是如何增强中国英语学习者的能力并将其母语和第二语言的文化和身份整合起来的问题。即使有人尝试解决这一关键问题，这个问题在中国的英语教学中也并没有得到很好的解决，至少是没有得到认真的解决。本项研究就是为了寻找解决这些问题的有效途径，探索出一种新的批判写作教学法，寻找一个同时满足语言学习者个人和社会需求的“第三空间”[2]，令英汉两种语言能够实现真正的平等对话。

---

〔1〕 Jin, L., Cortazzi, M., & Zhang, H., Cultivate student's comprehensive English competence from multiple levels—College English creative series: Multi-dimensional participation approach: Public lecture notes, 2005.

〔2〕 Kramsch, C. J., *Context and culture in language teaching*, Oxford: Oxford University Press, 1993.

第三章

二语写作文献综述

本书主题是为中国英语学习者赋能，帮助他们提高英语写作、创新能力和跨文化交际能力。因此，在回顾相关文献和研究时，本章从批判理论入手，然后根据教育目标将文献分为三大类：（1）二语写作教学法；（2）二语写作中的创造力；（3）二语写作中的跨文化研究。希望以此能更好地展示本书所涉及的国内外研究基础和背景，因为这些文献在赋能和解放的共同主题下，具有密不可分的内在的联系。

3.1 写作与读写的批判理论

在批判理论中，所有教学都属于意识形态。知识、教育和话语永远不可能保持中立。[1]因此，教育总是服务于多种目的，这些目的之间甚至会相互对立。例如，教育既可巩固原有的权力模式，也可以挑战这种模式。[2]在语言教育中，权力、差异、获取和支配的问题一直是批判性研究者、教师和决策者关注的中心问题。[3]近年来，教育逐渐被重新定义为要服务于人们的自身利益。全球化趋势下要求教育促进共存，反对“非此即彼”的思维模式。[4]

---

〔1〕 Fairclough, N. , *Language and power*. London, New York: Longman, 1989.

〔2〕 Rizvi, F. , Speaking truth to power: Edward Said and the work of the intellectual. In J. Satterthwaite, M. Watts & H. Piper (Eds.), *Talking truth, confronting power*, 2008, p113-126.

〔3〕 Pennycook, A. , *Critical applied linguistics: A critical introduction*. Mahwah, N. J. : L. Erlbaum, 2001.

〔4〕 Said, E. W. , *Humanism and democratic criticism*, New York: Columbia University Press, 2004.

语言类教师成了教育挑战的核心，他们面临着两种选择：是要教授与社会和文化问题无关的纯语言技能，还是要肩负参与社会、文化和政治变革的重大使命。

批判教育学，或“基于社会变革的教育”[1]旨在回答上述问题。批判教育学家应该共同致力于为弱势群体赋能，寻找应对和改变社会不平等现状的途径。因此，学校作为批判教育的主要场所，应该通过培养学生的批判性写作、阅读和思考能力，重构社会大环境中的组织和秩序。[2]尤其是写作教学，它涉及传授学生语言之间的关系，并通过批判性写作改变他们的生活边界，换句话说就是如何“书写和纠正世界”[3]。为此，批判性教师需要发展对语言意识形态维度的元意识，包括与文本、体裁、社会互动相关的实践。[4]

语言，特别是英语，与社会、经济和政治的全球化进程息息相关。Pennycook使用“全球英语”一词来定位英语在全球化批判理论中的传播和使用情况：

无论用现代帝国主义国家中心模式，还是用传统的隔离模式来理解它（英语）都是不充分的。我认为将英语置于一个更为复杂的全球化视野中更为妥当。这种视角能够以批判的眼光看待英语的力量、控制作用和破坏性，并审视其对新形式的反抗、转变、占有和认同的复杂性。这意味着我们需要超越关于同质性或异质性以及帝国主义和民族国家的争论，转而关注跨地区和跨文化的流动。

此外，Pennycook 使用了“跨文化流动”这一术语来讨论全球化的文化内涵和文化形式在不同语境下的移动、适应、转变和重塑的方式。从这个意义上来讲，英语可能代表的不是单一的文化，而是各种文化的汇总。因此，Horner 和 Trimbur 呼吁从国际角度看待书面英语与当地语言和全球化动态之间的关系，从而把学生从单一语言的英语观点中解放出来。Canagarajah 对二语

---

〔1〕 Pennycook, A., *The cultural politics of English as an international language*, London; New York: Longman, 1994.

〔2〕 Canagarajah, A. S., *Resisting linguistic imperialism in English teaching*, Oxford: Oxford University Press, 1999.

〔3〕 Wilson, L., *Writing to live: How to Teach Writing for Today's World*, Portsmouth, NH: Heinemann, 2006.

〔4〕 Ramanathan, V., *The politics of TESOL education: Writing, knowledge, critical pedagogy*, New York: Routledge Falmer, 2002.

学生在语言使用上必然会犯错误这一普遍假设提出了质疑，从而进一步强化了这一观点。他认为语法是一种思想意识，因此英语非标准用法的每个例子不一定都是一种无意识的"错误"或"糟糕的英语"；相反，二语学生可以根据具体修辞、文化和思想意识方面的目的来积极协商语法意义。

Pennycook 指出，在批判性写作教学法中，写作者"声音"（voice）的概念不仅仅是一种非沉默或个人情感的表达。它提倡一种以关注学生为出发点的教学法，不是通过那种老生常谈的人文主义的"以学生为本"的方法来让学生表达他们的"内心感受"，而是通过探索学生的历史和文化定位，探讨语言和话语的局限性和可能性。当要求学生寻找和表达自己的"声音"时，写作教师需要首先被赋能，以认识自己声音的主观性、本位性和偏向性。〔1〕

一些研究者认为英语的全球传播与语言和媒介帝国主义、与世界文化的美国化和同质化有关。〔2〕对此，Pennycook 表示，文化流动产生了新的本地化形式和新的全球身份认同形式。他提倡一种后殖民主义语言观，这种非本质主义语言观要求对语言的使用要有历史的理解，强调语言的互混与融合，关注语言的当地语境。

我完全赞同上述观点。英语教学中的单语取向否定了学生的能动性，抑制了学生在写作中的创造性和批判性思维。相反，语言符号的创造性啮合以及地方变体与"标准书面英语"的融合，正是世界英语逐渐走向多元化的积极举措。〔3〕

此外，批判性学者还讨论了读写的意识形态本质，以及通过在学校读写教育和课程体系中纳入学生的声音来赋予学生力量的重要性。读写通常被理解为"一种社会实践，即个体在其生活的各个领域所参与的社会实践和交流

〔1〕 Kamler, B., & Fine, M., *Relocating the personal: A critical writing pedagogy*, Norwood, S. Aust.: Australian Association for the Teaching of English, 2001.

〔2〕 Canagarajah, A. S., *Resisting linguistic imperialism in English teachin*, Oxford: Oxford University Press, 1999.

〔3〕 Canagarajah, A. S., *The place of world Englishes in composition: Pluralization continued*, College Composition and Communication, 57 (4), 2006, p586-619.

实践”。[1]例如，在中国传统文化中，政治与文化有着直接而明显的联系，这一点从孟子的“劳心者治人，劳力者治于人”中便可看出。读写能力不是一个单一的、中立的概念，而是一种互动的、复杂的个人能力，与历史、社会、意识形态息息相关。因此，需要对实际读写实践进行研究，以便在学校开展更广泛的读写活动，倾听学生的个人呼声。[2]

界定“读写”的斗争反映了一个被广泛接受的概念，即“读写”发展和存在于权力结构中，并反映不同权力集团的利益。正如 Bourdieu 所指出的，学校强调一种特殊形式的文化资本，将其制度化为教育资格证书，并以吸收与这种资本形式相关的特定文本和实践为基础。同样，Giroux 也表示，目前，学校在界定和复制读写能力上发挥了核心作用。学校往往给某些知识、言行和处事方式以合法地位，把与之相关的学习行为作为获得教育文凭的要求，这可能会使那些与主流文化资本只有微弱联系的学生处于明显劣势。此外，学生对读写能力的认识和需求往往被漠视，在教与学的过程中不能发挥能动作用，在制定他们自己发展方案的时候，他们成了“隐形人”和“聋哑人”。[3]

批判教学法要求学校的读写教育密切联系学生个人兴趣，以赋予学生写作力量。这就需要重新分配机会，以实现创新写作教育。关于这些方面的文献将在下一部分进行讨论。

3.2　二语写作教学法的发展与创新

3.2.1　二语写作教学法

在二语写作的发展过程中，学者们提出了一系列的写作方法或写作方向，每一种写作方法或写作方向都代表着对写作本质的不同理解（Matsuda，

〔1〕 Hamilton, M., *Sustainable literacies and the ecology of lifelong learning*, Paper presented at the Global Colloquium on Supporting Lifelong Learning (online), from http://www.open.ac.uk/lifelong-learning/, September 20, 2009.

〔2〕 Street, B., *The Implications of the 'New Literacy Studies' for literacy education*, English in Education, 31 (3), 1997, p45-59.

〔3〕 Grainger, T., Goouch, K., & Lambirth, A., *Creativity and writing: Developing voice and verve in the classroom*. London; New York: Routledge, 2005.

2003)。其中有五种比较具有影响力（按时间顺序排列）：①表现主义写作；②控制写作法；③现实-传统修辞派；④过程写作法（也称为认知写作法）；⑤学术英语写作（也称为跨学科写作）。首先，本节将简要回顾这些教学方法，并讨论学习者是如何通过这些写作方法被赋予或剥夺权力的。

第一，表现主义写作。表现主义写作在20世纪前期开始发展，并于六七十年代达到顶峰，[1]它认为写作是“一种创造性的行为，作者是探索意义过程中的焦点”[2]。在这种方法中，写作被认为是“一种艺术，是一种创造性的行为，在这种行为中发现真正自我的过程与表达的结果同等重要”[3]。教科书旨在鼓励学生通过写日记和抒发个人情感的文章等作业发现自我，进行自由、不加批判的写作。尽管有人批判表现主义写作天真地以自我为中心，[4]但其许多实践已经被过程教学法所接受，例如头脑风暴和同伴反馈。

第二，控制写作法。针对表现主义写作的批判，控制写作应运而生，这种方法更倾向于表现形式语言特征而不是表达独创的观点。二语写作学习被看作是一种习惯的养成，旨在避免表面上由第一语言干扰引起的语言错误。Pincas是控制性教学法的倡导者之一，他认为语言是对由模仿学到的固定模式的操纵，只有在熟练掌握这些固定模式后，才可能对其进行灵活操纵，或者对其中的变量进行创造性的选择。但控制性写作一直受到强烈反对，因为它将写作简单化归为固定模式的模仿和操纵。虽然控制性写作表面上已不再适用于ESL（English as a Second Language）和EFL（English as a Foreign Language）课堂教学，但事实上，这种教学法在许多二语写作课堂和教科书中仍普遍存在。

第三，现实—传统修辞派。20世纪60年代，伴随着对比修辞学的发展，

---

〔1〕 Johns, A., L1 composition theories: Implications for developing theories of L2 composition. In B. Kroll (Ed.), *Second language writing: Research insights for the classroom*, Cambridge: Cambridge University Press, 1990.

〔2〕 Connor, U., *Contrastive rhetoric: Cross-cultural aspects of second-language writing*, Cambridge [England]; New York: Cambridge University Press, 1996.

〔3〕 Berlin, J., *Rhetoric and Ideology in the writing class*, College English, 50 (4), 1988, p477-494.

〔4〕 Pincas, A., Structural linguistics and systematic composition teachring to students of English as a foreign language. In T. J. Silva & P. K. Matsuda (Eds.), *Landmark essays on ESL writing*, Mahwah, N. J.: Hermagoras Press, 1962.

现实—传统修辞派开始把学生的注意力集中在“语篇形式的逻辑建构与组织”上。与控制性教学法相比，它更关注大段语篇（结构和组织形式等）。因此，写作学习是一种组织管理，即将现成的或生成的内容填入预定的模式中。[1]这种方法虽因未能培养创造性思维的写作而受到严厉抨击，但在今天的英语写作辅导材料和课堂实践中仍然占主导地位。

第四，过程写作法。过程写作法（也称为认知写作法）将重点从文本特征转移到写作过程本身，[2]认为写作是一个复杂的认知过程，一个“非线性的、探索性的和生成性的过程，作者在此过程中发现并重新形成观点”。这种新的教学方法强调创新、修改和形成反馈。产生于20世纪70年代，过程教学法向二语教师传授了许多认知心理学理论与母语作文理论，使得作者本身和写作过程得到更大的重视，受到普遍欢迎。

关于写作过程研究的最大的贡献就是认识到写作不仅是展示学习内容的手段，更是一种求知的手段。换句话说，写作不仅记录先前形成的想法，也有助于创造和形成思想。此外，Raimes 指出，学习写作的主要目的是学习如何用写作表达思想，而其他目的则是“辅助性的”。她还指出，与大多数人的认识不同，足够的词汇量并不一定是写作的先决条件，只要有适当的语境、准备、反馈和修改的机会，任何程度的学生都能通过写作去发现意义。虽然过程教学法将学生和教师从以往规定性的、以成果为导向的实践中解放出来，但因其忽视写作的社会背景而受到批判。[3]20世纪80年代，二语写作的关注焦点从作者转向读者，随即产生了学术英语写作。

第五，学术英语写作。作为对过程教学法忽视社会需求的回应，学术英语写作或跨学科写作要求初学者既要学习语言和写作的惯例，也要学习公认的学科价值和实践方法 。因为该教学法认为，体裁是由思想意识驱动的，

---

〔1〕 Silva, T. J., Second language composition instruction: Developments, issues, and directions in ESL. In B. Kroll (Ed.), *Second language writing: Research insights for the classroom*, Cambridge: Cambridge University Press, 1990.

〔2〕 Raimes, A., *Problems and teaching strategies in ESL composition: If Johnny has problems, what about Juan, Jean, and Ywe-Han?* Arlington, Va.: Center for Applied Linguistics, 1979.

〔3〕 Corbett, J., *An intercultural approach to English language teaching*, Clevedon, Buffalo, Toronto, Sydney: Multilingual Matters, 2003.

任何文本，即便是在学校，都不能摆脱其作者的价值观和信仰。[1]从社会建构主义来看，人们不是为写作而写作，而是为了在不同的语境中达到不同的目的。[2]也就是说，写作是工具而非目的。因此，写作不应与修辞功能分开教授。

该教学法虽然受到研究者和教师的普遍欢迎，但因限制学生写作的创造性和艺术性而受到质疑。[3]例如，Spack 批判该教学法只将写作限制在固定的、有章可循的任务上，而没有积极引发学生思考，培养其智力和促进其道德发展。针对类似观点，Johns 回应道，在体裁为主的写作课中学生应把语言和文本看作是可以不断变化和能够协商的，从而将写作变得更加个性化或易于把握。

尽管存在局限性，但这种社会建构主义教学法告诉我们，在跨文化语境下分析写作作品时，还应该考虑写作任务的语境、情境、受众知识和写作目的。Trimbur[4]以术语"后过程法"来指代 20 世纪 80 年代的"社会转向"。他认为，后过程法、后认知主义理论和教育学将读写视为意识形态，并将写作作为一种文化活动。

除以上几种英语写作法外，仍需关注英语写作的最新发展趋势。多元读写、二语写作技术和二语写作练习、二语写作研究中的话语分析以及二语写作中的元学科探究是过去十年中影响二语写作领域的一些重要思潮。

3.2.2 关于二语写作教学法的讨论

二语写作教学史上一直存在实用性与批判性之间的较量。其主要争议之一是教师的角色定位问题。写作教师的主要任务是教授学生实用的写作技能，

---

〔1〕 Johns, A., Genre and ESL/EFL composition instruction. In B. Kroll (Ed.), *Exploring the dynamics of second language writing*, Cambridge; New York: Cambridge University Press, 2003.

〔2〕 Halliday, M. A. K., & Matthiessen, C. M. I. M., *An introduction to functional grammar* (3rd ed.), London: Arnold, 2004.

〔3〕 Cremin, T., Creativity, uncertainty and discomfort: teachers as writers, *Cambridge Journal of Education*, 36 (3), 2006, p415-433.

〔4〕 Trimbur, J., Taking the social turn: Teaching writing post-process. *College Composition and Communication*, 45, 1994, p108-118.

还是引导他们探索写作的社会政治功能，从而通过写作来改变世界。[1]此外，社会和个人声音的表达也是争论的焦点，同其他因素一起推动二语写作教育的发展。本节讨论中，有人可能会问，中国英语学习者写作的目的到底是什么？是让学生发现个性，像表现主义和个人写作法那样注重个人的主观感受，还是提高社会整体的读写能力，以便于学生适应未来社会生活，或者两者兼而有之。

针对这些问题，Johns 认为，虽然个人写作可以表达自己的声音和身份，更好地激励学生参与到写作当中，但这些成功和乐趣可能会造成学生以后难以融入社会生活。因此，Johns 呼吁语言教育工作者在二语写作课堂上采取社会化教学法，使学生今后在社会和专业生活中获得最多的机会，从而能够更好地融入更广泛的社会环境。我国著名外语教育专家文秋芳强调在中国应更加看重学生的社会需求而非个人需求。她敦促老师要迎合学生更深层、更基本的需求，使学生成长为更全面合格的社会人，而不是仅满足肤浅的教学需要，如营造快乐有趣的班集体氛围，或组织丰富多彩的表演或课堂活动。

这些论点反映了当今英语写作教育面临的主要争议，促使我们思考学生在英语写作中的真实需求。首先，学生要对写作充满信心和兴趣，否则很难成为有能力的写作者；其次，学生需要学会写作以满足未来生活的需要；再次，学生要通过写作来提高创造力；最后，学生要提高跨文化能力，以便在全球化的世界中作为社会存在取得成功。为保护学生写作中个人声音的表达和创造性的发挥以及告诫学生所有人都受语言的社会性影响，我们要鼓励学生在新的社会环境中学会创造性地协商和处理写作问题。

在目前关于写作方法的辩论中，这些需求似乎是相互对立的。然而，在 EFL（English as a Foreign Language）教学中，它们是否真的存在冲突？二语写作研究人员和实践者是否必须归入实用主义或社会性批判派别？是否有“第三空间”能够成功地整合这些需求？这些问题促使我寻求一种能够满足学生写作中多重需要的教学法，而不是以其他目标为代价仅仅实现其中一个目标。尽管上述写作教学法的发展主要是在北美地区进行的，但对包括中国在

〔1〕 Casanave, C. P., *Controversies in second language writing: Dilemmas and decisions in research and instruction*, Ann Arbor: University of Michigan Press, 2004.

内的世界其他地区的二语写作方法产生了巨大的影响，引发了一系列的教学创新和课程改革。

3.2.3 二语写作教学创新

2008年，第六届全国英语写作教学与研究国际研讨会在北京召开。其中五位主要发言人中有两位提出了相似问题。美国著名二语写作研究者、《语言学习》杂志执行主任 Alister Cumming 提出："为什么研究如此关注学生的写作和文本，而不是教师的行动和课程组织？" 北京师范大学著名教授和研究员武尊民也提出："对于如何在整个英语课程中组织写作教学，似乎缺乏研究，包括对写作教学内容的选择和组织以及与写作教学有关的教育问题。"

的确，有关英语写作教学和课程的文献并不充分，有关在英语语境下进行教学创新或课程改革的研究更是少之又少。近年来，对英语创新写作教学法的研究，尤其是英美写作教学法，主要集中在国外写作教学法的本土化发展上，许多研究员曾尝试将过程性教学法[1]和体裁教学法[2]引入中国的大学课堂。

有关中国英语写作语境下的教学法的研究同样相对较少。Lo 和 Hyland[3]进行了一项关于在香港实施新的 ESL（English as a Second Language）项目的研究。这个新项目旨在通过让学生写自己感兴趣的话题和提供真实而非想象的读者，来增强学生的积极性和参与度。Brien[4]研究了一门由澳大利亚教学团队针对香港大专学生开启的强化写作课程。本课程旨在嵌入以学生为中心的学习活动，增强学生的创造力和创造性思维。Smith[5]提出在中文研究

---

〔1〕 Pennington, M. C., Brock, M. N., & Yue, F., Explaining Hong Kong students' response to process writing: An exploration of causes and outcomes, *Journal of Second Language Writing*, 5 (3), 1996, p227–252.

〔2〕 Kong, J., *Applying the genre based approach in teaching writing to non–English majors*. Paper presented at the Sixth National Symposium on English Writing Teaching and Research, Beijing, 2008.

〔3〕 Lo, J., & Hyland, F., Enhancing students'engagement and motivation in writing: The case of primary students in Hong Kong. *Journal of Second Language Writing*, 16 (4), 2007, p219–237.

〔4〕 Brien, D. L., Developing and enhancing creativity: A case study of the special challenges of teaching writing in Hong Kong *Journal*, 11 (1), 2007. Retrieved from http: //www. textjournal. com. au/april07/brien. htm

〔5〕 Smith, K. J., "The thoughts we have learned: Internally persuasive discourse in Chinese post–graduate journals", University of Melbourne, 2007.

生课程中撰写反思日记，以帮助学生针对新的理解和重要概念进行思考。

以上关于创造性写作教学法的研究，大多集中在新方法的内容或学生的创新反应上，很少讨论教师在教学变革中所经历的变化或这些尝试涉及的更广泛的社会文化背景。当前的教学法研究表明，它远远超出了课堂策略或活动的范围，涵盖了教师的信念、理论、认识论、能动性和实践。〔1〕例如，Shi，L. 与 Cumming，A. 发现，英语写作教师将他们的个人信仰融入加拿大学校的教学创新中。针对这一情况，Gebhard〔2〕等人提倡教师教育方案，以支持写作教师对理论、研究和实践的理解，从而实践二语教学的批判教学法。

此外，广东外语外贸大学教师欧阳护华指出，作为其他社会变革的缩影，教学法的改革往往伴随着意识形态和权力关系的重建。因此，语言研究"应该比以往更贴近社会研究的节奏"。〔3〕游晓晔在 2004 年发表的论文《别无选择：中国大学英语写作教学》中得出结论，要想成功地将西方的写作方法引进和融入中国语境，需要考虑广泛的社会和文化因素。Liu，Y.〔4〕对台湾学生与进口写作教学法谈判的研究中也反映了这种观点。她认为，在将英美教学法应用于当地时，批判视角对于研究和理解学生的协商至关重要。

除了教学创新的社会政治背景外，Liu，Y. 就中国英语教师的信念和教学法研究指出了解释教师课堂实践的五个因素：建构教学决策的先验知识、对形式和内容在写作中的作用的态度、教学目标、对学生作品的反馈以及教师定位。对于二语写作教师，Casanave〔5〕提出在二语写作课上决策的三大依据分别是教与学的哲学、二语写作知识和当地实际情况。尤其是对教师责任的

---

〔1〕 Burnard, P., & White, J., "Creativity and performativity: Counterpoints in British and Australian education", *British Educational Research Journal*, 34 (5), 2008, p667-682.

〔2〕 Gebhard, M., Demers, J., & Castillo-Rosenthal, Z., "Teachers as critical text analysts: L2 literacies and teachers'work in the context of high-stakes school reform", *Journal of Second Language Writing*, 17 (4), 2008, p274-291.

〔3〕 Fairclough, N., *Language and power*, London; New York: Longman, 1989.

〔4〕 Liu, Y. & Gao, S., Exploring Chinese EFL teachers' beliefs and practices in writing instruction, Paper presented at the Sixth National Symposium on English Writing Teaching and Research, Beijing, 2008.

〔5〕 Casanave, C. P., Uses of narrative in L2 writing research. In T. J. Silva & P. K. Matsuda (Eds.), *Second language writing research: Perspectives on the process of knowledge construction*, Mahwah, N. J.: Lawrence Erlbaum Associates, 2005, p17-32.

信任被认为是影响学生写作动机和写作表现的关键因素。Lee 和 Schallert[1] 还发现，建立教师与学生之间的信任关系，可能是有效利用教师反馈的基础。因此，他们鼓励重新构想修正的认知过程模式，并增加了师生关系作为重要影响因素的作用。

综上所述，在中国英语教学中，写作教师一直在根据当地的需要和情况进行教学创新。然而，这种本土化的尝试在二语写作领域并没有得到足够的重视。此外，在中国英语教学创新领域的文献中，大多数研究者倾向于强调语言层面，而忽略了社会和教育层面的哲学内涵。特别是缺乏深入的民族志研究，以考察教师研究者形成和塑造写作教学法的过程，以及参与社会制度实践时经历的个人转变。

3.3 二语写作的创造性

中国与远东国家认为未来个人、社会和经济的成功都取决于创造性思维，故而非常注重创造性课程。

——Fisher

本研究的主旨之一是通过赋予学生力量让学生摆脱写作恐惧，从而释放写作创造力。因此，本章将回顾有关创造力和写作之间关系的文献，以及能够增强学生创造力和想象力的写作方法。

Sternberg[2]认为创造力是一种可以发生在每个人身上的“多方面的现象”。在所有现有的对创造力的定义中，有一种形式的创造性行为可以被描述为“表达能力”，即以一种自身独有的方式表达自己的能力。这种形式的创造力不是由一个人的智力决定的，而是取决于一个人的精神自治、内在动机、容忍模棱两可的意愿和克服障碍、承担风险、争取认可的意愿。Robinson 认

---

〔1〕 Lee, G., & Schallert, D. L., Meeting in the margins: Effects of the teacher-student relationship on revision processes of EFL college students taking a composition course, *Journal of Second Language Writing*, 17 (3), 2008, p165-182.

〔2〕 Sternberg, R. J., A three-faceted model of creativity. In R. J. Sternberg (Ed.), *The nature of creativity: Contemporary psychological perspectives*, Cambridge: Cambridge University Press, 1988, p125-147.

为人类的智慧本质上是具有创造性的。我们不仅找出世界的意义，还通过解释的力量来创造世界，通过“象征性思维”来诠释世界，包括文字、图像、声音、动作等。Robert Fisher 发现创造力的重要性后，坚持认为创造性应该是课程的中心，而不是一个边缘化的“补充”。创造力是人类繁荣的关键，尤其是在不确定、有问题的时代。由于创造力的概念在文化、政治和社会经济方面存在差异，Craft 认为应在文化情境教学法中对其进行批判性的审视。

Glaxton 认为，写作的本质是具有创造性和戏剧性的。探索性写作和探索性谈话的特定形式有助于“认知进化”，在该过程中“模糊的想法有时间孕育展开成为新的言语与思想形式”[1]。例如，通常被叫作讲故事的“叙述”，是一种打开心灵之窗的重要的符号学模式，还有关于对写作创造性的阐述。早在 20 世纪 70 年代，Zamel[2]就指出，写作的首要重点应该是表达和创造的过程，所以写作行为可以成为表达个人情感、经历或反应的真实需要的结果。同样，Richardson[3]的“写作是一种研究方法”强调了写作的探索性功能。在她看来，写作不仅仅是调查结束时的“扫尾工作”，而且是一种“求知方式”，即“一种发现和分析的方式”。以不同的方式写作，可以发现主题的不同方面和各方面之间的关系，并对主题和自身产生新的认识。

虽然写作和创造力之间存在内在联系，但在现实中，这种联系往往会因为对读写技能的过度强调而被切断。培养学生的知识和技能可以提高他们的创造性写作能力，但我们不能以牺牲创造性和写作机会为代价来教授读写能力。Nolen[4]认为，写作动机的一个核心组成部分是作者对表达自己的感情、想法和看法的兴趣。如果能将创造性的自我表达分享给真正的读者，而不仅仅是写作老师，将会极大地增强作者的动力。许多中国学者和作家也强调，好的

---

〔1〕 Claxton, G., Thinking at the edge: developing soft creativity, *Cambridge Journal of Education*, 36 (3), 2006, p351-362.

〔2〕 Zamel, V., Teaching composition in the ESL classroom: What we can learn from research in the teaching. In T. J. Silva & P. K. Matsuda (Eds.), *Landmark essays on ESL writing*, Mahwah, N. J.: Hermagoras Press, 1976, p27-36.

〔3〕 Richardson, L. W., Writing: A method of inquiry. In N. K. Denzin & Y. S. Lincoln (Eds.), *The SAGE handbook of qualitative research* (2rd ed.), Thousand Oaks, CA: Sage Publications, 2000, p923-948.

〔4〕 Nolen, S. B., Young children's motivation to read and write: Development in social contexts, *Cognition and Instruction*, 25 (2), 2007, p219-270.

写作是对公式的敌视，作家必须超越固定的格式，形成灵活的、有机的形式概念。

西方人花费大量精力来研究创造性写作。例如，Fisher[1]指出，创造性写作需要平衡传统和个人主义的潜在对立需求。他解释说：

> 写作是一种约定俗成的活动。一方面，拼写、标点和对不同文本类型的规约意味着书写方式的对错。另一方面，最好的作家却能够以创造性和个人的方式使用和颠覆传统。

有学者认为，在写作中培养创造性远不止是一个教学问题。由于社会建构和文化嵌入，关于创造性写作的研究必须考虑到创作实践产生的广泛的社会文化语境。为了给学生准备"创造空间"[2]，研究人员和教育工作者需要一个适应性的教育环境。于是提出了有计划的干预措施，涉及使用促进技术和教学法来改变目前的教育制度。例如，使用计算机和互联网可以有效地激活写作过程。Qi[3]也强调了当代技术在提高创造力中的重要作用，并提出了一种创造性的教学策略，即利用多维互动模式，促进学生之间、师生之间、学生和网络资源之间在英语写作课堂上的协作。

同样，Mai[4]也提出了基于学校网络系统的写作策略。学生可以通过网页获得写作任务、阅读教师所提供的写作范例、通过多媒体平台获取必要的背景信息、在写作过程中分享自己的想法和问题、获得反馈并在写作完成后公布自己的作品。该模式的优势在于：第一，网站提供了大量超出课堂学习时间和空间限制的信息；第二，通过互联网高效的通信促进了学生与教师之间的沟通，从而使学生在写作过程中能够主动地进行交流；第三，作为一个

---

〔1〕 Fisher, R., "Whose writing is it anyway? Issues of control in the teaching of writing", *Cambridge Journal of Education*, 36 (2), 2006, p193-206.

〔2〕 Loi, D., & Dillon, P., "Adaptive educational environments as creative spaces", *Cambridge Journal of Education*, 36 (3), 2006, p363-381.

〔3〕 Qi, G., A multi-dimensional interactive teaching model for English major's writing class, Paper presented at the National Symposium on English Writing Teaching and Research, Beijing, 2008.

〔4〕 Mai, X., Task based English writing strategy through the platform of school web system, Paper presented at the Sixth National Symposium on English Writing Teaching and Research, Beijing, 2008.

发表渠道，学生可以通过网站来分享作品，与读者进行互动；第四，可以很容易地建立一个写作档案和语料库，从而对学生的表现进行系统的存储和评估。

关于阅读与写作的关系问题，Leki〔1〕强烈主张将阅读与写作纳入同一课堂，让学生意识到阅读与写作的社会维度，从而提高阅读与写作的能力。值得注意的是，Vandrick〔2〕和Grainger〔3〕等人建议用文学作为一种丰富而具挑战性的手段刺激优秀写作和促进学生进入学术、知识和教育生活世界。Sturgell〔4〕进一步建议建立"试金石文本"图书馆，让孩子们沉浸在高质量的文学中，让他们的创造力从读书逐渐融入写作中。

各种艺术形式在培养学生的创造力方面都能够发挥重要作用。例如，戏剧可以激发深刻的思考，刺激学生的创造力和学习的热情。〔5〕通过让学生从角色本身出发，进行思考，为学习者的创造性和批判性思维的发展提供了巨大的潜力。这种角色扮演也能够成为打破教师与学生之间"无形之墙"和从多个角度产生思考的有效手段。〔6〕

对学生写作的反馈和干预始终是创造性写作教学的核心问题，尽管其方法一直存在争议并发生了重大变化。〔7〕就评估而言，许多研究人员表示需要其他形式的评估来确定创造性写作教学方法的有效性。〔8〕等级和评价不应以

---

〔1〕 Leki, I., Reciprocal themes in ESL reading and writing. In T. J. Silva & P. K. Matsuda (Eds.), *Landmark essays on ESL writing* , Mahwah, N. J.: Hermagoras Press, 1993, p173-190.

〔2〕 Vandrick, S., Literature in the teaching of second language composition. In B. Kroll (Ed.), *Exploring the dynamics of second language writing* , Cambridge ; New York: Cambridge University Press, 2003, p263-286.

〔3〕 Grainger, T., Goouch, K., & Lambirth, A., *Creativity and writing: Developing voice and verve in the classroom*, London ; New York: Routledge, 2005.

〔4〕 Sturgell, I., Touchstone texts: Fertile ground for creativity, *The Reading Teacher*, 61 (5), 2008, p411-414.

〔5〕 O'toole, J., *Doing drama research: Stepping into enquiry in drama, theatre and education*, City East, Qld: Drama Australia, 2006.

〔6〕 Cahill, H., Profound learning: Drama partnerships between adolescents and tertiary students of medicine and education, *NJ*, 29 (2), 2005, p59-71.

〔7〕 Ferris, D., Introduction. In L. L. Blanton & B. Kroll (Eds.), *ESL composition tales: Reflections on teaching*, Ann Arbor: University of Michigan Press, 2002.

〔8〕 Hamp-Lyons, L., Writing teachers as assessors of writing. In B. Kroll (Ed.), *Exploring the dynamics of second language writing*, Cambridge; New York: Cambridge University Press, 2003.

表面误差为依据，而应在一段时间内参照多个写作样本。基于“写作者即思想者”的观点，也出现了一种用认知发展级别来评价写作者的倾向，强调写作在发展批判性思维中的作用。一些人主张使用作品集作为写作的形成性进行评价，[1]以增强写作者的信心和掌握程度。Godinho 和 Wilson 对实证主义和建构主义范式中的作品集进行了区分。前者的目的是评估受外部定义和规范约束的学习结果；而后者的目的是为学习者的学习活动构建意义提供一种手段，这可能是一个不断发展的过程。因此，重点应该放在如何从学生视角，选择那些能反映他们个人成长和进步的作品上。

为了支持学生作为写作者的创造性发展，教师不仅需要知识、技能和理解力，还需要具有容忍不确定性、承担风险等情感能力，最重要的是，教师本人也要成为有艺术性和创造性的写作者。

综上所述，在本研究中，创造性主要表现在写作中的表达能力上。它更多地依赖于一个人的学习风格和个性，而非智力。因此，它可以通过教育在每个人身上得到极大的发展和丰富。本节回顾了创造性写作的各种概念，特别是在二语语境中的概念，包括创造力与传统之间的紧张关系、创意写作的社会文化本质、创意写作和创造性的空间之间的联系，还包括教师机构和现代科技、文学、艺术和戏剧的作用以及评估方法。

3.4 二语写作中的跨文化研究

由于“文化”是本研究的一个关键概念，而“文化”一词在文学中的定义也一直存在争议，所以在介绍有关二语写作的跨文化研究文献之前，有必要澄清“文化”和“跨文化能力”的含义。

3.4.1 文化观念的转变

根据 Scollon and Scollon[2]的研究，“文化”一词在英语中有两种常见用

〔1〕 Mai, X., *Task based English writing strategy through the platform of school web system*, Paper presented at the Sixth National Symposium on English Writing Teaching and Research, Beijing, 2008.

〔2〕 Scollon, R., & Scollon, S. W., *Intercultural Communication: A discourse approach* (2nd ed.). Cambridge, Mass.: Blackwell, 2001.

法：高级文化和人类学文化。高级文化侧重于知识和艺术成就，而人类学文化则指某个群体的思想、交流或行为的任何方面，这种文化赋予他们独特的身份，并用于组织其内部的凝聚力和归属感。后一种定义符合 Connor[1]对“已接受”的文化观的定义，这种观点主要以地理和国家主体为基础。Scollon and Scollon 的研究确定了四种对跨文化交流最为重要的文化因素：意识形态、社会化、话语形式和面子系统。

然而，后现代理论更倾向于“抹去所有群体身份的界限”[2]，并将它们分裂成个体。一方面，Corbett[3]认为，所有的文化都是“相互牵扯在一起的，没有一种文化是单一的和纯粹的，它们都是混杂的、异质的、大相径庭的、非单一化的”。因此，文化的概念成为一个充满疑问的研究对象。此外，Corbett 认为，尽管从长远来看，全球的交流模式可能会削弱文化差异，然而，与此同时，这些文化差异呈现出新的活力，虽然在固定社会中看不到这种新的活力，但随着社会解体和文化的分裂会变得“明显”可见，并象征着区域对全球化的抵制。

Li, X. 的研究表明，即使文化能够接受变化，它也未必会失去其独特的文化身份。但是，这一身份并不是静态的或完全具有约束力的，相反，它具有内在的开放性和固有的不一致性。[4]例如，中国领土广阔且历史悠久，任何描述中国和中国文化的尝试都充满了泛泛而谈的危险，上海一位受过教育的年轻企业家、四川山区不识字的老农夫、马来西亚和澳大利亚的华人移民对中国和中国文化的描述会有很大的不同，但这不能否认大多数中国人确实存在一些共同点。中国文化和文明的许多传统是普遍的，并不取决于社会和地区的具体情况，中国学生必然会对这些传统有一定了解。

值得注意的是，从事文化研究的学者对于文化还有一些迥然不同的理解。Raymond Williams 是文化研究领域的一位杰出人物，他认为文化既不是“崇高

---

[1] Connor, U., *Contrastive rhetoric: Cross-cultural aspects of second-language writing*, Cambridge [England]; New York: Cambridge University Press, 1996.

[2] Li, X., Composing culture in a fragmented world: The issue of representation in cross-cultural research. In T. J. Silva & P. K. Matsuda (Eds.), *Second language writing research: Perspectives on the process of knowledge construction*, Mahwah, N. J.: Lawrence Erlbaum Associates, 2005.

[3] Corbett, J., *An intercultural approach to English language teaching*, Clevedon, Buffalo, Toronto, Sydney: Multilingual Matters, 2003.

[4] Eagleton, T., *The idea of culture*, Malden, MA: Blackwell, 2000.

而文明的成就”，也不是“奇特而独特的身份”，而是“平凡的、自然的、无理性的和理所当然的”。他把文化称为“一种完整的生活方式”，强调文化的直接和普遍存在。Richard Hoggart 是大众文化的积极倡导者，他通过新媒体和文化研究为重新评价“文化”开辟了道路。他将文化的定义从文学经典中的“伟大传统”扩大到包括流行文化的所有方面，如时装、舞蹈、电视等。

总之，全球流动性和群体间的“跨国化”给教育和研究带来了新的重大挑战。[1]在文化的诸多方面中，作者的目的是最直接地关注那些已经被证明影响跨文化交际的方面。本书中，作者认为日益全球化的世界更像是一个“文化拼盘”，而不是一个“大熔炉”[2]，并赞同把文化看作是“互动的习惯模式，社会实践的常规形式，符号的反复使用，价值和信仰的积淀体系”[3]。然而，在这个多元的社会中，作者将以一种更动态、更全面的视角来看待文化，并在解释文化对写作的影响中加入更多的文献依据。

3.4.2 语言与文化的关系

社会语言学家已经确认语言和文化之间存在紧密联系，这可以在新合成词“语言文化”（*linguaculture*）中得到最好的说明，这个词显示了语言与文化之间的密切联系。这种观点认为，文化渗透在语言使用中，是“日常语言使用的不变背景”。Kramsch 认为，语言以多种复杂的方式与文化联系在一起，因为语言“表达、体现和象征着文化现实”[4]。语言被视为是一个具有文化价值的符号系统，反映了文化的先入为主，限制了人们的思维方式。但是 Kramsch 也指出，人的语言和自身文化身份之间不存在一一对应的关系。

然而，过去的文化观倾向于将群体的一般行为和价值观与他们的语言知识和理解相分离。这些观点打破了文化和语言之间的联系，可能会导致教学

---

〔1〕 Rizvi, F., Global mobility and the challenges of educational research and policy. In T. S. Popkewitz & F. Rizvi (Eds.), *Globalization and the study of education*, Malden, MA: Blackwell Pub, 2009.

〔2〕 De Lacey, P. R., & Poole, M. E. (Eds.), *Mosaic or melting pot: Cultural evolution in Australia*. Sydney: Harcourt Brace Jovanovich Group (Aust.), 1979.

〔3〕 Corbett, J., *An intercultural approach to English language teaching*. Clevedon, Buffalo, Toronto, Sydney: Multilingual Matters, 2003.

〔4〕 Kramsch, C. J., *Language and culture*. Oxford: Oxford University Press, 1998.

和研究的两难境地：语言学经常忽视文化，跨文化研究经常忽视语言。因此，越来越多的人呼吁在语言教育中纳入文化因素，换句话说，就是将语言教学转变为“渗透着文化的交流实践”[1]。全球化的加速推进，增大了对具有更广泛的世界观和跨文化交际能力的多语种人才的需求。

美国有许多依靠跨文化能力或双文化、多元文化能力性质的学科。关于跨文化能力的构成，新的共识倾向于将其视为一组认知、情感及行为技能和特征，能够在各种文化背景下进行有效自如的交流互动。[2]跨文化能力是通过学习外国语言文化来超越自己单一世界观的能力。理解世界观的形成是跨文化能力的一个核心方面，换句话说就是理解语言和文化如何塑造一个人的世界观和其他人的世界观。

跨文化能力并不能通过“文化渗透”获得，双语化过程也不一定会产生二元文化，[3]跨文化能力是从学习外语和学习语言与文化如何在第一和第二语言互动中得到发展的。由于跨文化能力是本研究的一个关键概念，下文将继续对其进行讨论。

3.4.3　二语写作的跨文化研究

二语写作的跨文化研究主要集中在对比修辞领域。对比修辞学最初基于语言相对性的观点，即每种语言都对其使用者强加一种世界观，试图通过理解文化特殊性和语言共性来识别和解释二语作家所遇到的问题。自Kaplan1966 年首次进行二语写作的跨文化研究以来，便已发现英语和汉语写作之间的差异，并从社会政治和文化的角度探讨了产生差异的原因。对比修辞学家认为，不同的文化对写作有着不同的期待，这些期待被内化为不同的话语模式。不同的读者期望是跨文化写作差异产生的主要原因。因此，了解

---

〔1〕 Lo Bianco，J.，Preface. In J. Lo Bianco & C. Crozet（Eds.），*Teaching invisible culture*：*Classroom practice and theory*，Melbourne：Language Australia，2003，p4.

〔2〕 Bennett，J. M.，Transformative learning：Designing programs for culture learning. In M. A. Moodian（Ed.），*Contemporary leadership and intercultural competences*：*Exploring the cross-cultural dynamics within organizations*，Los Angeles：SAGE，2008.

〔3〕 Ng，B. C.，& Wigglesworth，G.，*Bilingualism*：*An advanced resource book*，London；New York：Routledge，2007.

学生对英语学习的期望是非常重要的。例如，以英语为母语的读者往往会被事实、统计数字和论证中的例证所说服，他们希望得到具体的例子，而不是泛泛而谈，并且最好可以在想法之间建立明确的联系，表明他们高度重视创造性。

对比修辞学因其弊端受到了批判，例如它对文化的静态和狭隘的理解、[1]过分强调书面文本，[2]以及不鼓励二语写作学生表达自己的语言文化特性的意识形态倾向。[3]后现代理论认为所有类别的身份都是“不稳定的、可渗透的、多元的”，这对对比修辞研究提出了特殊的挑战。针对这些批评，当前的对比修辞学正对其目标和方法进行修订，以更好地应对批判理论对文化研究的新影响、增强对地方特色和写作活动特殊性的敏感度、更多地关注权力和意识形态对各种环境的影响。

因为对二语写作教学中的应用研究非常有限，所以接下来的部分将主要回顾跨文化语言教学方法的文献。这些文献在西方和中国之间进行比较，以区分这一领域的理论差距和教学差异。

3.4.4 西方：英语教学的“文化转向”

近年来，文化元素融入外语教学的重要性得到了广泛认可。从 20 世纪 80 年代中后期开始，二语教学的跨文化教学法“促使人们重新审视关于语言的作用和语言课程目标的最基本假设”[4]。在不同文化间迁移的语言学习者是一种跨文化的学习者，因此便需要一种跨文化的学习和教学方法。通过这种方式，学习者不仅能够成为另一种语言的熟练使用者，而且能成为文化间的协调者，即文化外交官。

然而，目前形成的共识认为文化并不是通过自然浸泡而习得的，而是需

---

〔1〕 Kubota, R., & Lehner, A., “Toward critical contrastive rhetoric”, *Journal of Second Language Writing*, 13 (1), 2004, p7-27.

〔2〕 Scollon, R., “Contrastive rhetoric, contrastive poetics, or perhaps something else?” *TESOL Quarterly*, 31 (2), 1997.

〔3〕 Ramanathan, V., & Atkinson, D., “Individualism, academic writing, and ESL writers”, *Journal of Second Language Writing*, 8 (1), 1999.

〔4〕 Barthes, R., *The semiotic challenge*, Berkeley: University of California Press, 1994.

要通过努力才能被获得、被注意和被教授。[1]因此，在我们的教育中需要通过有意识的努力将无形的和普遍的宏观文化分解为具体的、可教授的材料。这就涉及教师角色和教学内容的复杂转变。学生对新知识的好奇心，[2]以及他们对经验和学习的批判性反思对于跨文化能力的发展至关重要。[3]

因此，语言教学行业正在经历一个重要的转变：从教授语言进行跨文化交流，即交际语言教学法（Communicative Language Teaching），到视语言为文化的跨文化语言教学法（Intercultural Language Teaching）[4]。交际语言教学法将语言视为弥合“信息鸿沟”的一种手段。它假定语言学习者如果能发展语言知识和技能，就能最终获得母语者的交际能力。这种语言观切断了语言学习中语言和文化发展之间的联系。与此相反，跨文化交际教学法意味着语言教学不再仅仅是讲授另一种语言文化，它还通过与目标语言文化的对比，向语言学习者讲授他们的母语文化。

跨文化语言教学法在承认语言的重要交际功能的同时，也强调其社会功能——跨文化的理解和调解。语言学习者应该接受培训，以便能够从知情理解的角度看待不同的文化。跨文化交际教学法将语言学习定位为一种双重努力，即学习者通过比较外国和本国文化，可以了解语言文化形成的原因，从而有机会重新审视自己认为“理所当然”的文化习惯和思想，了解到这不过是众多世界观中的一种，而不是“唯一”的一种，从而拓展语言教学的传统界限。因此，了解世界观的形成是跨文化能力的一个核心方面。从这个意义上来讲，语言教学对当代世界具有重要的社会意义。

跨文化语言教学法的一个主要目标，是在多元化的世界中创造一个真正

〔1〕 Crozet, C., & Liddicoat, A., The challenge of intercultural language teaching: Engaging with culture in the classroom. In J. Lo Bianco, A. Liddicoat & C. Crozet (Eds.), *Striving for the third place: Intercultural competence through language education*, Melbourne: Language Australia, 1999.

〔2〕 Bennett, J. M., On becoming a global soul: A path to Engagement during study abroad. In V. Savicki (Ed.), *Developing intercultural competence and transformation: Theory, research, and application in international education* (1st ed.), Sterling, Virginia: Stylus, 2008.

〔3〕 Hoff, J. G., Growth and transformation outcomes in international education. In V. Savicki (Ed.), *Developing intercultural competence and transformation: Theory, research, and application in international education* (1st ed.), Sterling, Virginia: Stylus, 2008.

〔4〕 Garcia, O., “Review”, *The Modern Language Journal*, 85 (2), 2001, p332-334.

跨文化的“第三空间”。这是一个“来自不同文化和语言背景的交际者相遇并成功交流的无边界交汇点”[1]。可以通过跨文化的“探索”来实现，即在个人和人际间的创造过程中就差异进行协商。[2]跨文化语言教学法的最终目的是帮助学习者抵制文化、语言和话语霸权，并通过学习外语文化来超越他们单一的世界观，逐步提高跨文化能力。这个目标可以从三个层面来说明：学习文化、比较文化和跨文化探索。

总之，外语的教与学始终是“一个跨文化的过程”，教师向学习者介绍“挑战和改变他们对世界的看法以及他们在特定社会和群体中的文化身份”的学习方法。[3]这就赋予了语言从业人员巨大的责任，并要求对教师进行适当的教育。对学习者而言，培养跨文化能力不仅仅是学习文化和对比文化，也是一种探索本国语言文化和外国语言文化能够实现真正的平等和对话的“第三空间”的能力。

3.4.5 中国：跨文化教育和语言教育现状

直至20世纪80年代，培养学生跨文化意识和能力的重要性才引起了中国语言研究者和教育工作者的关注。[4]1980年，许国璋发表了第一篇关于跨文化研究的里程碑式的文章，他在文中考察了一些“文化负载词”及其与英语教学的关系。不久，语言教学中出现了更多关于文化主题的文章，一些教材也开始增加文化注释。[5]自80年代中期以来，一些大学开始开设跨文化交际课程，并出版了更多有关跨文化知识和实践的专著和教科书。1995年，第

---

〔1〕 Crozet, C., Liddicoat, A., & Lo Bianco, J. Introduction: Intercultural competence: From language policy to language education. In J. Lo Bianco, A. Liddicoat & C. Crozet (Eds.), *Striving for the third place: Intercultural competence through language education*, Melbourne: Language Australia, 1999, p1-20.

〔2〕 Crozet, C., & Liddicoat, A., The challenge of intercultural language teaching: Engaging with culture in the classroom. In J. Lo Bianco, A. Liddicoat & C. Crozet (Eds.), *Striving for the third place: Intercultural competence through language education*, Melbourne: Language Australia, 1999, p113-125.

〔3〕 Sercu, L., & Bandura, E., *Foreign language teachers and intercultural competence: An international investigation*, Clevedon, Buffalo, Toronto: Multilingual Matters Ltd, 2005.

〔4〕 曹洁：“高中英语教材中文化内容设计的问题及改进建议”，载《英语教师》2009年第8期。

〔5〕 Hu, W., *Crossing cultural barriers* (1 ed.), Beijing: Foreign Language Teaching and Research Press, 2002.

一届全国跨文化交际研究会在哈尔滨召开，此后每两年召开一次全国性会议。

基于对语言教学中文化成分认识的提高，课程教材研究所研究员和教育工作者曹洁对英语教材的编写提出了一些实用的建议：①除了引进外来文化外，还需要对我国本土文化和目标文化进行比较，以加深学生对本土文化的理解；②我们要像研究构词法中的前缀、后缀和词根一样挖掘语言符号的文化渊源，激发学生学习的兴趣，扩大词汇量，加深他们对语言和文化之间联系的理解；③在理解练习中，增加与文化理解相关的问题或活动，锻炼学生思维，增强文化意识。总之，曹洁鼓励英语教材编写者在教材中明确文化成分，要努力提高教师的文化意识，为教师提供新的教学手段，此外还应将文化因素纳入教学评估。

其他学者也倡导在语言教育中培养跨文化意识。胡文仲在《超越文化的屏障》一书中对跨文化交际进行了简要的概述，一方面，强调跨文化意识的重要性，并指出跨文化交际的一些障碍。另一位学者胡超就如何提高跨文化交际能力给我们提供了非常实用的建议。他指出，语言教学要以案例为基础，教材应将重点放在问候、恭维、商务谈判、幽默分享等文化行为上，并建议通过课堂活动、话题讨论、问题自查和资源补充对这些技能进行反思和练习。另一本由王振亚所著的《以跨文化交往为目的的外语教学》一书中基于韩礼德的功能语法，特别是语篇理论，阐述了跨文化语言教育的若干关键问题，包括跨文化教育的现状、语言与文化的关系、跨文化能力、教材的选择与安排、国外理论、教学程序与评价等。此外，经济学家郎咸平还撰写了一些期刊文章，论述在中美商业互动中认识跨文化交流中的文化差异的重要性。

有学者提醒我们，在外语教学和外语文化教学中，有两种危险是需要警惕的，就是既不能过分强调也不能低估差异。因为人们，尤其是初学者，在接触“外国”事物时，容易产生“思维障碍”。如果教师错误地过分强调文化之间的差异，可能会给学习者增加更多的心理负担，使他们在利用现有知识解决这些差异时犹豫不决。相反，过分强调共同特征也可能是危险的，因为它可能误导学生将自己的行为视为唯一的常态的文化标准，并将自己的行为准则强加于与自己交往的人。培养高水平的文化意识的有效方法是让学生了解文化差异以及造成这些差异的文化和历史渊源。

总的来说，跨文化意识的重要性在文献中被广泛讨论，但其在实际教学中的应用还远远滞后于修辞。王振亚认为，这是因为文化教育中的一些重大问题没有得到解决。第一个问题是关于文化教材的选择。虽然一些教学大纲提出了培养学生跨文化交际能力和意识的必要性，但并没有列出语言教学中需要涉及的文化话题。所以老师们只能自己决定教什么和怎样教。文化教学中“随便”的态度削弱了文化教学在语言教学中的地位，因此，在过去的几年里没有取得显著的进展。第二个问题是如何将文化知识融入语言教学中。目前缺乏语言与文化教育相结合的理论和方法，所以通常的做法是“让语言和文化分道扬镳”。这样的文化教育就显得不足和肤浅。第三个问题是跨文化教育缺乏“文化描述”教材。没有对特定文化中的文化现象进行充分的描述，就很难对不同的文化进行比较。

总之，跨文化教育是基于语言规划的国家建设的重要组成部分。[1]我国的课堂教学尚处于未成熟期，迫切需要理论和方法来指导课堂教学。特别是如何通过英语写作教育培养学生的跨文化意识，在西方和中国都是一个有待深入研究的课题。

3.4.6 小　结

通过对上述文献的回顾，我们可以得出以下几个结论：

第一，在中国外语教学中，很少有关于批判性教学的文献和报道。尤其是缺乏深入的民族志研究来指导中国学校在实际教学过程中进行写作探索。因此，急需研发能够激发个人意义和身份建构的文化教学法。

第二，中国教育工作者和实践者已经认识到培养学生的创造力和跨文化意识的重要性，并努力在英语写作的教学和学习中引入更有创造性的方法。然而，这些努力并没有产生足够的影响以改变目前全国范围内写作教育的状况。其原因既可能是缺乏深入的民族志研究，也可能是我们的研究需要更坚实的理论基础。因此，这些研究往往不为其他群体所知，也不为其他群体所

〔1〕 Lo Bianco, J., Advantage and identity: Neat discourse but troubled union: Singapore's medium of instruction policy. In V. Vaish, S. Gopinathan & Y. Liu (Eds.), *Language, capital, culture: Critical studies of language in education in Singapore*, Rotterdam/Taipei: Sense Publications, 2007.

接受。

第三，跨文化语言教学，特别是如何在二语写作教学中应用跨文化教学，在国内和国际上都是一个较少研究的领域。因此，对这些方法进行理论建构，并设计具体的英语写作教学法是非常必要的。

总之，现有文献既提出了批判性教学法的需求，又为进一步研究批判性教学法和创造性写作实践提供了概念框架。然而即使在西方国家，这也是一个相对较新的领域，[1]其中一些理论仍然存在激烈的争论，[2]应当采取一种批判的态度来审视它们在目前和进一步研究中的有效性。

---

〔1〕 Feldman, D. H., & Benjamin, A. C., "Creativity and education: an American retrospective", *Cambridge Journal of Education*, 36 (3), 2006, p319-336.

〔2〕 Matsuda, P. K., & Silva, T. J., Introduction. In T. J. Silva & P. K. Matsuda (Eds.), *Landmark essays on ESL writing*, Mahwah, N. J.: Hermagoras Press, 2001, p241-256.

第四章

方法论与研究方法

一场幕后进行的方法论战争正在打响。

——North[1]

在本节开始之际，作者首先叙述了自己在博士研究过程中选择方法论的心路历程。这是一个登山新手的旅程，她面对眼前错综复杂的小径感到困惑迷茫，不知该走哪条路才是正确的选择。

4.1 作者对于方法论的探索

研究刚开始时，我对方法论和方法之间的区别感到困惑。渐渐地，我意识到研究方法是实际的研究技术，如调查、访谈、观察和实验；而方法论就像一副眼镜，通过眼镜你可以看到并进行你的研究。那么方法论从何而来呢？它源于“指导行动和产生研究的基本信念集”[2]的探究范式，而这些信念反过来又植根于哲学根源。

认识到哲学基础的重要性后，我转向了研究范式的阅读，并立即被实证

〔1〕 North, S., *The making of knowlege in composition: Portrait of an emerging field*, Upper Montclair, NJ: Boyton/Cook, 1987, p352.

〔2〕 Silva, T. J., On the philosophical bases of inquiry in second language writing: Metaphysics, inquiry paradigms, and the intellectual zeitgeist. In T. J. Silva & P. K. Matsuda (Eds.), *Second language writing research: Perspectives on the process of knowledge construction*, Mahwah, N. J.: Lawrence Erlbaum Associates, 2005, p7.

主义所吸引。我的第一反应是和学生一起做一个教学实验，来测试我预想的英语教学理论。带着“客观性”“有效性”“公正性”“普适性”等光荣的使命，我下定决心要在英语写作中发现未知的真理，并将其传播出去。

我的导师Trevor和Julie委婉地打消了我的这种雄心壮志。他们认为，基于个人经历的知识是非常有限的，我应该把目光投向更广阔的领域。在从最初努力将注意力从自己转移到他人身上之后，我始终被实证研究所吸引。在当时的我看来，只有经验证据才是科学有效的，所有其他类型的调查都会产生主观臆断。由于我的研究主要采用定性研究的方法，博士研究的头几个月里，我一直沉浸在定性的课程和文献中，对案例研究、访谈和观察进行了深入的了解。与此同时，我也阅读了叙事和民族志方面的书籍，这对当时的我来说既令人兴奋又令人困惑。

我第一年期末论文提案的标题是“中国高校创造性写作实践的民族志案例研究”，并从以下几个方面论证了该方法：

“我的研究是对一所中国大学十年间对创造性写作的探究的描述和解释。从学科定位上看，该研究属于民族志个案研究的范畴。在进行案例研究时，应当指出，这类研究并没有一套固定的方法论。在该研究中，叙事民族志对我的影响尤为明显，在整个调查、材料收集、材料分析和表达的过程中，都使用了叙事的方法。此外，我对自我民族志、批判民族志以及后结构主义民族志都很感兴趣。”

老实说，当我写这份报告的时候，我并不知道如何将叙事学方法融入我的研究中，也不知道如何把新的研究模式（如自我民族志）和我的写作结合起来。我在提案中加入这些元素是为了挑战自己并展示研究中可能采取的方向。

但是民族志和案例研究方法的结合立刻遭到了两位导师的质疑。他们说，“你仿佛一只脚踏在后实证主义，另一只脚踏在后现代主义”。后来，他们写了一篇论文来澄清这两个概念。他们认为，在定性研究范式的连续统一体中，案例研究似乎处于保守的一端，其特点是“有界性和特殊性”。相反，当代民族志则属于后现代主义的一端，关注的是现实生活语境的连通性和自然性。此外，这两种方法在研究人员的立场上可能略有不同，材料收集、分析和写作的方法也有所不同。

这些理论和方法上的讨论使我受益匪浅，因为它有助于突出我研究的哲学基础的重要性，并澄清我认为重要的一些问题。首先是我应该如何着手获取这些材料。需要做的不是捕捉参与者的故事，他们不像“散落在沙滩上的贝壳”那样客观存在；相反，研究者与参与者共同创造研究资料，换句话说，参与者的故事不是被“发现”而是被“构建”的。可见，叙事性访谈技巧是至关重要的。

另一个重要的问题是如何记录我的研究。结构主义在报道研究时常使用大量叙事描述，通过它们来真实再现多重现实。〔1〕在教育环境中，叙事是教育者和学生理解自身经历的一种特别有力的方式。〔2〕此外，我意识到叙事不仅是一种写作方式，也是一种看待我们研究的方式。研究人员需要在文本中明确、诚实地定位自己，既是参与者故事的叙述者，也是故事的共同建构者。简言之，从整体设计、研究框架到具体的文本和分析细节，整个研究是研究者建构的一个故事。〔3〕

基于以上对叙事的理解，自我民族志应运而生。虽然我对 Ellis，Bochner，Richardson 以及其他一些将个人故事用于研究写作的研究人员的作品很感兴趣，但我并没有足够的勇气公开宣称这是我的研究方法之一。有时，我试探性地向同事们提到我的叙事写作和自我民族志，他们似乎认为这些方法过于“前卫”而不能被“接受”。然后我学会了对我的研究方法保持缄默并反复思考一个两难的问题：我如何才能以一种“安全”的创造性的方法来研究和表现我对创造性写作的探索？

2008 年 5 月，在美国参加一场国际写作会议时，中国汶川大地震的噩耗令我感到震惊。除震惊与痛心外，我偶尔听到的一则对地震的报道意外地使

---

〔1〕 Patton, M. Q., *Qualitative research and evaluation methods* (3 ed.), Thousand Oaks, Calif.: Sage Publications, 2002.

〔2〕 Casanave, C. P., Uses of narrative in L2 writing research. In T. J. Silva & P. K. Matsuda (Eds.), *Second language writing research: Perspectives on the process of knowledge construction*, Mahwah, N. J.: Lawrence Erlbaum Associates, 2005.

〔3〕 Richardson, L. W., *Writing strategies: Reaching diverse audiences*, Newbury Park: Sage Publications, 1990.

我增强了对叙事的信心。一天晚上，我在旅馆休息室中看到电视在跟踪直播一对夫妇如何在废墟中找寻自己的孩子。我看到他们疯狂地在倒塌的瓦砾中挖掘寻找自己2岁的儿子。漫长的等待和寻找，数小时的徒手挖掘，一次又一次对孩子的呼唤，一次又一次希望的破灭，经过18个小时的绝望找寻，他们终于找到了那个血迹斑斑的小布包，那是他们被压碎了的爱和对生命的希望。

这个现场直播给人的感觉是无法描述的。当我擦干脸上的泪水，环顾四周时，我看到旅馆接待员在哭泣，清洁女工在哭泣，路人都停了下来，为这悲伤的场景哀悼。一种强有力的叙事超越了时间和空间，超越了媒体和政府的所有数字和言辞，瞬间将不同国籍、不同肤色的人紧紧连在一起，共同关注着远在万里之外的遇难者。

怀着对叙事的坚定信念，我以全新的状态投入研究。我相信叙事，包括自己和参与者的第一人称叙述将成为本书的重要部分。创造性写作和研究方法不可避免地会出现不确定性和模糊性，我决心冒着被嘲笑和被敌视的风险迎接这些挑战。

4.2　研究方法论

本研究是对中国学习者英语写作实践和理论的批判性反思，包括对一所中国大学（广东外语外贸大学）写作教学法的考察，记录了作者在英语写作学习、教学、实践和研究方面的经验，从而使跨文化写作方法理论丰富了英语写作的创造性源泉。总之，这些主题构成了本书的多层次叙述。所采用的研究方法主要包括叙事理论、民族志、批判教育学和文化研究。

4.2.1　叙事理论

叙事理论起源于解释性社会科学方法论（interpretive paradigm），强调有意义的社会行为、社会建构意义和价值相对主义。[1]反过来，解释方法论也

---

〔1〕 Neuman, W. L., *Social research methods: Qualitative and quantitative approaches* (6th ed.), Boston: Pearson/Allyn and Bacon, 2006.

可以将其哲学根源追溯到社会建构主义，它假设现实是由社会互动和人们的信仰所创造和塑造的。建构主义支持帮助民族志研究者在论文中使用大量的叙述性描述，通过直接揭示和引用个人视角、经验来捕捉和再现多重现实。这一目标可以通过“讲述和重述同一个故事”来实现，以引出对同一个问题的多种观点和视角。

正因如此，Bochner[1]呼吁在定性研究中进行“叙事转向”，将故事作为教与学的基础。同样，Merriam[2]认识到叙事能帮助民族志研究的读者，因为它所叙述的故事，强调按时间顺序的描述，并且强调对时间和地点进行个性化描述，这能为读者提供丰富的素材和体验。

叙事分析现在已经成为研究组织机构的一种特殊方法，它通过教学故事、关于学生的故事、学生讲述的故事、项目参与者的故事等方式进行研究。通过讲故事，他们不仅启发读者的思考，而且能产生直观感受，因为这些故事与读者对日常课堂的体验紧密联系，所以便于理解，也易于接受和相信。[3]此外，Czarniawska[4]将组织研究的过程抽象为讲故事的过程，即在组织中不断构建意义的过程。例如，广东外语外贸大学的教学创新故事并不是有待收集的“现成的机构事实”，而是由叙述者创造的。就本研究而言，是其参与者的故事，以及作者通过复述、分析和解释在本书中构建的故事。

在国际教育的背景下，叙事往往被用来“从整体上捕捉学生的学习状况”，因为用学生自己的语言讲述的故事通常比抽象地讨论潜在的文化冲突更吸引人、更具有启发性。[5]

第一人称叙事在第二语言写作研究中得到了广泛的应用，并用来呈现民

---

〔1〕 Bochner, A. P. , Narrative's virtues. *Qualitative Inquiry*, 7 (2), 2001, p131-157.

〔2〕 Merriam, S. B., *Qualitative research and case study applications in education* (2nd ed.), San Francisco: Jossey-Bass Publishers, 1998.

〔3〕 Maxwell, J. A. , *Qualitative research design: An interactive approach*, Thousand Oaks, Calif. : Sage Publications, 1996.

〔4〕 Czarniawska, B. , Narrative, interviews, and organizations. In J. A. Holstein & J. F. Gubrium (Eds.), *Handbook of interview research*, Thousand Oaks, Calif. ; London: Sage Publications, 2002, p733-749.

〔5〕 Lou, K. H. , & Bosley, G. , Dynamics of cultural contexts: Meta-level intervention in the study abroad experience. In V. Savicki (Ed.), *Developing intercultural competence and transformation: Theory, research, and application in international education* (1st ed.), Sterling, Virginia: Stylus, 2008.

族志访谈的语料，因为“第一人称叙述者能更好地传达教学中最引人入胜、最具启发性的教学故事”[1]。Hay 把第一人称叙事中的“我”称为“内在的我”，而不是“被压抑的我”，因为它能够使叙述者在进行自我表达和在故事中表现身份时感到自在。哪怕是没有“艺术细胞”或自我表现力的教师，也可能在叙事中表现出创造力，将个人和职业身份联系在一起。所有这些都呼吁我们超越真实，追求“叙事”。同样原因，自传也因其情感、个性和叙事特质而日益引起人们对身份建构研究的兴趣。

在本书中，教师的叙事，尤其是第一人称叙事是对广东外语外贸大学项目进行重构的重要工具。当事人讲述的故事不仅生动地再现了过去数年的教学创新过程，而且揭示了塑造这种创造性教学法的因素。不同教师对同一教学故事的讲述和复述，既能反映不同观点，也能揭示其中的矛盾与冲突。

另外，作者与导师的邮件往来展示了作者对创造性写作的探索方法。这些电子邮件，加上作者对其修辞特征和理论基础的分析评论，构成了一种更具创新性的二语写作学习方式，研究者电子邮件中的跨文化叙事也展示了一种新的研究以及撰写研究论文的方法。最重要的是，这些电子邮件阐明了文化认同、跨文化交流和从英语学习者变为英语作者的身份转变之间的必然联系。

反对在研究中采用叙事方法的学者认为，语言学习叙事可能会缺乏准确性和真实性，[2]研究人员在表现文化“他者”时，往往过于直观。对于这些批评，Brodkey 回应道，所谓的“客观事实”不会、也不应该减少我们对叙事的兴趣：

> 一个人研究故事并不是因为它们是真实的，而是和人们讲述故事的原因一样，是为了了解别人如何理解他们的生活：他们所考虑的和不愿考虑的；他们认为值得思考的和不值得思考的；他们所提出的和不愿意讨论的生活问题和困惑。

---

[1] Hay, T., & White, J., Beyond authenticity. In T. Hay & J. Moss (Eds.), *Portfolios, performance and authenticity*, Frenchs Forest, N. S. W.: Pearson Education Australia, 2005, p74-87.

[2] Bailey, K. M., & Nunan, D. (Eds.). *Voices from the language classroom: Qualitative research in second language education*, New York: Cambridge University Press, 1996.

综上所述，中国英语学习者的整个二语写作实践可以看作是一种元叙事，由一系列叙事共同组成，包括广东外语外贸大学的教改故事，本人二语写作的学习、教学和研究的历程，研究对象的叙事等。

4.2.2 民族志

本研究采用民族志的研究方法。广义上讲，民族志是一种方法论策略，用来提供人类社会的描述性文化知识。[1]该研究方法的选择是基于作者的研究问题，涉及中国学习者的二语写作实践，特别是其与文化、社会政治语境之间的互动关系。因此，除了文献研究和文本分析，深入了解参与这种创造性实践的特定人群可能会为本研究提供令人信服的证据和见解。

民族志研究通常是注重整体性的，因为只有在尽可能充分的环境中，才可能对人类有最深刻的理解，[2]该方法能较好地揭示创新写作参与者的社会文化因素。在当代，民族志，即文化研究，已经走向了后现代化和跨国化，并成为一种强大的“赋能的声音”。

本书中主要有两种类型的材料，一种是中国一所大学（广东外语外贸大学）的创造性写作项目，另一种是作者在英语写作学习和教学中的经验。研究广东外语外贸大学项目的方法论属于教育民族志的范畴，而本人的研究属于自我民族志的范畴。

教育民族志

那么，在教育背景下进行民族志研究时，应该达到什么样的目标呢？Gregory 广泛总结了如下研究目标：

（1）发生了什么？

（2）如何发生的？

---

〔1〕 Hitchcock, G., & Hughes, D., *Research and the teacher*, London; New York: Routledge, 1989.

〔2〕 Denzin, N. K., & Lincoln, Y. S., Introduction: The discipline and practice of qualitative research. In N. K. Denzin & Y. S. Lincoln (Eds.), *Collecting and interpreting qualitative materials* (2nd ed.), Thousand Oaks, Calif.: Sage, 2003.

（3）参与者如何看待事件？

（4）作为该项目的成员需要什么条件？

（5）进行了哪些社会和学术学习？

因此，民族志学者应该描述以下研究内容：

（1）背景或语境；

（2）团队成员；

（3）具体的社会互动；

（4）互动的产物。

教育民族志与个案研究不同，后者以个体作家和学习者为研究对象，是"对写作和学习写作的高度个性化和特殊性过程的研究"[1]。而教育民族志"定义了一个群体，以及成为群体成员意味着什么和参与特定群体会发生什么"[2]。进行课堂民族志研究的教师研究人员面临的特殊困难是，民族志学者描述而非判断正在发生的事情。他们只考虑重复出现的行为模式，并推断出交互中的成员规则。

当然，民族志在教育研究方面也存在着局限性。例如，第一，学校不是完全"自然"的环境，因此可能不会产生纯"自然"的研究资料，尽管有些材料是个人形式的；[3]第二，民族志工作者的重点是提供一个群体的描述，而不是群体内的个人的描述；第三，民族志作为一种单一的研究方法可能不足以为研究问题提供一个完整可信的答案。辅以对特定个体的研究，比如对研究者本人的研究，将是对本书研究方法的必要补充。

自我民族志

教育民族志使我对过去数年在广东外语外贸大学发展起来的一种创造性

---

〔1〕 Bissex, G. L., & Bullock, R. H., Introduction. In G. L. Bissex & R. H. Bullock (Eds.), *Seeing for ourselves: Case-study research by teachers of writing* (1st ed.), Portsmouth, N. H.: Heinemann, 1987.

〔2〕 Gregory, E., Taking decisions. In J. Conteh, E. Gregory, C. Kearney & A. Mor-Sommerfeld (Eds.), *On writing educational ethnographies: The art of collusion*, Stoke on Trent, UK; Sterling, VA: Trentham Books, 2005a.

〔3〕 Kearney, C., Honor and authenticity: The methodology chapter. In J. Conteh, E. Gregory, C. Kearney & A. Mor-Sommerfeld (Eds.), *On writing educational ethnographies: The art of collusion*, Stoke on Trent, UK; Sterling, VA: Trentham Books, 2005, p107-120.

的写作教学法有了丰富的认识，而自我民族志则促使我既要向内看，也要向外看。[1]自我民族志利用“自我来解释文化”，将“个人自我”和“学术自我”连接在一个故事中，这个故事可以“作为一个理论或理论陈述”。它鼓励将“个人自我”融入学术写作中，使作者作为研究者和被研究者的身份在本书中得到反思性的呈现。

在过去数年里，自我民族志的价值得到了越来越多的研究者和教师的认可。从二语习得研究者的角度来看，这种自传体叙事是了解学习者元语言意识、学习过程和策略的窗口。从教师的角度来看，民族志可以提高学习者对自身学习过程的认识，并且因其易于掌握和操作，还可以成为强有力的教学工具。

Mansfield[2]断言，“把自我作为生活经验和可识别意义的中心，已成为现代和后现代文化的决定性问题之一”。他认为，在西方社会，对自我的描述“已经成为我们理解自己生活的关键方式”。几十年来，人们一直关注自我意识、自我建设和赋能。[3]Robinson[4]强调了情感对于教育和创造力发展的重要性。他说，“一个没有感情的世界是不人道的”，“只有通过感情和理性，我们才能找到真正的创造力”。

Chang[5]在她的新书《自我民族志研究法》中鼓励研究人员“打开记忆之锁，写下你过去的片段，为你的文化分析和解释建立数据库”。她建议人们将注意力从“清理”或“缝补”信息点转移到积极地“将它们转化为具有文化意义的解释”。这就要求作者明确阐释个人经历和文化理解之间存在的内在联系和力量，以及这些阐释如何导致社会变革。

因此，民族志论文常以个人的、自传性的介绍开始，从而引出问题的定

---

〔1〕 Bochner, A. P., & Ellis, C., *Ethnographically speaking*: *Autoethnography*, *literature*, *and aesthetics*, Walnut Creek, CA: AltaMira Press, 2002.

〔2〕 Mansfield, N., *Subjectivity*: *Theories of the self from Freud to Haraway.* St Leonards, N. S. W.: Allen & Unwin, 2000.

〔3〕 Holstein, J. A., & Gubrium, J. F., *The self we live by*: *Narrative identity in a postmodern world*, New York: Oxford University Press, 2000.

〔4〕 Robinson, K., *Out of our minds*: *Learning to be creative.* Oxford: Capstone ; John Wiley, 2001.

〔5〕 Chang, H., *Autoethnography as method.* Walnut Creek, CA: Left coast Press, 2008.

义或需要研究的大问题。[1]本书从作者对写作的恐惧开始，讲述了成为作家的梦想是如何被之前的教育所扼杀，因此刺激了作者对于创造性教学法的追求，以消除中国英语学习者对写作的恐惧。自传体的故事为这一章设定场景、找到并提出问题。除了开头的故事，作者的学习、教学和实践写作的经验也被用作主要的研究材料，因为作者也是中国英语学习者之一，也是其研究的一个对象。

特别是在第一章，作者对批判性和创造性写作教学法的研究视角转向了作者自身。作者与导师的电子邮件往来反映了作者的生活、研究和思想，作为一种自我民族志来说明和阐明作者的创造性和跨文化研究的方法和理论。这种研究方法体现了 Laurel Richardson“写作是一种研究方法”的主张。作者认为，写作是一种“跨文化和内文化”的探究。通过写作和反思这些电子邮件的写作，作者开始构思新的写作教学法——跨文化教学法。

研究人员在进行民族志研究时，应避免沉迷于自我的倾向，以免忽视研究的目的。[2]作者在研究中尝试将“批判性”和“自我民族志”结合，并尝试在措辞上尽量精准。这一点要通过不断地自我反省和质疑以及对照优秀教育研究论文的标准来完成。[3]

对我而言，自我民族志是更大的挑战。鉴于论文写作传统的保守性和政治性，作为一名来自不同学术文化和传统的二语写作者，论文写作的过程很可能就是“淹没”自我的声音的过程。[4]遵守惯例虽具有安全性，但会产生单调的作品；相反，个性和写作的多样性可能会带来风险和负面的读者反应。我内心的声音在鼓励我，去塑造不断演化的作者和研究者身份，细细品味丰富的混合文本，让我的作者声音和我的知识一起增长。

---

〔1〕 Gregory, E., Tracing the steps. In J. Conteh, E. Gregory, C. Kearney & A. Mor-Sommerfeld (Eds.), *On writing educational ethnographies: The art of collusion* (pp. ix-xxiv), Stoke on Trent, UK; Sterling, VA: Trentham Books, 2005b.

〔2〕 Rosaldo, R., *Culture & truth: The remaking of social analysis*, Boston: Beacon Press, 1989.

〔3〕 Richardson, L. W., & Pierre, E. A. S., Writing: A method of inquiry. In N. K. Denzin & Y. S. Lincoln (Eds.), *The SAGE handbook of qualitative research* (3rd ed.), Thousand Oaks, CA: Sage Publications, 2005.

〔4〕 Viete, R., & Ha, P. L., The growth of voice: Expanding possibilities for representing self in research writing. *English Teaching: Practice and Critique*, 6 (2), 2007, p39-57.

4.2.3 批判理论和文化研究

批判理论是作者除了叙事和民族志之外的主要研究方法之一。本研究借鉴了读写与教育学以及文化与媒体研究中的批判理论，贯穿全文的三个主要概念是“赋能”“解放”和“平等”。

首先，批判教育学的一个基本特点是，所有学生不仅需要了解语言学习所蕴含的力量，还需要认识到他们有权利或义务质疑、抵制和挑战现状。因此，二语教师承担着为学生赋能的社会责任，引导学生认识包括写作惯例在内的语言的社会文化和政治性质，并通过协商新的写作议程来启动社会变革。其次，将中国学生从社会文化的约束中解放出来，探索适合其个人和文化需要的混合身份，是解决当前写作教育问题的有效途径。最后，在写作中探索跨文化空间的关键是认识和纠正不同语言和文化中的权力不平等。通过跨文化视角和跨文化主题的写作，可以拓宽自己的世界观，加深对本土语言文化和目标语言文化的理解，成为促进和平与平等的社会力量。这为我的研究奠定了思想和方法基础。

然而，二语教学领域的一些学者和教育工作者倾向于认为第二语言的写作是中立和不受价值观影响的。他们认为，与长期受批判性读写理论影响的母语写作不同，二语写作的目标，特别是目前流行的学术英语写作法，是帮助学生学习第二语言学术写作的规范和惯例，而不是对此加以质疑或抵制。[1]在我看来，这种实用主义或“妥协主义”与语言教育的“社会”和“文化”转向背道而驰。正如Pennycook[2]指出的，目前二语课堂应首先了解“学生的语境，而不是让他们学习一些既有的概念”。

除了批判理论，文化研究的理论也在很多方面对我的研究有所帮助。首先，它为重新界定“文化”开辟了道路，将其狭隘的定义从大学阅读清单所

〔1〕 Santos, T., Ideology in composition: L1 and ESL. In T. J. Silva & P. K. Matsuda (Eds.), *Landmark essays on ESL writing*, Mahwah, N. J.: Hermagoras Press, 1992.

〔2〕 Pennycook, A., *Critical applied linguistics: A critical introduction.* Mahwah, N. J.: L. Erlbaum, 2001.

定义的“伟大传统”扩大到劳动阶层的文化或大众文化。[1]其次，文化研究促使我们关注某一特定现象与意识形态、国籍、族裔、社会阶级和性别之间的关系。[2]在21世纪，文化研究就已开始分析区域和全球抵制西方霸权的形式。最后，文化研究非常重视“自我”。正如Mansfield[3]所说，“我”这个再小不过的日常生活中最常用的词，已经成为文化研究中最激烈最复杂的辩论和分析焦点。

文化研究范围的扩大带来了新的媒体和读写研究，涵盖了大众文化的所有方面，如时装、舞蹈、电视、电影和报纸等。文化和读写概念的扩充，使我们能够在写作课堂上利用各种文学、文化和媒体产品作为资源，探索语言和文化，而不是主要依靠经典文学。此外，全球化带来的“霸权”等文化交流中的权力关系失衡，促使我们探索一个对话双方处于平等地位的跨文化空间。

4.3　材料收集、分析和展示

4.3.1　材料收集

本研究的主要材料可分为三种。第一种是关于我写作经历的个人故事，大多来源于记忆、日记和《研究手记》，是经过多年收集整理得来的；第二种就是我和导师之间的往来邮件，它们一直保存在电子邮件文件夹和我的《研究手记》里；第三种是关于广东外语外贸大学的创新写作教学法，其材料收集来自很多渠道。下面将介绍收集广东外语外贸大学项目材料时所采用的方法。

为什么选择广东外语外贸大学？这些材料和参与者都是经过有目的的筛选的，也得到了大学和参与者本人的同意。目的性抽样因其信息丰富、具有启发性而被广泛应用于定性研究中。抽样的目的不是经验性的概括，而是要从正

---

〔1〕 Hoggart, R., *The uses of literac: Aspects of working class life, with special reference to publications and entertainments*, Harmondsworth: Penguin, 1958.

〔2〕 Storey, J., *Cultural theory and popular culture: An introduction* (3rd ed.), Harlow, England; New York: Pearson / Prentice Hall; Longman, 2001.

〔3〕 Mansfield, N., *Subjectivity: Theories of the self from Freud to Haraway*, St Leonards, N. S. W.: Allen & Unwin, 2000.

在研究的案例中得到启发。[1]

在中国所有的大学中，我选择广东外语外贸大学作为研究的样本，原因如下：

（1）广东外语外贸大学是中国外语研究的领军大学，拥有一支强大的教学科研队伍，锐意进取、敢于创新。广东外语外贸大学还通过会议、出版物、师资培训等方式对中国其他院校产生了广泛的影响。

（2）广东外语外贸大学在教学创新方面的研究和实践传统也是我选择它作为研究样本的重要原因之一。它是对外开放程度最高、改革力度最大的大学之一。在过去的20年里，广东外语外贸大学在英语写作方面进行了持续地系统性研究和探索，建立了一套完整的课程体系、教材、技术支持等基础设施。

（3）广东外语外贸大学位于广州，具有地理优势，便于通过引进外国教师和专家、向海外派遣工作人员以及进行各种国际交流与合作计划，与其他国家保持积极的沟通交流。

（4）在广东外语外贸大学就读的学生来自中国各地，有着不同的家庭背景和生活经历，因此他们将为研究提供最佳的多元化视角。

（5）2003-2012年间，我亲自参与了广东外语外贸大学的一些创新项目，因此，我一直密切关注广东外语外贸大学在课程改革方面的发展。参与这些项目使我能够以一个研究员的立场、以内部人员的角度看待他们的观点。

总之，选择广东外语外贸大学作为样本组织可以最大限度地扩大我们在有限的时间和实地考察中可以学到的东西的范围。

为什么要研究十年的内容呢？首先，纵向研究将有助于对这一专题进行更深入和历时的研究；其次，1999年以来，广东外语外贸大学对创造性写作进行了系统的探索；再次，广东外语外贸大学过去20年的文件保存得很好，也容易得到毕业生的联系方式，因此，中国二语写作者教育史上的这一段时期能够被很好地呈现出来，以供研究；最后，我获得了广东外语外贸大学的同意，以获取关于研究的所有信息，不仅如此，他们还同意应我的请求提供

[1] Patton, M. Q., *Qualitative research and evaluation methods* (3 ed.), Thousand Oaks, Calif.: Sage Publications, 2002.

必要的援助与合作。

参与者

要全面了解广东外语外贸大学近年来对写作教学的探索，需要倾听和重视多种声音。这是因为从各种来源获得的多种感知构成了多重的“现实”，研究者可据此得出有效的结论。为此，我选择了广东外语外贸大学约10名教师作为研究的参与者，包括创新教学法的发起人，以及教师队伍中的主要成员。为了将内部和外部的关键利益相关者都纳入研究当中，我特意采访了没有参与这个项目的教师，特别是那些对这个项目有不同看法的教师。采取的一项关键方法是让参与者讨论同样的话题，以便就同一问题提出不同的观点。

材料收集方法

广东外语外贸大学民族志研究中，采用了多种不同的研究方法，主要包括文献分析、观察参与者和叙事访谈。在资料收集过程中我注意保持开放、敏感、尊重的心态，密切关注项目和情况变化并积极应对，随时收集新出现的定性数据。

文献和文本分析

本研究主要对广东外语外贸大学十年间的教改历史进行研究，故文献回顾是不可或缺的研究方法。由于各种渠道提供的信息可能并不相同，有些历史资料也可能无法通过其他方法获得，比如课程设计、教材、写作样本等，故文献和文本分析对本研究非常重要。[1]

为了对相关文件进行系统的审阅，我查阅了以下文献：

（1）教学大纲：包括国家、大学、学院和系等级别的关于大学生整体发展、关于英语、特别是关于英语写作的大纲。

（2）课程设计：包括英语总体课程体系和英语写作课程。

（3）教材：教材以及写作课程的个人和集体教学计划。

---

〔1〕 Hodder, I., The interpretation of documents and material culture. In N. K. Denzin & Y. S. Lincoln (Eds.), *The handbook of qualitative research* (2nd ed.), Thousand Oaks, Calif.: Sage Publications, 2001.

（4）产品：写作样本、考试材料、教师点评、自制网站、作品集等。

（5）出版物：教科书、期刊文章、课程杂志。

（6）其他：报纸文章、演讲稿、函件、报告、会议记录。

这些资料来源广泛，包括大学管理部门、教师和学生个人、互联网和图书馆等。其中部分资料涵盖了十年的发展历史。作者将文献分析的结果与其他来源的数据分析结论相对照，并在本章的后部对分析框架进行介绍。

叙事访谈

询问他人生活的过程，并尽可能仔细地倾听，以便故事能够被理解和重述，这是一个迷人的、令人疲惫的过程，但也是一个刺激的过程；提问、倾听、理解和复述过程的好坏决定了研究本身的质量。

——May

访谈被认为是机构研究中叙事产生和传播的主要场所。[1]好的访谈可以帮助检查观察结果的准确性，并补充在观察中遗漏的信息。本研究中，访谈是在先前建立的熟悉和信任的基础上，通过正式和非正式的方式进行的。

在正式访谈中，作者主要采用半结构化访谈的方式，鼓励被访谈者将开放式问题发展成自己的趣闻轶事和话题。此外，还进行了多次非正式访谈，使被访谈者能够完全采取主动的态度。这种互动多发生在个人聊天、午餐约会、傍晚散步或课间休息时，能够引导出非常丰富和有趣的叙事。

提出好的访谈问题需要创造力和洞察力，而不只是机械地把研究问题转化成访谈指南。[2]为此，首先，要尝试预测具体的访谈问题在实践中会如何发挥作用。其次，尽可能找与被访谈者亲近的人一起，对访谈问题进行预演，以确定这些问题能否达到预期目的，需要如何修改。最后，还要通过各种渠道对广东外语外贸大学进行广泛调研，以获得更多的背景知识和参与者信息，

---

〔1〕 Czarniawska, B., Narrative, interviews, and organizations. In J. A. Holstein & J. F. Gubrium (Eds.), *Handbook of interview research*, Thousand Oaks, Calif.; London: Sage Publications, 2002, p733–749.

〔2〕 Johnson, J. C., & Weller, S. C., Elicitation techniques for interviewing. In J. A. Holstein & J. F. Gubrium (Eds.), *Handbook of interview research*, Thousand Oaks, Calif.; London: Sage Publications, 2002, p491–514.

从而拟定有意义的访谈问题。在访谈中，采访者尽量对被访谈者的非言语行为保持敏感，包括对特定问题的犹豫和防御性反应，这可能为数据分析提供额外的素材。

当然，访谈这种方法也存在局限性。例如，被访谈者可能对某些话题感到敏感，尤其是与同事关系有关的话题，或者对新教学法的负面看法。被访谈者的陈述可能会受到采访者或其他被访谈者的影响。有时采访者可能会无意识地把话题转到采访者感兴趣的方面。因此在访谈中，我试图通过以下策略将这些影响最小化：

第一，我试图与被访谈者建立融洽的关系，尤其是师生关系。对于被访谈者，我说明了我作为研究人员而非检查员或评价者的角色，目的是了解更多关于二语写作的实践行为。我强调了我们拥有英语写作研究和教改的共同使命。我向他们保证，他们的身份和反应将只用于我的研究，并将受到法律的保护。这样，被访谈者在回答时可能会更加放松。

第二，我还试图创造一种鼓励学生和老师反思自己写作实践学习的氛围。为了参与这项有助于提高对英语写作理解的研究，被访谈者可能需要放弃一些个人兴趣爱好，从而为研究提供更积极和真实的反馈。

第三，为了避免被访谈者提供不真实的想法，作者特别关注收集资料中出现的不一致性。[1] 在本研究中，我有意捕捉并展示了这些不同的声音，因此我特别寻找了对创新不太积极的、对教学直言不讳进行批判的、在学习特别是写作等方面存在问题的学生。

电子邮件交流

电子邮件通信是我收集资料的一个重要工具。一方面，它为广东外语外贸大学项目提供了源源不断的资料；另一方面，我和导师之间的电子邮件可以用来阐明我从一个胆小怵写的二语学习者成长为一名优秀英语写作者的转变过程。

---

〔1〕 Maxwell, J. A., The value of a realist understanding of causality for qualitative research. In N. K. Denzin & M. D. Giardina (Eds.), *Qualitative inquiry and the politics of evidence*, Walnut Creek, CA: Left Coast, 2008, p163-180.

作为一种新兴的数据收集方法，许多研究者认为电子邮件通信是很有用的研究工具。[1]它非常适合本研究的方法论，原因如下：

首先，互联网具有更快、更便宜、能够接触更广泛的地理区域的优势。当我从实地考察回来时，它也起到了继续收集数据的作用。

其次，电子邮件可以轻松、廉价地转换成可用度极高的资料，比如叙事。White[2]认为电子邮件交流包含了一些信件、期刊写作的要素。它让参与者有时间思考自己的答案，因此它是让参与者提供大量深思熟虑的回答的一种可靠方式，并且它不会让人觉得咄咄逼人而感到压力。

最后，电子邮件通信的另一个重要特征是书写过程中权力关系的重新分配，以及可以通过电子邮件揭露多重身份。通过与一名日本学生的电子邮件互动，Casanave[3]发现，身份和权威是如何通过这个过程协商的，这个过程既强化了教师和学生之间的权力失衡，又能“平衡”这种失衡。这也是我能够在与导师的电子邮件交流中更自由、更大胆地写作的原因之一。

当然，电子邮件在数据收集方面也有缺点。例如，没有面对面的交流，采访者与被访谈者无法进行非语言行为的交流。因此，在开始电子邮件交流之前，如果能与被访谈者建立联系，能够在一定程度上弥补这一缺陷。

除了面对面访谈和电子邮件交流外，在一些情况下还可以采用电话访谈的形式，如对不能或不愿意参加面对面访谈的被访谈者、对计算机和互联网的使用有技术困难的人进行访谈时，或对访谈信息进行补充和核对时都可以借助电话来交流。

观察

除了文献分析和访谈，通过观察我看到了在广东外语外贸大学英语写作

---

〔1〕 Fontana, A., Postmodern trends in interviewing. In J. A. Holstein & J. F. Gubrium (Eds.), *Handbook of interview research*, Thousand Oaks, Calif.; London: Sage Publications, 2002, p161-175. Gaiser, T. J., & Schreiner, A. E., *A guide to conducting online research*, London: Sage, 2009. Heflich, D. A., & Rice, M. L., Educational research online: Lessons learned. *International Journal of Educational Telecommunications*, 7 (4), 2001, p393-340.

〔2〕 White, J., *Questions of identity: the researcher's quest for the beginning teacher*. Unpublished Thesis (Ph D), University of Melbourne, Dept. of Learning and Educational Development, 2004.

〔3〕 Casanave, C. P., *Controversies in second language writing: Dilemmas and decisions in research and instruction*, Ann Arbor: University of Michigan Press, 2004.

的日常现实中实际发生的事情。我还接触到了广东外语外贸大学项目的其他维度，比如师生之间的课堂互动，这是通过其他方法无法轻易接触到的。

我观察了使用和未使用新教学法的写作课堂，还亲自参加了一些课外写作活动，如戏剧表演和阅读交流会。与此同时，我也观察过老师们的会议和课后互动。在观察过程中，我尽量注意中心时间及其背景条件，为后续分析做好准备。在完成每一个观察后，我都做了详细记录，并尽快进行整理分析。作为一种开放式的探究，观察使我能够不断地重新审视和解释通过其他来源获得的数据，这使得我的发现更加全面、真实和充满冲突。

4.3.2 资料分析

由于所有的分析和解释都是"特定权力和知识体制的产物"[1]，资料分析的核心问题不是有效性和可靠性的方法论问题，而是如何忠实地、合乎道德地展示和分析我所得到的信息，如何在自己作为作者的约束和限制下尽可能地再现被访谈者的表达意图。

在教育民族志资料分析中，对事件进行解释的责任不仅在于研究者，也在于读者。Brice[2]阐述了二语写作定性研究中数据编码的难点，要求在研究报告中对数据进行详细的长篇描述。

由于我的大部分资料都是文本形式的，所以可以进行文本分析。文本分析的技巧有很多，例如用结构主义的术语分析叙事的传统方法。叙事结构，更准确地说，半叙事结构应理解为深层符号学结构，而不是表面结构。虽然后者表面上属于可观察的范围，但前者被认为是话语的基础。

文本分析将叙事访谈视为一种文化形式的记录，因为这样的故事是建立在已有的故事情节和讲述故事的方式之上的。[3]口头叙述中发现的思想、图

---

[1] Holstein, J. A., & Gubrium, J. F., Interpretive practice and social action. In N. K. Denzin & Y. S. Lincoln (Eds.), *Strategies of qualitative inquiry* (3nd ed), Thousand Oaks, CA: Sage, 2008, p192.

[2] Brice, C., Coding data in qualitative research on L2 writing: Issues and implications. In T. J. Silva & P. K. Matsuda (Eds.), *Second language writing research: Perspectives on the process of knowledge construction* (pp. 159-175). Mahwah, N. J.: Lawrence Erlbaum Associates, 2005.

[3] Passerini, L., *Fascism in popular memory: The cultural experience of the Turin working class*, Cambridge [Cambridgeshire]; New York; Paris: Cambridge University Press, 1987.

像和语言策略构成了 Passerini 所说的“日常生活的象征秩序”，而阅读访谈的象征秩序能够阐明参与者在其他方面看不见的主观体验。

对我来说，主要的分析策略是备忘录、分类（如编码和主题分析）和情境化（如话语分析、叙事分析）：

备忘录

备忘录是定性分析的基本技术。它不仅能捕捉研究人员对数据的分析思维，而且能促进这种思维，深化分析见解。[1]本人的《研究手记》既是备忘录也是日记，记录了我的研究和写作历程，以及我个人在写作过程中的体验和感想。我相信除了备忘录的功能外，《研究手记》还可以被视作研究材料，以说明本人的创作过程。同时，《研究手记》还可以解释我在研究中的身份和立场。

分类

我的主要分类策略是进行编码。首先，对材料进行分析并将其重新分类，以便于在这些类别内部和类别之间进行比较；其次，将数据分类为更广泛的主题和问题。为了不丢失原始上下文（常被称为“上下文剥离”），我将编码与相应的资料链接在一起。

情境化

在分析数据时，我的目的不是试图“发现”意义，也不是根据“隐藏”的真理来解释文本，而是最终“孕育、想象、体验文本的多元性、文本意义指向过程的开放性”。[2]为此，我将批评话语分析、语篇分析和叙事分析中的分析策略作为我的主要工具来将材料语境化。

---

〔1〕 Maxwell, J. A., *Qualitative research design: An interactive approach*, Thousand Oaks, Calif.: Sage Publications, 1996.

〔2〕 Barthes, R., *The semiotic challenge*, Berkeley: University of California Press, 1994.

根据 Fairclough[1]的三维分析框架，我的分析构成了对文本的语言和互文特征的描述，对话语实践的解释，以及对话语过程和社会过程的关系之间的解释。这种方法将对具体语篇样本的“微观分析”与对话语变化的“宏观”分析联系起来。由于它将语言使用、文本解释和社会文化解释联系起来，所以这种方法对文化分析非常有价值。

它不仅关注文本或话语，还关注话语与社会生活其他要素之间的关系，关注过程及其随着时间的推移发生的变化。[2]在文本分析中，应该特别注意理解文本的“未说”、缺失和隐含的内容，因为它们通常可以“对被认为是给定的、常识的东西提供有价值的见解”。本人在分析广东外语外贸大学的话语实践中，强调了常规与创新之间的冲突，即语篇形式体现出的不同程度的同质性或异质性，因为正是这种文本的特性，使其成为社会文化过程和变化的敏感指标。

Fairclough 提醒我们，语篇分析是分析原文语篇样本的最有效方法。本研究中，有一些中文资料需要翻译成英文。在分析这些数据的时候，我特别注意了原文的文本特征，如果这些特征在翻译过程中丢失了，就要回归原英文版本中加以识别。

如果 Fairclough 的方法可以被看作是分析的一个“垂直”维度，将注意力从表面的文本特征引向更深层次的话语和社会层面，那么 Scollon and Scollon[3]的分析框架为分析提供了一个“水平”蓝图的有效补充。

广东外语外贸大学教师欧阳护华在对中国教师教育项目的研究中，成功地运用了 Scollon and Scollon 提出的提纲，其理论基础是话语系统的四个主要元素：思想意识、社会化、话语形式和面子系统。因此，笔者提出了四个关键问题，以及一些在话语系统研究中要解决的次要问题：

（1）思想意识：该群体的历史、社会、思想意识特征是什么？

---

〔1〕 Fairclough, N., *Language and power*, London ; New York: Longman, 1989.

Fairclough, N., *Critical discourse analysis: The critical study of language*. London ; New York: Longman, 1995.

〔2〕 Fairclough, N. , *Language and globalization*, Abingdon, OX; New York, NY: Routledge, 2006.

〔3〕 Scollon, R., & Scollon, S. W., *Intercultural communication: A discourse approach* (2nd ed.), Cambridge, Mass.: Blackwell, 2001.

（2）社会化：如何认识成员身份？

（3）话语形式：首选的交际形式是什么？

（4）面子系统（社会结构）：首选或假定的人际关系是什么？

综上所述，批评性话语分析、语篇分析等分析工具可以为课题研究提供一系列理论视角和分析方法，使我们能够在全球化的社会分析中纳入文本分析。通过关注“话语”，我们注意到预先构建的结构特征，以及群体在特定方向上将其改变的战略行动，这是批判研究的主要关注点之一。

4.3.3 表现方式

本研究采用多层叙事的方式进行报道。它是将作者置于文本之中，将文本置于社会科学文献和传统之中的一种策略。[1]作为“CAP 民族志”(creative analytical practices)，即创造性分析写作实践的一种形式，多层叙事被包括 Lather & Smithies[2]和 Ellis[3]在内的许多研究者青睐，它通过重视研究人员的立场和经验，改变了传统的社会科学写作。后现代理论认为写作总是局部的、当地的和情境的，写作者不管多么努力地压制自己，总是会在写作中出现。“CAP 民族志”则认为研究产品，也就是写作不能与作者、写作方式或认识方法分离。

民族志研究的表现形式引起了人们的广泛关注。一方面，它可能产生太多的详细叙述，太大的阅读量；另一方面，叙事民族志因模糊了社会科学和文学写作之间的界限而受到批判。[4]对此，Richardson[5]表示，民族志研究

---

〔1〕 Richardson, L. W., & Pierre, E. A. S., Writing: A method of inquiry. In N. K. Denzin & Y. S. Lincoln (Eds.), *The SAGE handbook of qualitative research* (3rd ed.), Thousand Oaks, CA: Sage Publications, 2005.

〔2〕 Lather, P. A., & Smithies, C., *Troubling the angels: Women living with HIV/AIDS*. Boulder, Colo.: Westview Press, 1997.

〔3〕 Ellis, C., & Bochner, A. P. (Eds.), *Composing ethnography: Alternative forms of qualitative writing*. Walnut Creek, Calif.: AltaMira Press, 1996.

〔4〕 Crotty, M., *The foundations of social research: Meaning and perspective in the research process*, St Leonards, NSW: Allen & Unwin, 1998.

〔5〕 Richardson, L. W., & Pierre, E. A. S., Writing: A method of inquiry. In N. K. Denzin & Y. S. Lincoln (Eds.), *The SAGE handbook of qualitative research* (3rd ed., pp. 959-978). Thousand Oaks, CA: Sage Publications, 2005.

是建立在认真研究和实地考察的基础上的，而创作部分主要在于写作，写作应该坚持“高而难的标准”。为判断这种非传统的个人和创造性的民族志写作的质量，她提出了以下四个具体标准：

（1）实质性的贡献。这篇文章有助于我们理解社会生活吗？作者是否展示了一种言之有据的社会科学观点？这篇文章看起来是“真实的”吗？它对“真实”的文化、社会、个人或集体意识的描述可信吗？

（2）审美价值。这并非表示降低标准，而是增加了另一个标准。这部作品在审美上成功了吗？创造性分析实践的使用是否对文本进行了解释？文本是否达到了具有艺术性、令人满意、深刻且不枯燥的程度？

（3）反思性。具有主体性的作者是如何成为本书的生产者和产物的？是否有足够的自我意识和自我曝光，让读者就观点作出独立判断？作者是否主动对研究标准和表述水平承担责任？

（4）影响力。它能在情感和知识上对“我”产生影响吗？它是否提出了新的问题，或促使“我”去进行研究、思考、写作或者采取行动？

Richardson 的写作标准将成为我评价自己研究和写作的主要标准，尽管我知道这需要熟练的创造性写作、敏锐的观察和直面自我、质疑自我的勇气。

4.4　方法论的局限性

在进行民族志和叙事研究时，我们应该意识到这些方法固有的局限性，并努力将其最小化。

4.4.1　普适性

定性研究方法（包括民族志和叙事研究）的一个重要问题就是普适性。但本研究比较注重特殊性，而不是普适性，因为生活中有些普适性之外的特殊经历，“我们总是渴望了解这些‘真实’的经历，因为它们散发出真实的特殊芳香”。[1]

---

〔1〕 Rosen, H., Stories of stories: A postscript by Harold Rosen, In B. Rosen (Ed.), *And none of it was nonsense: The power of storytelling in school*, London: MGP, 1988, p163-172.

此外，后现代理论深刻地影响了我对理论化的理解。今天，对理论的宏大叙事的探索已经被对更局部、更微观知识的关注所取代，理论被认为适合于特定的问题和具体的情况。[1]我们从日常细节中研究社会碎片，而不是元理论。通过小的知识碎片，我们可以对以前的概括性理论进行修订和补充。

4.4.2 系统数据

定性研究的另一个主要关注点是如何系统地开发研究证据。这需要在可能的情况下强调多种方法。作为一名研究人员，我总是问自己：在不同的情况下，数据是以不同的方式从足够多的参与者那里以不同的甚至冲突的视角获取的吗？令我欣慰的是，大多数时候答案都是肯定的。

同时我也意识到“证据在道德或伦理上从来都不是中立的”[2]，这些数据是通过我对理论和研究兴趣的过滤来选择的，而我的选择很大程度上是基于对研究性质的理论预设。也就是说，基于对研究性质的理论预设我选择了研究主题，决定以广东外语外贸大学作为样本；选择了要采访的教师和要观察的班级；我提出的面试问题引导讨论朝着某个特定的方向进行；我作为最后书稿的唯一作者，在论文中采取或抛弃哪些数据。

在阐明这一立场时，我并不是在宣称自己的研究如何客观独立；相反，我知道自己对研究结果不可避免地产生影响。总之，与强调研究发现和结果的传统研究不同，本研究的研究过程是结果的一部分。

还有一个问题是，我的理论预设可能会影响数据的选择和分析。诚然，没有一个研究者能够以完全“开放”的心态进行科学研究，并且必须有初步的理论来检验、质疑、支持、否定证据。为了尽量减少这种担忧，我试图保持尽可能广泛的初步理论框架，以便探索新的领域或新的理论结构。此外，自省式的自我民族志是检验和展示先前想法、表明研究中的价值观和立场的有效方法。

---

〔1〕 Fontana, A., Postmodern trends in interviewing. In J. A. Holstein & J. F. Gubrium (Eds.), *Handbook of interview research*, Thousand Oaks, Calif; London: Sage Publications, 2002.

〔2〕 Denzin, N. K., & Giardina, M. D., The elephant in the living room, or advancing the conversation about the politics of evidence. In N. K. Denzin & M. D. Giardina (Eds.), *Qualitative inquiry and the politics of evidence*, Walnut Creek, CA: Left Coast, 2008, p12.

4.4.3　研究成果

质疑研究合理性的一个原因是担心其可能将情况过于简单化或复杂化，因此传递给读者一种扭曲的世界观。[1]针对这一担忧，我采用了各种经历和视角，运用分析理论进行系统分析，并说明结论的主观性和不确定性。与此同时，我尽量避免逻辑上的单一性、绝对性和封闭性，强调矛盾性、碎片化、自我反思和多元性。[2]

此外，征求他人的反馈可以有效减少影响研究信度的因素，包括研究人员的偏见和假设，以及逻辑或方法上的缺陷，这是一种极为有用的策略。所以我已经和各种各样的人，包括局外人和局内人，讨论了我的数据和结论。尤其是同行检验，这是减少错误解释可能性的重要方法。

跨文化研究中的一个主要问题是种族中心主义，它假定一个人的文化世界观是所有现实的中心。与种族相对主义（对不同行为和文化具有同理心）相反，种族中心主义通常会导致对他人语言和文化的诋毁或形成负面刻板印象。Connor[3]提出，避免这种问题的方法之一是在进行跨文化研究时，与母语为其他语言的人合作。对我而言，我的两位导师，还有其他的老师和同学，在研究的每个阶段都帮助我对文化感知保持敏感性。

简言之，为了应对后现代世界的挑战，我们可能需要从“三角检验法”（使用多种研究方法以提高信度）向“水晶多面性”转变，考虑从远远超过“三面”的角度来接近和尊重真理瞬息万变的本质。因此，我把重点放在多重研究方法和解释上，而不是只检验某一种解释。

在下一部分，笔者将视野投向更广阔的二语写作领域，对该领域的常用研究方法做一综述，以期为二语写作研究者提供参考借鉴。

---

〔1〕 Merriam, S. B., *Qualitative research and case study applications in education* (2nd ed.), San Francisco: Jossey-Bass Publishers, 1998.

〔2〕 Alvesson, M., *Postmodernism and social research*, Phildelphia, Pa.; Buckingham, U. K.: Open University, 2002.

〔3〕 Connor, U., *Contrastive rhetoric: Cross-cultural aspects of second-language writing*. Cambridge [England]; New York: Cambridge University Press, 1996.

4.5 二语写作研究方法综述

国内外众多专家学者对二语写作的研究中不乏兼具深度和广度的相关发表文献。然而针对二语写作研究方法分析所发表的文献少之又少，但研究方法又是科学研究所不可或缺的重要工具。尤其是近年来，随着国内外学者对实证研究的重视程度提高，对这一领域的研究方法进行深入了解的需求急剧增加。研究者只有对这一领域常用的各种研究方法有深入的了解并能够在研究中根据自己的研究课题选择合适的研究方法，才能在更大程度上得出相对科学的、可信度更高的结论。本节旨在为二语写作领域的研究者及教师介绍这一领域几种主要的研究方法及其适用范围，以期为研究者进行科研及教师更好地了解学生提供方法上的借鉴。

4.5.1 二语写作研究方法概览

《第二语言写作学术期刊》（Journal of Second Language Writing）于 1992 年创建，是语言学及语言教学领域同行评审学术期刊，亦是这一领域国际权威核心期刊之一。据期刊引用报告（Journal Citation Reports），该期刊 2017 年影响因子为 3.321，在 182 本语言学期刊中名列第二。因此，本书选取 2011 年至 2018 年《第二语言写作学术期刊》上发表的 146 篇相关文献进行统计分析，以期为各位研究者使用二语写作研究方法提供借鉴。

通过阅读这 8 年间发表的论文发现，《第二语言写作学术期刊》发表的文献中既包括实证研究，也包括理论研究和综述性研究，本篇主要对该领域实证研究的研究方法进行总体性介绍，故而剔除了相关理论研究 11 篇及综述性研究 16 篇，主要分析其中包含实证研究方法的 119 篇文献。二语写作实证研究方法种类繁杂，主要有测试研究、个案研究、语料库等研究方法，本节亦对不太常见的研究方法（如日志法、有声思维、人种志等）进行了简单介绍，以期尽量全面囊括二语写作领域的所有实证研究方法。

二语写作实证研究方法一览表

研究方法 \ 年份	对照实验	个案研究	文本分析法	行动研究	测试研究	语料库研究法	有声思维	问卷法	访谈法	日志法	人种志	总计
2011	1		1	3	3	2					1	11
2012	1	3	1	2	2	3			1			13
2013	2	4	2	2	2	2		1	3			18
2014	1	5	3	1	3	4				1		18
2015	1	6	1		7	2	1	1				19
2016	1	1	1		2	6		1	1			13
2017	2	3	1	1	2			1				10
2018	2	2	1	3	4	2		1	1	1		17
总计	11	24	11	12	25	21	1	5	6	2	1	119
百分比	9.2%	20.2%	9.2%	10.1%	21.0%	17.7%	0.8%	4.2%	5.1%	1.7%	0.8%	100%

由上表可知，二语写作领域的实证研究方法众多，其中最主要的研究方法是测试研究，占所有发表文献的21.0%，受到国内外学者的广泛青睐；与之使用频率不相上下的研究方法是个案研究（20.2%），个案研究作为典型的定性研究方法，通过对小数量群体的深入观察追踪，从而实现对某一二语写作变量整体规律的把握；使用频率位列第三的研究方法是最新的语料库研究方法（17.7%），这一研究方法随着计算机科学及语料库语言学的发展，逐渐走向成熟；行动研究（10.1%）和对照实验（9.2%）这两种研究方法的使用频率相对较小，但常常与其他研究方法混合使用；文本分析法（9.2%）是较常用的研究方法之一，且近年来常与语料库的研究方法结合使用，通过大规模分析二语写作文本，从而得出一定结论；问卷法和访谈法是较为常见的二语写作研究方法，且通常结合使用以达到定量研究和定性研究的有机统一；

日志法（1.7%）、有声思维（0.8%）和人种志（0.8%）这三类研究方法在二语写作领域使用频率均较低。下面本节将详细介绍几种主要研究方法并简单介绍几类不太常见的研究方法。

4.5.2 国内外二语写作主要研究方法评述

测试研究、行动研究与对照实验

测试研究是二语写作领域另一种重要的实验方法，旨在通过实验测试某种方法是否适用于二语写作课堂教学活动及其适用程度和范围，或是探索二语写作中某些因素对二语写作的影响。Hu 和 Lam 设计了为期 12 周的学术英语课堂写作任务，以测试同伴反馈对二语写作的影响。[1] Hui-Chun 和 Shelley 通过一个学期（5 个月）的电子阅读器辅助学术英语写作课堂教学测试，探究电子阅读器对二语学术英语写作的有效性。[2] Liao 通过测试实验探索面对面口头交流及网上交流两类课前活动对以汉语为母语的二语写作者写作的影响。[3] 桑紫林通过为期 18 周的课堂合作教学写作测试训练，指出合作产出模式有助于提高学生二语写作的准确性。[4] 雷鹏飞通过设计为期 8 周的写作任务重复教学实验，探讨任务重复对英语写作的影响。[5] 测试研究这一研究方法一般适用于持续时间较长的二语写作测试实验，通过长期课堂教学活动产生出对结果的数据统计，分析某一特定方法对提高学生二语写作能力的影响。

行动研究是指“以某些行动对组织系统的影响为主要研究对象、实验社

---

〔1〕 Hu, G., Lam, S. T. E., Issues of cultural appropriateness and pedagogical efficacy: exploring peer review in a second language writing class, *Instructional Science*, 38 (4), 2010, p371-394.

〔2〕 Hui-Chun H., Shelley S. Y., The Effectiveness of Adopting E-Readers to Facilitate EFL Students' Process-Based Academic Writing, *Journal of Educational Technology & Society*, 18 (1), 2015, p250-263.

〔3〕 Jianling L., The impact of face-to-face oral discussion and online text-chat on L2 Chinese writing, *Journal of Second Language Writing*, 41, 2018, p27-40.

〔4〕 桑紫林：“合作产出对英语学习者书面语准确性发展的影响研究”，载《外语与外语教学》2017 年第 4 期。

〔5〕 雷鹏飞、徐锦芬：“任务重复对学术英语写作的影响：以动态系统理论为视角”，载《外语界》2018 年第 5 期。

会心理学的一种研究方法，其中包括诊断性研究、参与性研究与实验性研究三种方式”。[1]这一研究方法最初运用于社会心理学领域，后来运用于教师研究。国内外二语写作领域学者使用行动研究方法进行的研究均较少。莫丹通过制定教学行动方案，严格实施教学计划，通过问卷调查、访谈、教学对象写作文本及教师和同伴反馈等数据搜集，研究“教师+同伴”的反馈模式对提高留学生汉语水平写作能力的影响。[2]李莉文通过设计为期 16 周的教学行动方案，通过搜集英语专业二年级学生作文文本、教师教学日志、讨论教学录像等探讨学生读写意识和思辨意识在英语写作中的培养。[3]Harman 通过为期 8 个月对其五年级学生进行以文本类型为基础的教学指导，探究学生如何通过文本类型为基础的教学指导提高其二语写作水平和能力。[4]

对照实验是二语写作的重要研究方法之一，国内外学者对它的使用均达到较高水平。这一研究方法通过控制除实验目的外的其他所有变量，设计对照组与实验组，观察分析实验数据，分析某一特定因素对研究课题的影响。国内二语写作研究中，对照实验方法研究的范围主要包括对特定二语写作方法有效性的探讨，如不同任务类型对二语写作者词汇丰富性的影响、[5]追踪修正法和单词处理器对英语写作反馈纠正的有效性测试[6]及 CLIL（Content and Language Integrated Learning）教学模式对降低学生二语写作焦虑的有效性研究。[7]国外运用对照实验方法进行二语写作研究的范围更加广泛，既包括

---

〔1〕 行动研究，https://baike. sogou. com/v690151. htm？ fromTitle =%E8%A1%8C%E5%8B%95%E7%A0%94%E7%A9%B6，最后访问日期：2019 年 1 月 30 日。

〔2〕 莫丹：“基于反馈的留学生汉语多稿写作教学行动研究”，载《语言教学与研究》2018 年第 5 期。

〔3〕 李莉文：“英语写作中的读者意识与思辨能力培养——基于教学行动研究的探讨”，载《中国外语》2011 年第 3 期。

〔4〕 Harman R.，“Literary intertextuality in genre-based pedagogies：Building lexical cohesion in fifth-grade L2 writing”，*Journal of Second Language Writing*，22，2013，p125-140.

〔5〕 肖莉：“任务类型对中高级汉语二语者写作词汇丰富性的影响”，载《语言教学与研究》2018 年第 6 期。

〔6〕 苗佳：“基于追踪修正和单词处理器的英语写作纠错反馈研究”，载《东北大学学报（社会科学版）》2018 年第 6 期。

〔7〕 钟含春、范武邱：“CLIL 模式对英语专业学生写作焦虑影响的定量追踪研究”，载《解放军外国语学院学报》2018 年第 4 期。

对某一特定二语写作方法有效性的探索，[1]又包括将不同实验对象设置为研究对象的差别性研究。[2]值得注意的是，国内外采用对照实验方法的二语写作研究一般持续时间较长，搜集的数据除了被试者的写作文本外，还包括对被试者的问卷调查、访谈等。利用这些数据评估被试者英语能力水平、记录实验使用教学方法的感受等，以减少实验变量，提高二语写作方法研究的信度。

这三种研究方法既有相同点，亦存在不同之处。其相同点在于都是采用实验对二语写作进行深入探讨，且常常结合其他研究方法，如课堂观察、调查问卷、访谈、日志法、个案分析等对实验对象及其文本进行数据搜集，来更加全面及深入地分析研究者的研究课题。三者的不同之处在于：行动研究这一研究方法通常适用于教师教学行动研究，通过制定教学行动方案并实施为期较长的教学行动以观察二语写作过程中某一学习方法是否适用于学生及其可适用的程度和范围；测试研究主要通过测试实验探索某一方法对二语写作课堂的影响，相对于对照实验对变量的严格控制，测试研究中可存在多个变量；对照实验主要通过设置对照组和实验组、控制变量，以探究某一写作方法等对二语写作的有效性。

个案研究

个案研究方法在西方研究者中普及较早，中国国内早前更为关注量化研究，通过分析比较较大数量的研究内容，从而得出其一般规律，因此个案研究在国内起步发展较晚。近年来，这一研究方法越来越受到中国学者的关注，中国学者开始关注虽数量较少但具有较高质量的个案分析，以期为未来发展提供一些借鉴。二语写作领域个案研究方法的适用亦遵循这一规律。

---

〔1〕 Zhang X. Z. X.，“Reading-writing integrated tasks，comprehensive corrective feedback，and EFL writing development”，*Language Teaching Research*，2017，p217-240. Ruegg R.，The relative effects of peer and teacher feedback on improvement in EFL students' writing ability，*Linguistics and Education*，29，2015. Jiang W.，Measurements of Development in L2 Written Production：The Case of L2 Chinese，*Applied Linguistics*，34，2013，p1-24.

〔2〕 Dobao A. F.，Collaborative writing tasks in the L2 classroom：Comparing group，pair，and individual work”，Journal of Second Language Writing，21（2012）. Shehadeh A.，“Effects and student perceptions of collaborative writing in L2”，*Journal of Second Language Writing*，4，2011，p286-305.

二语写作领域个案研究方法的适用对象可以是老师，如牛瑞英和张蕊以一位经验丰富的英语教师为个案，分析其对所教授的19名英语专业学生的英文写作的反馈，以期为教师给学生提出反馈提供一定的借鉴；[1]也可以是学生，如刘春燕对我国香港地区某高校的一名学生进行为期4年的个案研究，以考察二语课程中的语言输出与语言发展的关系。[2]个案研究追踪观察的时间跨度通常在一个学期以上，[3]但也存在时间跨度较短的个案分析，如Yang通过对两名韩语学习者的访谈和有声思维法及刺激回忆法搜集的其二语写作过程的数据，探究其在写作过程中的思维活动。[4]个案研究方法的共同点在于所研究的对象较少，一般不会超过6个人，且通常采用如问卷、访谈、有声思维法等方式和方法，搜集研究对象在二语写作过程中及写作后的感受等，以更好地实现研究目的。

语料库研究与文本分析

随着科技水平的发展，计算机越来越普及，成为家庭和工作中必不可少的重要伙伴。语料库语言学这一新兴领域也随之而生。用计算机技术进行大规模快速分析的生动语料为研究者提供更为具有代表性的语言示例，[5]获得学者的广泛青睐。二语写作领域的学者同样借助语料库研究大规模分析学生写作文本，探索二语写作词法、句法等的特点。二语写作领域的语料库大致可分为两类，一类是学者根据自己的课题研究目的，自行建立语料库，对文

---

〔1〕 牛瑞英、张蕊："二语写作教师书面反馈焦点、策略及成效个案研究"，载《解放军外国语学院学报》2018年第3期。

〔2〕 刘春燕："二语课程中的语言输出与二语发展——香港高校本科生课程英语写作的个案研究"，载《外语界》2014年第3期。

〔3〕 Yu S., Lee I., Understanding EFL students'participation in group peer feedback of L2 writing: A case study from an activity theory perspective, *Language Teaching Research*, 2015, p572-593. Yu S., Lee I., Exploring Chinese students' strategy use in a cooperative peer feedback writing group, *System*, 2016, p58.

〔4〕 Yang L., Examining the mediational means in collaborative writing: Case studies of undergraduate ESL students in business courses, *Journal of Second Language Writing*, 2014, p23.

〔5〕 Biber D., Gray B., Poonpon K., Should We Use Characteristics of Conversation to Measure Grammatical Complexity in L2 Writing Development?, *TESOL Quarterly*, 2011, p5-35.

本进行分析；[1]一类是学者选用符合研究课题的现有语料库进行分析，从而得出结论。[2]二语写作领域的语料库语言学将随着计算机的进一步发展，在未来研究中占据更为重要的地位，发挥更大的作用。

文本分析法一直是二语写作中的一种重要的研究方法，通过搜集文本并借助一定的理论模型，或是依据研究者课题研究的重点，实现对二语写作者写作水平和写作能力的分析。Rinnert，Katayama 和 Kobayashi 通过分析 19 名英语母语者的日语写作文本及 21 名日语母语者的英语写作文本的修辞特征（rhetorical text features）、论证类型（argumentation subtypes）、首段介绍和尾段结论的组成（introduction/ conclusion components）以探究日语学习者根据自己母语构建二语写作的动态转换（transfer）过程。[3]何欣忆、黎曜玮等人采用二语句法复杂分析器并结合随机森林和逻辑回归机器学习算法分析非英语专业大学生英语写作议论文 2300 篇以探究高分组学生在句法层面的重要写作特征。[4]随着有声思维法、民族志等新兴研究方法的出现，文本分析法在二语写作研究方法中的地位逐渐下降，越来越多的学者倾向于采用其他研究方法或文本分析法与其他研究方法相结合的分析方法，探究二语写作模式及其特点等。

近年来，计算机发展带来的语料库语言学发展常与较为传统的文本分析法相结合，研究者首先根据自己的研究目的选择或建立语料库，再结合文本分析模型或研究者研究的重点，分析写作者所写文本词法及句法特征，并由

---

〔1〕 赵丽萍、张丽婷：“多媒体环境下二语在线写作中话语立场标记语特征阐析——基于态度立场标记的自建语料库研究”，载《外语电化教学》2014 年第 1 期。Mancilla R. L.，Polat N.，Akcay A. O.，“An Investigation of Native and Nonnative English Speakers'Levels of Written Syntactic Complexity in Asynchronous Online Discussions”，*Applied Linguistics*，1，2015，p112-134。鞠玉梅：“二语报纸专栏评论写作互动元话语使用考察”，载《外语研究》2018 年第 4 期。

〔2〕 Fei Xiao L.，“Corpus-based evaluation of syntactic complexity measures as indices of college-level ESL writers'language development”，*TESOL Quarterly*，2011.

〔3〕 Rinnert. C.，Katayama A.，Kobayashi H.，“Argumentation Text Construction by Japanese as a Foreign Language Writers：A Dynamic View of Transfer”，*The* Modern *Language Journal*，99 2015，p213-245.

〔4〕 何欣忆等：“高分组英语写作文本的句法特征探究——基于句酷批改网英语写作文本的数据挖掘”，载《现代教育技术》2018 年第 12 期。

此分析写作中二语写作水平能力的提高程度等。[1]

问卷法与访谈法

问卷法与访谈法在二语写作领域通常被同时使用，研究者首先运用调查问卷方法大规模搜集数据，得出相关领域的一般规律，再运用访谈法对问卷调查中的典型代表进行访谈，以补充大规模量化统计中所没有注意到的细节，优化研究结论，提高研究信度。[2]下面将逐一介绍这两种研究方法。

问卷法是研究者通过控制式的测量对所研究的问题进行度量，从而搜集到可靠的资料的一种方法。[3]其优点在于标准化程度较高、成本较低；缺点则是问卷设计难度较大，且无法保证问卷回收质量。国内外二语写作领域对问卷法使用程度均较高，如马洁和董攀通过对 260 名非英语专业大学生进行问卷调查，探究了大学生英语写作焦虑程度及自我调节策略的使用情况；[4] O'Donnell 通过 2009 年及 2010 年两次对中级和低级二语学习者同伴反馈写作进行问卷调查，考察同伴反馈对二语写作者写作水平的影响。[5]问卷法适用于研究对象较多的量化测试，但由于其自身存在的缺陷，常常配合其他研究方法共同使用，以提高研究成果的可信度。在正式发放问卷前，通常需要对问卷进行预调查，并根据预调查结果完善问卷，以提高问卷回收质量。

访谈法亦是二语写作领域较为传统的研究方法。但由于访谈法所选用的样本较少，成本较高，且无法控制访谈过程中被访谈者受访谈者影响等，常常结合其他研究方法共同考察研究者的研究课题，很少单独使用，如 Zhao 通

---

〔1〕 Crossley S. A.，"Mcnamara D. S.，Does writing development equal writing quality? A computational investigation of syntactic complexity in L2 learners"，*Journal of Second Language Writing*，2014，p26。吴继峰、周蔚、卢达威："韩语母语者汉语二语写作质量评估研究——以语言特征和内容质量为测量维度"，载《世界汉语教学》2019 年第 1 期。

〔2〕 刘兵、王奕凯、ZHANG Jun Lawrence："任务类型对在线英语写作任务准备和产出的影响"，载《现代外语》2017 年第 1 期。Ferris D.，Brown J.，"Hsiang S. L.，et al.，Responding to L2 Students in College Writing Classes: Teacher Perspectives"，*TESOL Quarterly*，45 2011，p207-234。

〔3〕 问卷调查法，https://baike.sogou.com/v354201.htm? fromTitle=%E9%97%AE%E5%8D%B7%E8%B0%83%E6%9F%A5%E6%B3%95，最后访问日期：2019 年 2 月 3 日。

〔4〕 马洁、董攀："大学生英语写作焦虑自我调节策略研究"，载《外语界》2017 年第 5 期。

〔5〕 O'Donnell ME，"Peer Response with Process-oriented，Standards-based Writing for Beginning-level，Second Language Learners of Spanish"，*Hispania*，97 2014，p413-429.

过文本分析法、刺激回忆法及访谈法实现二语写作者对同伴和教师的反馈理解与使用之间不同的区分；[1] Jill V. 通过结合有声思维法及访谈法分析教师如何运用“声音”（voice）作为学生二语写作的评价标准等。[2]访谈法适用于小样本的研究，且访谈者在访谈过程中应尽量保持中立，尽可能保证被访谈者真实反映自身态度及观点。

其他研究方法

日志法、有声思维法、民族志等亦是二语写作领域的重要研究方法，但由于三者在二语写作研究中使用频率不高，因而笔者将简单介绍这三种研究方法，以期为有志于这一领域的研究者提供些许借鉴。

日志法兴起于 20 世纪 90 年代。按照记录日志工具的不同，日志法大约可分为两类：一类是借助电脑输入日志软件（如，Inputlog）搜集写作数据并对学生写作过程中的停顿次数、时长、位置等进行分析，借助电脑深化对二语写作的认知；[3]另一类则是学生在接受二语写作课程并完成写作任务后，撰写反思日志，并基于此分析数据。[4]日志法通常需要借助电脑软件（如 SPSS、SAS）才能完成对日志记录数据的分析，从而得出研究结论。

有声思维法（Think-aloud）是指在实验过程中，参与者被要求将脑中产生的所有想法全部实时大声说出并由记录者记录下来用以研究人类思维模式的一种研究方法。[5]这是目前了解、掌握受试者大脑思维过程的一种有效方式，也是目前能被接受并对受试者完成任务影响最小的心理测试方法。[6]有

---

〔1〕 Zhao H. Z. H. G.，“Investigating learners'use and understanding of peer and teacher feedback on writing: A comparative study in a Chinese English writing classroom”，*Assessing Writing*，1 2010，p3-17.

〔2〕 Jeffery J. V.，“Subjectivity, Intentionality, and Manufactured Moves: Teachers ‘Perceptions of Voice in the Evaluation of Secondary Students’ Writing”，*Research in the Teaching of English*，46 2011，p92-127.

〔3〕 徐翠芹：“输入日志和屏幕录像的交叉运用——计算机辅助二语写作过程研究新视野”，载《外语电化教学》2011 年第 5 期。

〔4〕 张晓鹏：“读后续写对二语写作过程影响的多维分析”，载《外语界》2016 年第 6 期。Han J.，Hiver P.，“Genre-based L2 writing instruction and writing-specific psychological factors: The dynamics of change”，*Journal of Second Language Writing*，40 2018，p44-59.

〔5〕 Rankin, J. M.，“Designing thinking-aloud studies in ESL reading”，*Reading in a Foreign Language*，4 1988，p119-132.

〔6〕 Ericsson K. A.，H. A. Simon，*Protocol Analysis: Verbal Reports as Data*，The MIT Press，1993.

声思维法参与者必须提前接受相关训练才能达到相关实验任务要求。有声思维法通常被用于探究二语写作过程中母语对二语写作的影响，[1]分析二语写作过程中写作者处理词汇、语块问题的思维模式，[2]有声思维法亦可用于考量二语写作焦虑、二语写作成绩与母语使用量之间的关系[3]及多语言学习者先前学习的语言知识对解决其他语言写作问题的影响等。[4]有声思维法研究的对象数量亦较少，且多与访谈法等方法结合考察二语写作过程中写作者思维的运行模式。

民族志这一研究方法要求学者在调查地区居住较长时间，深入了解和学习当地的语言和文化，且尽最大可能投入到当地人的日常生活之中，与此同时还要保持一个观察者的不偏不倚的立场，[5]从而实现对某种文化的全面了解。二语写作领域中，民族志观察者通常是授课教师，被观察者通常是其学生，教师通过为期一个学期甚至更久的民族志研究，结合课堂观察法、话语分析、讨论、访谈及学生习作分析学生二语写作过程。[6]民族志研究作为田野研究的一种方法，能够深入了解某地的文化，获得第一手资料，从而具备整体的、跨文化的视角；然而其不足之处在于研究成本较高，且数据整理难度大、主观性强等，这些也是限制其发展的主要原因。[7]

---

〔1〕陈晓湘、王阳：“二语写作过程中母语使用的量化分析”，载《湖南大学学报（社会科学版）》2010年第6期。van Weijen DDVH, van den Bergh HHVU, Rijlaarsdam GGCW, et al., L1 use during L2 writing: An empirical study of a complex phenomenon, *Journal of Second Language Writing*, 4, 2009, p235-250.

〔2〕徐昉：“英语专业学生二语限时写作提取语块的思维特征”，载《外语与外语教学》2010年第1期。Murphy LLUE, Roca De Larios JJUE, Searching for words: One strategic use of the mother tongue by advanced Spanish EFL writers, *Journal of Second Language Writing*, 2, 2010, p61-81.

〔3〕周保国、唐军俊：“二语写作焦虑对写作过程影响的实证研究”，载《外语教学》2010年第1期。

〔4〕Tullock B. D., Fernández-Villanueva M., The Role of Previously Learned Languages in the Thought Processes of Multilingual Writers at the Deutsche Schule Barcelona, *Research in the Teaching of English*, 47, 2013, p420-441.

〔5〕民族志，https://baike.sogou.com/v8019882.htm? fromTitle=%E4%BA%BA%E7%A7%8D%E5%BF%97，最后访问日期：2019年2月3日。

〔6〕Zheng C. Z. C., Understanding the learning process of peer feedback activity: An ethnographic study of Exploratory Practice, *Language Teaching Research*, 1, 2012, p109-126.

〔7〕民族志，https://wenku.baidu.com/view/e045462bbd64783e09122bec.html，最后访问日期：2019年2月3日。

结论

二语写作领域研究方法较多，每一种研究方法都有其独特的适用范围及其优缺点。研究者若想用有限的研究成本得出最公正客观的结论，必须详细了解每一种研究方法的特征，从而选择最适合的研究方法。

从适用条件看，行动研究、对照实验、测试研究、语料库研究、个案研究、民族志、有声思维法这几种研究方法通常会结合其他研究方法共同使用，将其他研究方法作为辅助研究手段，以保证得出客观的研究结果。日志法、文本分析法、问卷法、访谈法、观察法这几种研究方法则很少单独使用，通常被作为辅助研究手段，与其他研究方法共同使用。

从研究题材来看，测试研究、对照实验、行动研究多用于对某一种教学方法的有效性的探讨；而语料库研究、文本分析法则专注于文本结构特征，分析二语写作者所写文本词法、句法特征，探究写作者二语写作能力和水平等问题；民族志研究方法常从整体视角观察写作者写作过程以深刻描述二语写作；而有声思维法则更关注人在二语写作过程中思维的运行模式及母语对二语的影响等。

从研究对象的数量上讲，语料库研究、民族志、文本分析法、访谈法这几种研究方法的研究对象的数量一般较大，故而借助电脑软件等进行分析可大大减少研究成本，其缺陷在于无法从微观了解二语写作这一过程；个案研究、有声思维法、日志法、访谈法等几种方法研究对象的数量较少，但是成本较高，通常研究对象应具有代表性，因此选择时需谨慎对待。

二语写作领域研究者选择实证研究方法时，应切实结合自身研究目的和研究成本，选择合适的研究方法。在实证研究过程中，各种研究方法通常会混合使用，以保证研究成果的可信度。同时，研究者应详细介绍被试者身份、能力等对研究影响较大的因素，亦应仔细介绍研究过程，从而提高研究结论的可信度。

4.5.3 小 结

本部分首先对作者所选择的研究和表现方法进行批判性的叙述。从一个机械的初学者、一个困惑和迷惘流浪者，到如今一个更成熟的登山者，完成了对研究方法论的学术探索。

许多方法论为本研究提供了有效方法。本研究整体上采用民族志研究方法，对广东外语外贸大学和作者自己的英语写作实践进行了描述，重点考察了这一实践的社会文化背景以及参与实践的成员之间的互动关系。在数据收集、数据分析和描述中采用叙事的方法，目的是为整个项目提供一个直接、生动、多方面的画面。不同来源的叙事，包括广东外语外贸大学的叙事、我的叙事和其他参与者的叙事，共同构成了一个关于中国英语写作教育的叙事。

在分析这些叙事的时候，我运用了批判的理论来阐明这些创造性写作方法的形成因素。在叙述和文本分析中，文本分析工具也被用于分析这些写作故事，以揭示更深层的含义。作为对上述方法的补充，我在本文的一些章节中还使用了文化研究、批评媒体研究和批评读写研究的理论。

此外，本章还为二语写作领域的研究者及教师介绍了这一领域的主要研究方法及其适用范围，以期为研究者进行科研及教师更好地了解学生提供方法上的借鉴。

第五章

广东外语外贸大学对外语写作的探索

一个蕴含丰富创新教学经验的宝库，却无人问津，原因在于其未被翻译成故事。

——Rosen[1]

为进行批判性和创造性写作教学法研究，我参观了中国各地的许多著名大学，但到目前为止，广东外语外贸大学（本章以下简称“广外”）的教学方法改革给我留下了最深刻的印象。20世纪末以来，广外一直在探索创造性写作的教学方法，并取得了丰硕成果，其中包括一系列创新写作活动、全面的课程改革和一整套基础设施的建立，如教科书、课程杂志、网站等。广外的项目在中国高校中影响广泛，且多年来一直被视为写作教学改革的圣地。

本章将对广外的创新写作教学进行全面论述。本章的第一部分介绍其社会政治背景，并概述其写作教学法，包括写作教改的发展阶段、各种写作活动的共同特点，以及教学创新的影响和挑战。本章的主要部分结合教育学、语言学和批判理论，介绍广外教改的主要特色，并通过教师自己的声音对教师作为“赋能者”和“被赋能者”的角色进行探讨。本章的最后一部分是作者对该教改实践的理论解读。

---

〔1〕 Rosen, H., Stories of stories: A postscript by Harold Rosen. In B. Rosen (Ed.), And none of it was nonsense: *The power of storytelling in school*, London: MGP, 1988.

5.1　“以写促学”理念及实践概述

由广外英文学院的教研团队创造的“以写促学”教学法从诞生至今已近20年，在中国外语教学特别是写作教学界引起了巨大反响，并产生了深远影响，可谓我国写作教学改革的先行者和示范者。笔者将通过对“以写促学”教学法多年的研究，结合该教改参与者的研究成果，进一步认识这一创新教学法的本质，有意识地进行总结和反思，更好地推广和提升这一重要的外语教学方法。

5.1.1　“以写促学”教学法诞生的社会背景

“以写促学”教学法诞生于20世纪末，当时世界发展开始逐步进入全球化时代，创造力和世界意识的培养逐渐成为各国教育的重要目的之一，国际外语教学正面临着后现代思潮影响下的“社会转向”和“文化转向”等趋势。在二语写作界，写作教学的目的是长期以来存在的争论之一：实用主义认为教师应该教授学生写作技能，而批判教育家认为教师的使命是培养学生的批判思想，让他们认识到写作的社会政治功能，从而通过写作来改变世界。这个分歧和其他因素一起，推动了二语写作的发展，从自由写作（expressivist approach）到控制作文（controlled composition），从现实—传统修辞法（current-traditional rhetoric）到过程法，再到现在流行的学术英语写作，写作教学越来越重视语言教学的社会功能，强调文体、文本与社会意识形态和价值观之间密不可分的联系。[1]与此同时，教育界也越来越重视跨文化交际意识。在一些西方国家，外语教学开始逐步从语言交际教学法向跨文化交际教学法过渡，把培养学生的世界意识和跨文化交际能力作为外语教学的最终目的。[2]

经过40年改革开放，中国日益强大，逐渐成为世界政治、经济和文化强国，在全球化市场和各种国际事务中发挥着越来越重要的作用。这对我国的

---

〔1〕 Halliday, M. A. K., & Matthiessen, C. M. I. M., *An introduction to functional grammar* (3rd ed.), London: Arnold, 2004.

〔2〕 叶洪、Trevor Hay：“中国文化保护与跨文化的‘第三空间’”，载《求索》2010年第7期。

教育，尤其是外语教育，提出了前所未有的机遇和挑战，具有外语交际能力、创新能力和跨文化交际能力的外语类毕业生迅速成为人才市场的宠儿。为了满足时代对新型外语人才的需求，教育部1998年委托高等学校外语专业教学指导委员会对《高等学校英语专业英语教学大纲》进行了修订，强调培养复合型人才的重要性，特别强调要注重培养外语类学生获取知识的能力、独立思考的能力和创新能力，并提高其思想道德素质、文化素质和心理素质。遗憾的是，20世纪90年代末我国的英语教学仍面临“投入多，产出少”的困境，尤其是英语写作教学，受到20世纪80年代以来“听说领先”的交际教学法思潮的影响，写作课没有得到足够的重视，以考试为目的的写作教学常常用模式化训练代替正常教学，导致学生写作水平低、厌恶写作、害怕写作、公式化写作和抄袭盛行，抑制了学生对外语学习的兴趣和信心，不利于学生思维能力和创造力的培养。研究表明，学习者的情感因素在外语学习中具有重要作用，它像一把双刃剑，既能阻碍学习动机，也能成为学习的发动机。教育者必须打通学生情感通道，才可能获得理想的学习效果。这需要教师细心关注和保护学生的情感需求，通过增加英语输入和大量的写作练习克服“怵写”心理。可是在现实中这几乎是不可能的。从20世纪90年代末中国大学开始全面扩招，导致师资的严重不足。尤其是写作教师，因为需要大量时间批改学生作文，他们不堪重负，很难有精力关注学生情感，更不可能给学生大量练习写作的机会。写作，成为教师最不愿意教和学生最不愿意学的课程之一。

“写长法”就诞生在这样的背景之下。他的创始人王初明教授提出“写长作文”应该成为中国人学外语的突破口之一，这是因为以下几个原因：首先，“写”比“说”更易于消除紧张自卑的情绪，尤其是对于口语较差和性格内向的学习者。其次，中国人在学习外语的环境中听说的机会较少，读写机会较多；写作，特别是写长作文能给学生以成就感，从而激发他们学习外语的兴趣和信心。再次，写作能将被动的外语“输入”转为积极的“输出”，有利于知识的内化，并因需求增加而产生进一步的“输入”。最后，提醒教师给学生积极鼓励而不纠缠于学生写作中的错误能保护学生的学习信心，也利于教师把时间和精力集中于更有效的写作教学活动中，比如写作任务的设计等。

这一最初的“写长”理念是王初明教授以心理语言学和 Swain 的输出理论等为依据，结合中国学习者当时的实际情况提出的。在之后的十多年中，这一理念得到了系统的发展，并在广外英文学院郑超教授领导的写作团队中得以实践，总结出了一整套教学理念与实践方法，形成了“以写促学”外语教学法。

5.1.2　“以写促学”教学法的发展历程及主要内容

“以写促学”教学法的诞生以 2000 年王初明教授等在《外语教学与研究》(第 3 期) 上发表的论文“以写促学——一项英语写作教学改革的试验”为标志，这项试验中王教授及其团队在英语系一年级学生中进行了为期一个学期的“写长”尝试，并获得了显著成果。当年这一教学试验获得广外优秀教学成果特等奖、2001 年这项教学改革获得广东省高等教育教学成果一等奖。2002 年 3 月，“以写促学”的教学改革开始在广外英语系一、二年级推行，标志着该系全面课程改革的开始。2002 年，由郑超教授领导的教学团队和学生共同创办了《以写促学》杂志和网站，同年这项教改成功获得全国教育科学“十五”规划重点课题立项。2002 年是教学改革的关键一年，也是教学改革的转折点，该项目的领导工作也移交给了郑超博士（当年是王初明教授的博士生，后成为广外教师和英语系主任）。随着这些变化，教学法的名称也从最初的“写长法”改为“以写促学”。同年，“以写促学”项目被确立为国家教育科学重点研究项目。2003 年第一届全国写作改革研讨会在广外召开，“写长法”作为这次会议的主题，其影响逐步扩大到全国，有许多高校开始仿效广外进行“写长法”的试验，有关的论文也开始在各种期刊上频频出现。2004 年，以“写长”为主要特色的“中级写作教学法”获得广外优秀教学成果一等奖；也是在 2004 年，收集了数篇“写长法”研究论文和学生作文的编著“Write to Learn”出版；2005 年该教改获得高等教育国家级教学成果二等奖。在“以写促学”理念基础上广外英文学院进行了写作课程的整体改革，将中级英语写作分为四个阶段：“笔随心动”“立论谋篇”“品味创作”“走进报刊”，分别着重于记叙文、论说文、自由创作和报刊特写等写作训练。2008 年系统反映“以写促学”教学理念和实践的教材《英语写作通用教程》出版并投入使用；2010 年，广外以“写长法”为核心理念的“中级英语写作”入选国家精品课程。

过去 10 年中“写长法”经历了许多变化和调整，并且因教师不同在课堂上也有不同的使用方法，但有四个基本原则一直贯穿其发展的各个阶段，使得“写长法”有别于其他的外语教学法。

精心设计写作任务

“以写促学”教学理念认为学生写作成败很大程度上取决于写作题目是否合适。好的写作题应该与学生的生活密切相关，能激发学生兴趣，或能帮助巩固和应用其他科目所学的知识（例如英语精读）等。这些题目需要经常更新以避免重复和枯燥，学生也可自己设计喜欢的写作题目。

课内示范和课后写作相结合

写作课上教师通过介绍写作题目、引荐相关的阅读和视听材料、评点学生范文等来帮助学生了解作文要求、增加信息输入；课后给学生充足的时间写长写好。

以积极鼓励代替纠错。教师反馈应以积极鼓励为主，而不纠缠于学生的语法句法错误。通常教师会标记出学生作文中好的句子、观点和全班一起分享，这样既保护了学生的自信心和对写作的兴趣，也减少了教师改错的时间。但这不等于教师对错误视而不见，典型的错误被教师收集起来在班上进行讨论，并在教材中进行归类整理，以供学生参照修改。同样，写作方法和规则也主要通过学生大量练习写作来总结和归纳，而不是由教师直接灌输给学生，以便保护学生的创造力和探索精神。

灵活的评分体系

“写长法”的评分体系主要包括四个方面，其中作文长度占分最多，为 40%；文章结构、内容和准确性各占 20%。如果某作文得分为 40+18+15+18，则表示作文长度达到了要求、结构合理、内容比较有趣、准确性较高。作文长度的要求可以根据学生水平而变化，起初 200-300 个单词即为合格，到学期末可逐渐增加到1000个单词以上，并且作文长度不设上限。

5.1.3　“以写促学”教改的影响和挑战

从1999年至今，“写长法”在发展中不断演变和完善，并且在广外及其他院校的应用中被教师和学生创造性地加以发挥作用。它一方面把许多英语学习者从“怵写”的困境中解脱出来，让他们变得“想写”“敢写”和“会写”，对中国的英语写作教学产生了广泛而深远的影响，对提高学生写作水平和整体英语水平做出了积极的贡献。我国著名的教育家和学者秦秀白先生在评价“以写促学”的课程体系时这样总结：这项教改以先进的教育理念为基础，符合教育部颁发的《高等学校英语专业英语教学大纲》要求，获得了多项国家和部省级大奖，反映了“以学生为中心”和“任务式写作”等先进的写作教学理念，并综合使用了现代化的教学手段，如使用媒体教具、创办教学网站和（电子）杂志等。[1]

“以写促学”教学法虽然在外语界产生了较大影响，解决了当时外语学习的一些迫切问题，但是由于种种原因，它曾受到过来自广外内外的质疑和挑战，总的来说反对主要来自以下几个方面：（1）某些写作教师不理解或质疑“写长法”的教学理念，认为“写长”和“不改错误”不符合传统教学理念，是对学生不负责任的行为。（2）有些学生认为写作课老师如果不详细教授写作方法和纠错，便无法学到知识；有些学生甚至公开对抗教改。但这些反对者中有许多随着对“写长法”的了解增加和教学改革成果的陆续实现而改变了认识，其中有一些人还积极投身到了这项教学改革中。（3）广外写作教改团队内部也存在分歧，例如对于如何使用教材和范文，如何给学生反馈意见，是否应该遵循统一的教学计划等还有很多不同意见，尤其是应该如何要求学生写作的“长度”，怎样让学生保持写作热情和兴趣等问题仍然是许多广外教师感到头疼的问题。（4）尽管广外通过学术教学会议、网站、杂志和发表文章、出版教材等方式将“以写促学”教学法的影响力辐射到了全国，但是有

---

〔1〕 秦秀白：“‘中级英语写作’课程鉴定和推荐意见”，载http://www.writetolearn.com/Article_Show.asp? ArticleID=852，最后访问日期：2009年3月20日。

些学者和教师对“写长法”仍持有异议，特别是针对其试验的效度问题和促学的理论依据等方面（文秋芳，2005）。从2005年起我国重要学术期刊上出现了围绕“写长法”的辩论与争鸣（例如文秋芳，2008；王初明，2005，2008；周频，2008），这些文章一方面暴露出“写长法”的一些弱点，另一方面也促进了“写长法”的自我反思与完善。希望本书对“写长法”促学理论和思想的论述能为这些讨论提供建设性的参考。

5.2 写作语境：打破与重塑

在接下来的部分中，我们将更深入地了解广外在教学和课程创新方面的探索方法，并说明这些方法是如何对学生作者进行赋能的。有观点认为，这些方法的一个共同特点是对二语写作中的一些教学惯例提出了挑战，例如任务设计、错误修正和评估机制，实行统一的写作课程，在学生真实生活兴趣和写作实践之间建立联系，将学生从错误的写作理念和思想意识中解放出来，转变师生关系和探索二语写作的社会文化意义，为学生作家创造新的写作语境。为了使这些观点更清晰，除了批判教育学、二语写作和创造力教育的理论之外，我还使用Kramsch的“语境”概念作为分析广外项目的框架。

毋庸置疑，语言的使用发生在语境中，所以书面或口头文本与语境是不可分割的。人们也普遍认识到，有意义的语境对语言学习是至关重要的，[1]因此我们应该在语言教育中同时教授文本及其语境。然而，常识性的感知往往会忽略了上下文中的全部可能性。教师如果忽视或未能挖掘这样的语境潜能，往往会无意中将课堂话语限制在肤浅的语言交流上。因此，必须重视语境教学，以创造一种“促进直接和间接传播知识，不仅重视事实，而且重视事实之间的关系，鼓励经验的多样性和对多样性的反思的教学法”[2]。Bernstein也将语境化与教学知识的解放联系起来。但如何运用语境来改善语言教学，对这方面的研究仍然不足并存有争议。

---

〔1〕 Saville-Troike, M., *The ethnography of communication: An introduction* (3rd ed.), Malden, MA: Blackwell Pub, 2003.

〔2〕 Kramsch, C. J., Context and culture in language teaching, Oxford: Oxford University Press, 1993.

5.2.1　解放：长度、反馈、评价

王初明教授是“写长法”的发起人。1977年毕业于四川外国语大学，1981年在广外获得英语语言文学硕士学位，之后一直在广外担任教师和研究员工作。王教授1986年获得英国雷丁大学应用语言学硕士学位，1996年获香港中文大学语言学博士学位。他的座右铭之一为：“教学思想是教育的关键。教育工作者的主要任务之一是发现学生的优点，并用鼓励来强化这些优点。”

采访王教授时，他将发展“写长法”的因由归结为以下几点：[1]

在我看来，英语学习有两个主要障碍：一是焦虑；二是母语的干扰。至于解决办法，首先我们需要消除心理障碍，鼓励学生勇于尝试和不怕丢脸；对于胆小的人，使用比较平和的交流方式，如书面语言。这可以有效减少学习者的焦虑，增强他们学习英语的信心和兴趣。此外为了减少母语的干扰，我们可以通过创造二语环境来增加英语的使用，例如阅读英语小说（越厚越好）和写长篇英语短文。

因此，“写长法”不仅是一种写作教学法，而且是一种促进英语学习的方法。它给予学生更多的机会来使用英语，以获得信心和成就感，用书面作品来促进进一步的学习。王教授认为，我们同样也可以“读长”“听长”“说长”。简而言之，探索更有效的学习策略的关键在于满足学生的自尊需求，并通过增加产出来促进学习。

而学生对“写长法”有何反应？一名学生在课堂杂志上写下了她第一个月的学习感受：

在过去的一个月里，我们写了五篇多于300词的作文。开始的时候，我的确觉得这是强制性要求，不知道如何动笔。但当下笔时，我的大脑仿佛被激活了一样，开始追踪脑中发生的事情。有时我不甘于写简单的句子和结构，

[1] Wang, C., Interview transcript (interview transcript ed.), Guangdong University of Foreign Studies, 2008c.

经过仔细思考，灵感就会迸发出来。在那一刻，脑海里自动浮现出一些自己以前收集的词汇，令我产生一种愉悦的成就感……

除了长度要求外，王教授还强调了“写长法”的基本原理，并解释了教师反馈中语法更正应该减少的原因：

“写长法”有两个基本原则：第一，写得越长越好，修改越少越好；第二，教师的工作应该集中在设计激发性的写作任务，而不是纠正错误。

学生的写作错误会随着学习的积累以及英语的频繁使用而自动消失。学习英语口语和母语也是如此。在英语口语学习中，我们鼓励学生尽量多说，而不是一味地纠正错误，错误会随着重复使用而自动消失。那么在英语写作上又有什么不同呢？

一些人认为，如果不改正，写作错误就会“固化”。但我相信学习，甚至生活本身，都是一个自我纠正的过程，一个经验学习的过程。哪位伟大的作家是老师批改出来的？

的确，在母语和二语的写作研究中，几乎没有证据表明对学生写作的错误纠正能够产生预期的积极作用，[1]并且如果它把学生和老师的注意力从写作过程的其他关键方面转移开，甚至可能产生消极作用。[2]但由于长期以来纠错一直是写作教师的“命中注定的工作”，因此对教师来说，打破常规可能很难，尤其是对年轻、没有权威的教师来说。广外项目团队中的一名中年女教师无奈地告诉我们：

我们还需要批改学生的作文吗？是的，不论长短都要批改。老师们不仅要指出表面的错误，还要强调其他问题。这仍然需要很多时间。但是，修正的效果是非常有限的。

---

〔1〕 Leki, I., *Understanding ESL writers: A guide for teachers*, Portsmouth, N. H.: Boynton/Cook Publishers, 1992. Truscott, J., The case against grammarcorrection in L2 writing classes, *Language Learning*, 46 (2), 1996, p327-369.

〔2〕 Ferris, D., & Hedgcock, J., *Teaching ESL composition: Purpose, process, and practice*, Mahwah, N. J.: Lawrence Erlbaum Assoicates, 2005.

我们必须纠正学生作文中的错误，否则学生会不满意。但纠正的有效性却一直受到质疑。例如，一位同事跟我讲的他的亲身经历，一名学生在作文中写了“standed”而不是“stood”，老师将这个错误提出来并加以警告。但接下来的写作中，学生的文中出现了更多的“standed”，这一现象令这位老师感到非常绝望！

因此，老师的错误纠正并不总能如愿地帮助到学生。当二语写作领域中还在为纠正和反馈的有效性激烈争论时，广外已经对其表示质疑，并做出了改变。

正如上述介绍的一样，在该项目的评分方案中，学生的作文长度是最重要的，这样才能鼓励他们进行广泛写作。相应地，广外对整个写作课程的评价也进行了改革。传统封闭式考试要求学生在有限的时间和空间内参加笔试，不同的是，广外的考核标准由三部分组成：学生每周作业占30%，期中考试占20%，期末考试占50%。期中考试的内容是要求学生在80分钟内写一篇作文（至少450个单词）；期末考试相对来说任务较复杂，要求学生调查某一主题并撰写草稿，自我修改直到对自己来说完美为止，然后交由老师进行批改，最后将分数计入学生的期末成绩中。

评分方案基于以下几点考虑：第一，写作构思。写作构思需要有足够的时间去交谈、阅读、玩耍、想象、思考和分享想法，以及起草和重构。然而这一点很难实现，学生大多数情况下写作任务很繁重，如果写得太仓促，文章就会显得非常肤浅，因此评分的前提是给学生提供一个较为充分的写作过程。第二，写作是通过创作的生成和反思性过程形成的，是作家创作和批判作品的过程。给予和接受批评，并相应地修改自己作品的能力是写作中必不可少的一部分，需要在课堂上仔细培养。通过多次起草、讨论和协作，广外学生能够全身心沉浸到写作之旅中。第三，传统的评分标准强调结构清晰、多用副词和形容词、标点符号准确、连接词多、复合句多等易于观察和检验的特点，而忽视作者的参与程度、写作的内容、意义、风格和声音。[1]这会导致学生停留在充满条条框框的狭窄道路上，丧失自发的创造力和写作的乐

〔1〕 Grainger, T., Goouch, K., & Lambirth, A., *Creativity and writing: Developing voice and verve in the classroom*, London; New York: Routledge, 2005.

趣。广外项目中，学生有了更多的时间和空间来关注自己的个人需求、激情和个性。将学生的认知和情感需求置于学习过程中，而不是一堆可衡量的技能之上，旨在帮助他们成长为作家，而非成功的应试者。

5.2.2 赋能：新课程

“以学生为中心，以需求为动力，放手写长”

“写长法”的初步成功为其进一步发展铺平了道路。2001 年，教学新方法开始融入广外英语系更多的写作课程中。基于 1999-2000 年第一个实验项目的经验，在“写长法”的基础上增加了更多的教学策略。研究小组组长郑超在其报告“以写促学，让学生写出自信和成就感”中，将修订后的教学法总结为“以学生为中心，以需求为动力，放手写长”的教学。经过演变的教学法可概括如下：

（1）归纳先于演绎。

传统的英语写作教学方法是先教授最小的写作单元——措辞，然后是句子和段落的写作，直到最后教授一篇完整的作文。与大多数中国学校传统的教学方法不同，新的教学方法是从直接写整篇文章开始的。在广泛的写作实践过程中，学生能够体验到不同文体的特点，并尝试各种写作技巧。基于学生从写作中获得的经验知识，教师可以简要介绍一些修辞策略，以提高写作质量。

（2）通过自我纠正避免低级错误。

在新教学法看来，错误可以分为两种类型。所谓的“零级错误”是指那些学生自己就可以很容易避免或改正的语法错误。另一种错误是在措辞、句法和语篇层面上的非习惯用法。后者在学习过程中是不可避免的，随着学生语言能力的逐步提高，有可能会被消除。学生自检之前的写作（例如在四周前或更早之前写的作文）能够有效处理这类错误。

（3）长度长，速度快，避免重复。

写长文是“写长法”的基本特征，但追求长篇大论并不意味着要以简洁为代价。因此，在此阶段，之前的评分系统中又增加了一个标准——简洁性。

在原有的“写长法”和新策略的基础上，郑老师对广外英语系一、二年级英语专业的学生进行了全面的课程改革，共包括两到三个学期的英语写作课程，分为四个发展阶段。每个阶段有 6 个写作任务（第四阶段除外，该阶段包含 2 到 3 个较大的任务）。在前三个阶段，每项任务需要 4 个课时（英语专业学生每周 2 小时）：

第一阶段，“笔随心动”。

这是写作之旅的开始阶段，这一阶段鼓励学生们自由地书写生活中感兴趣的话题。其主要目标为培养学生的写作兴趣和广泛的写作习惯。这一阶段的话题通常比较灵活和个性化，比如“意外之财”“身边趣事”等。

第二阶段，“立论谋篇”。

经过大约 12 周的广泛写作练习，学生们开始了第二阶段的论证写作，这也是四级和八级考试（英语专业的两大国家能力测试）的主要写作类型。在课堂上分享以往学生的写作模式，通过讨论探讨总结写作策略。这是让学生了解写作的结构、逻辑流程、衔接等基本形式和技巧的关键阶段，也是培养学生简明准确地写作的阶段。

第三阶段，“品味创作”。

这个阶段的重点是文学体裁，包括散文、随笔、故事续写等。教学的目的是培养学生对文学创作的热爱，提高审美情趣，学习各种文体的写作技巧。这一阶段的另一个重要目标是让学生大量接触文学阅读材料，以便他们能够吸收文学作品的精华，消除母语对英语写作的负面影响。

第四阶段，“走近报刊”。

在这个阶段有两到三个较大的写作任务，可以合并成一个项目。主要目标是激励学生为实际目的写作，比如为报纸或杂志写作。由于涉及文献综述、社会调查和数据收集，可谓是学生写作之旅中的一个巨大飞跃。这一阶段的写作任务也更为复杂，即在大学第三学年和第四学年的学术论文写作任务。

讨论：认知和情感赋能

四个阶段的写作课程与传统的写作课程有很大的不同，主要表现在它将全文写作优先于语言形式和元素的学习，并根据学生的认知和情感需要，精心为学生安排了一个连贯的学习节奏。

在传统的写作教学中，语言分析作为一种抽象的对象主导着写作课程，通常遵循词语—句子—段落—文本的写作模式。很多时候，学生还没到最后一个阶段，写作热情就已经被文本形式的机械练习耗尽了。从学生的角度来看，命名和了解写作“知识”似乎比在有意义的语境中理解和运用语言更为重要。

实践证明，广外课程高度重视作文和优先考虑整体语篇写作，效果显著。教材《以写促学：英语写作通用教程》，是广外十年研究的丰硕成果，同时也是广外在写作教育中通过满足学生认知和情感需求来增强学生能力的最好例证。

教材《以写促学：英语写作通用教程》

该教材于2008年8月出版，反映了“写长法”的研究成果，以广外英语写作课程的全面改革为主要特色。当我通读这本书的时候，对其中一些特点印象深刻，在我看来，这些特点与普通的写作教材有很大的不同。

第一个引人注目的特点是亲近和惊奇的写作风格，可能是由于书中生动的对话式教学形成的。例如，在序言中王教授给“我们的学生——永恒的朋友”写了一封简短的信，他在信中鼓励学生“多写、广写，以提高英语水平和自信心，最终创造出绚丽多彩的人生”。在“激情写作阶段”的“课程展望”中，编辑这样写道：“我们的策略旨在‘引诱’学生写出优秀的长篇作文，其秘诀在于培养学生‘自我欣赏’的兴趣。”

任务A-3“写一个意料之外的故事”的要求如下：

当听到结局出人意料得好笑的故事时，你一定会捧腹大笑。现在轮到你来写这样一个令人惊喜的故事了。进行真正的文学创作吧！

这种逼真的对话形式在书中随处可见。此外，每个单元的末尾都设置了一个名为“小笔吧”的部分，以非常生动的方式展示了相关的写作知识和技巧。另一个有趣的专栏叫作“防火墙”，以生动幽默的方式展示和讨论学生们在写作中常见的错误，并进行警示。

教材的第二个特点是每个写作任务的各部分之间、不同任务之间以及四个写作阶段之间的紧密联系。以任务 A-5“创建虚构情节”为例，其教学过程分为以下几个步骤：先以美国幽默作家 Art Buchwald 的作品“Fresh Air Will Kill You”为例，并对其结构、措辞、讽刺语气等特点进行评析；在范例阅读之后，学生的写作任务为“写一篇至少 300 个单词的反映人与自然或社会发展冲突的短篇故事，试着模仿范例作品的讽刺风格，但不要重复其情节”。

布置完任务后，对以前学生的范文进行评析，评价其优点和有待改进的地方。以此为基础，让学生产生大致想法，了解任务所要达到的预期效果以及思考如何进行写作。然后，“小笔吧”部分会指导学生如何通过阅读、复制和应用，从英语书籍、期刊、报纸和词典中收集的好句子来提高写作质量，并简要介绍了小说与非小说的区别，分析了学生写作中常见的错误。这些教学内容相互关联，为学生提供了有效的输入，从而让学生在写作中得到有效的输出。

除了理顺每个写作任务内部的联系外，还要仔细寻找不同写作任务之间的连贯过渡。在任务 A5 的开头，编辑回忆道：

我们练习写作已一月有余。也许你还没有意识到自己已经学会了运用写作技巧和想象力来写文章，甚至你们中的一些人可能已经拥有了幽默感。然而，这一切仅仅是开始，我们不能对此感到满足。当前，我们的焦点正从以自我为中心的写作向以读者为中心的写作转变。

类似过渡语同样存在于写作阶段之间。王教授在“创作写作阶段”的“课程展望”中这样写道：

在 A 阶段，我们进行了叙事写作的练习，在这一阶段，我们并未特别强调写作技巧，因为我们的主要目的是激发学生的写作欲望。在 B 阶段，我们几乎把所有的时间和精力都花在了准确性和逻辑流程的论证上，我相信即使是最勤奋的学生也可能会对此感到厌倦。现在让我们从逻辑思维回归想象，从证据回归故事情节，从理性回归感性。让我们以更放松的心态回归文学创作。

这样的指导有助于在写作阶段、写作任务和教学过程之间形成有机的联系，为教材使用者提供一个清晰的蓝本。它还可以增加书的实用性，使学生和老师更容易接受教材中的信息。

在上述特点的基础上，我发现教材有一个明显的特点，那就是多样性。前言中明确指出，“这样一个动态的改革，不需要静态的教科书”。的确，教材中充满了动态变化。从写作的四个阶段可以看出，写作要求有很大的差异，从描述性写作到逻辑论证，从文学创作到报刊文章。除了内容不同，书的结构也会根据需要而变化。例如，除了任务 A1“意外之财”，几乎所有的写作任务都伴随着一篇由英国本土作家写的范文。因为这是第一堂写作课，要求学生们跟随自己的直觉，记下自己脑中所想。没有写作范本的约束和压力，学生们在写作的最初阶段也不会泄气。

后几阶段为学生提供的写作范例中，有些是根据不同的教学时间提供的，有些是在课堂上进行头脑风暴时提供的，有些是为快速写作练习提供的，还有一些是在学生之间进行讨论或反思后提供的。在教学过程中，教师也会加入到教学过程中的各个环节中，对学生进行指导。一般来说，教师遵循归纳—演绎的顺序，也就是说，他们倾向于等待学生发表自己的意见，揭露自己的弱点，提出问题，然后再介入其中给予帮助。

结论

在教学方向方面，“写长法”和后来的“以写促学”教学法与“过程写作”有许多共同的特点。它鼓励二语作者通过写作和修改过程来发现和探索，同时尽量避免语言层面问题的影响。在某种程度上，它类似于“流利第一”的方法，目标是流利第一，然后是清晰，最后是正确。这种教学法也呼应了“表达主义运动”的精神，在这种运动中，写作行为把学生作者从受到严格限制的、有章可循的学术作业和评价中解放出来，并帮助他们探索个人的重要问题。广外项目借鉴了“自由写作”“头脑风暴”“日记写作”“个人随笔写作”等表现主义传统，为学生提供“启发性话题”，这些话题来自学生自身生活、真正感兴趣的话题，鼓励学生以无拘无束、富有创造性的方式表达自己。

因此，对“写长法”的批判主要围绕多年来关于过程和表现主义方法争论的问题，即流畅性与准确性的争论、关于错误纠正的价值的争论、过程与作品的争论。[1]针对这些批评，“写长法”自我修正为“以写促学”教学法，这是一种综合了“写长法”优点的教学法，同时试图调和上述问题中的一些争论。

可见，广外教学法在许多方面偏离了过程写作或表现主义方法。第一，“自由写作”的形式并不是项目的最终目的，而是写作冒险的开始。从写作课程的课程设计中可以看出，写作课程分为四个阶段，其中“激情写作”只是第一阶段，是让学生对写作产生“迷恋”的阶段，旨在为后续任务的训练做好准备。第二，通过评分方案调节学生作文的长度，使写作教学对教师来说更加可控和易于管理。第三，纠错并非完全被排除在外，而是以一种积极、鼓舞人心的方式进行，要求注重学生作品的优点而非问题。语法教学以更友好、更有趣的方式出现，例如教科书中的“防火墙”或“小笔吧”。第四，除了个人和自我探究的文章，学生还需要学习在学术环境中生存的写作类型，如论文考试，以及有助于深入思考的写作，如说明文、议论文和专项写作，这也是项目的重要组成部分。此外，如何在这些任务之间形成一个连贯一致的过渡，也是创新写作课程中需要考虑的问题。

总之，广外的课程改革取得了可喜的成果。创造性写作教学法在提高学生英语写作的自信心和能力，提高学生的创造力和思维能力方面取得了显著的成效。郑超表示，该项目还能够帮助学生应对国家英语水平考试（英语专业四级和八级）。这些测试中包含的写作模块过去常常让老师和学生都感到担忧，而对这类任务的训练过去常常占据课堂的大部分时间。但是现在只要一到两周的练习，学生们就可以轻松地完成这些任务，因为大量的写作练习使这些任务变得轻而易举。

---

〔1〕 Casanave, C. P., *Controversies in second language writing: Dilemmas and decisions in research and instruction*, Ann Arbor: University of Michigan Press, 2004.

5.2.3 增进相关性：主题设计、流行文化和批判读写

主题设计

通常来讲，写作教师面临的主要挑战之一是如何吸引学生。许多人发现在课堂上很难调动学生的兴趣，使其对写作任务做出积极的反应。广外为解决这一问题也做了大量的努力，为“吸引”学生写作采取了诸多策略，其中包括设计鼓舞人心的主题、给予积极的反馈、提供出版渠道、将流行文化引入写作课堂等。这些策略不仅能够满足学生的情感需求，还将学生的写作与现实生活兴趣紧密联系在一起，从而激发出了学生的内在写作需求。这一部分，我们将结合读写、教育学和媒体研究中的批评理论，说明广外为激发学生写作兴趣所使用的方法。

学生要为自己写作，并根据自己的需要和兴趣选择主题和形式。正如Grainger[1]所说：

> 人类写作出于多种原因：思考和理解自身经验，理解自己和他人，交流和分享信息，赋予自身权力并进行改变，在自由写作中获得乐趣。

写作应该融入与作者息息相关的生活和工作中，否则当学生看到写作的主要目的不过是向教师展示自己所学知识时，就会减少对写作的热情和投入。在广外，“相关性”一直是选择写作课话题和范例的关键原则之一。

关于设计写作题目，王教授说道：“主题设计是该教学法的重中之重，而优秀话题需要足够的时间进行设计。”

广外认为，优秀主题应必备以下几个因素：第一，主题与学生过去或现在的生活密切相关。例如，在“我第一次……的经历”这个主题上，学生们描述了自己首次参加游泳比赛、做饭、抽烟、考试和照看孩子等经历。同样，学生们也能够谈论其他个人话题，如“我为什么上大学”“破碎的梦”“住院”

---

〔1〕 Grainger, T., Goouch, K., & Lambirth, A., *Creativity and writing: Developing voice and verve in the classroom*, London; New York: Routledge, 2005.

等。第二，优秀的话题通常与学生其他课程学到的知识有关，从而学生能够通过写作充分发挥自身能力，整合来自各个学科的知识，如语文课等其他专业课程，使之成为写作主题，这是一种内化知识的有效方式，也是促进进一步学习的必要条件。在某种程度上，它反映了跨学科写作的最新趋势。此外，课程还会要求学生对自己在文学或阅读课上学到的文学作品发表评论，或将口头传说改编成话剧。第三，优秀的话题能够激发学生的创造力和想象力。在“如果世界上没有……”主题中，学生展开丰富的想象力，提出“如果世界上没有动物”“如果世界上没有美女”“如果世界上没有想象力”等话题。广外还尝试了一些旨在培养学生创造性思维的话题，包括“意外之财”“结局出乎意料的故事”“生活有趣的一面”等。除了刺激性的话题，广外还鼓励学生尝试其他形式的写作，如诗歌、小说和杂志、报纸的专题写作。第四，优秀的话题能够促进社会和文化理解。在“谈节日”中，学生们介绍了许多中国节日，如元宵节、中秋节、春节和清明节等。此外，还介绍了许多中国习俗，如“茶文化”和“庙会”。广外鼓励学生走出“象牙塔”，关注校园外的社会经济，尝试“家庭关系”“人与事业”“青年与社会”等话题。课程杂志有一期专门讨论了“中国评论网”中的内容，包括学生对社会问题的讨论，如就业市场的关键需求、青少年抑郁和自杀倾向、自由职业、沉迷虚拟生活、过度消费、吸毒、职业道德、社会变革和挑战等问题。

不仅如此，学生还可以自由选择主题。我读过一些非常有趣的文章，例如“为什么我还没有女朋友”“课堂最后十分钟”“生活在4453年的小男孩”。关于广东外语外贸大学设计和使用的所有主题，请访问网站 http://www. writetolearn. com。

写作任务与学生生活密切相关，大部分作文范例都选自广外学生的写作档案。选取这些范例的好处在于其是由学生而非著名作家撰写，因此语言水平、文化背景和生活经历等方面都与学生一致，学生更容易从范例中吸取优点，并以此为鉴，提高写作水平从而取得进步。

出版渠道

除激发写作兴趣和提升参与度外，无论课堂内外，学生作品都应进行分享并给予相应地位，以便学生提醒自己是作家群体中的一分子。通过这种方式，学生既能体验到写作的艰辛，也能够在创造性应用写作中获得成就感，从而促进英语写作学习。

广外宣传渠道众多，如网站、朗诵会、《优秀作文作品集》[1]和课程杂志等。其中，课程杂志主要由学生编辑和投稿，通过邀请学生投稿并将其部分作品进行修改完善，能有效提高写作能力，增强写作兴趣。此外，杂志为讨论、交流创意写作经验和作品提供了平台。

第一期《以写促学》杂志于2002年4月出版。从此每年发行一次。其中除论文外，还包括学生的文章、诗歌、评论、社会调查、写作技巧和错误更正等。这些作品大多选自学生作品或由教师推荐。老师和学生都为这本杂志付出了诸多努力，其中写作团队组长郑超老师还担任了插图作者。

网站（http://www.writetolearn.com）

由广外建立的"以写促学：英语写作教学中写长法的辐射网"网站，既是学生作品的宣传渠道，也是动态互动平台。作为教科书和杂志的延续和补充，该网站包含了学生最新作品，关于教学法的研究论文以及写作新主题和技巧。

该网站主要分为十个专栏。第一部分为学生最新论文范例（最近这个专栏被名为"跨太平洋写作交流"的新计划所取代，该计划将于本章5.3.6中进行讨论）；第二部分为广外项目的学术讨论和研究论文；第三至第六部分为写作四阶段内学生写作作品集合；第七部分为"小笔吧"（语法讨论）；第八部分"战斗训练"为专业四级和专业八级考试（大学英语专业两大考试）写作模块的技巧讲解；第九部分为更多课后练习的主题和示例；第十部分为教科书《以写促学：英语写作通用教程》的简介。值得注意的是，除示例文章外，"小笔吧"和"战斗训练"部分的内容大多为学生投稿，并配有生动活泼的幻灯片对观点进行阐述。

除了十个主要专栏外，还有一个小专栏叫作"写作竞技场"。在其中我发

---

〔1〕 欧阳护华主编：《广东外语外贸大学英语专业学生优秀作文选》，北京大学出版社2003年版。

现了学生和网站管理员之间一些有趣的对话，如有位读者问道："我已经非常努力了，但写作时为什么还是不断犯错?"管理员郑超老师幽默地回答说："摆脱母语束缚要进行一生的努力。避免犯错的唯一办法就是去犯错。通过揭露错误，用大脑进行分辨和纠正，避免再犯。如果一个人不去犯错，就永远不能避免犯错。"（"以写促学"网站："写作竞技场"，2009）

网站管理员郑超告诉我，为了与新出版的教材保持同步，该网站于2008年进行了更新。他希望该网站能够成为广外与国内外其他机构交流的平台，共同探讨经验和挑战。同时，网站也是广外师生了解项目最新进展的重要窗口。

朗诵会

朗诵会、课程杂志和网站，为学生提供了展示作品的平台。与其他两种平台不同，朗诵会强调学生的书面写作和表现，特别是其创造性。

为决出优胜者，学生们在课堂上朗读自己的作品，进行初步选拔，选出两个故事（允许合著者）作为代表参加跨班比赛。决赛时会邀请写作老师作为观众和评委，教师也会受邀在比赛开始前朗读作品，比赛间隙还会准备节目表演，此举能缩短老师和学生之间的距离，使学生更加放松和自信。比赛结束后，老师会进行点评，决出最佳情节、最佳原创、最佳写作和最佳表演奖。

与其他课余活动相同，朗诵会由学生自发组织，极大地提高了沟通能力和管理能力，老师常常赞叹不已。正如郑老师所说："一切都井井有条，我受邀出席时，上台路线都安排得很妥当。"

除写作课和练习课外，广外还将活动融入课程中，以提高学生写作兴趣和写作能力，培养学生独立深入思考的能力。这些活动不仅能够增强学生的自信心，还能丰富社会经验，激发创造力。除了朗诵会，广外话剧表演和读书清单活动也给我留下了深刻的印象。

戏剧：才艺表演

2003年，我在广外参加首届全国英语写作教学与研究国际研讨会时，有幸观看了英语系一年一度的英语戏剧表演。作为课程的重要组成部分，该活动旨在让学生有机会在写作和表演中发挥自身才能和创造力。这次活动大部分由学生自己组织，也是学生学习生活中最激动人心、最难忘的经历之一。

从选择戏剧故事开始，阅读剧本，根据自己的需要重写；挑选演员，任命导演、制片人和舞台经理。关键的一步是为演出寻找赞助商，提供资金支持。学生在整个过程中表现出了惊人的热情和创造力。投入的精力和时间是巨大的，结果往往也能够证明它是有价值的。

当帷幕徐徐升起时，我惊叹于绚丽的舞台，不敢相信这仅仅是学生的舞台。男女主角都是英语系的学生，但看起来年轻又老练。接下来的表演更让我惊喜不已，情节耐人寻味，演技精湛，语言效果和舞台布置令人惊叹。事实上，当夜会务组有一场聚餐，这场精彩的戏剧表演足以让人放弃聚餐美食。

阅读清单：文学赋能

我参加的另一项活动是阅读清单活动。英语系一年级的学生邀请了四位颇有声望且受欢迎的教授推荐阅读清单。这四位教授具有不同的学科背景，提出了非常实用的建议。如学生必读的书有哪些，大学四年中应该读多少书等；还有一些实用技巧，例如如何查找书籍、记笔记、处理生词以及撰写评论。这些可敬的教授们在阅读问题上意见并不一致，我觉得趣味横生。例如，一位教授建议学生在阅读时跳过生词，因为生词多次反复，其含义会在阅读中慢慢清晰。而另一位教授并不同意，相反，他认为要利用电子设备等设备查找生词的确切含义后才能继续阅读。从这些生动坦率的讨论中，我意识到，并没有固定的、通用的阅读技巧，每个人都有自己的方法。这将开阔学生们的眼界，让他们看到各种各样的可能性，并努力尝试各种方法，最后找到自己的解决方法。

这些老师推荐的阅读清单也很有趣。从圣经到美学，从中文到英文，从小说到科技，都曾对这些教授的认知和成长有过深刻影响。同时，我也惊讶于老师和学生之间的积极互动。问题接踵而至，老师无法顾及，一些学生甚至站起来举手，企图让自己更显眼以吸引老师的注意。热情是有感染力的，我为学生的参与热情和学习激情所折服，那一刻我觉得又回到了大学一年级，那种感觉令人兴奋不已。

媒体和流行文化

强大的深层文化潮流，尤其是低端流行的文化，实际上决定了作家的创造力，但这些潮流仍未被揭示，甚至连研究人员也完全没有意识到它们的存在。

——Bakhtin

读写能力的变化凸显了流行文化对学生作文的影响，学生在作文中创造性地吸收他人的话语和声音，并在写作中对此进行修改。[1]最近的研究明确展示了学生们是如何从他们想象中所接触的流行文化和文学中汲取灵感，以及他们接触到的文学文本是如何“鼓励他们以不同的方式写作，走出‘固有风格’，进入新语言境界”[2]。

在中国思想史上的大部分时间内，考试制度是维护儒家正统思想的“死亡之手”，“阻碍了通俗文学融入当代文学”。学生们没有机会公开讨论“课堂以外的神圣而重要的东西”[3]。教师可能被排除在学生实际生活之外，与学生相比，他们对大众文化的理解仍处于初级阶段。但是老师们能够鼓励学生灵活地混合多种多样的符号为写作提供材料和想象力。

广外教师敏锐地意识到流行文化的吸引力。教师了解学生在大众传媒中获取的知识，鼓励学生将电视和漫画世界与写作联系起来，激励学生进行创作，例如卢老师介绍道：

我发现学生开始对规定的写作题目产生厌倦。所以前几天，我给他们播放了一部肥皂剧《换换爱》的一个片段。对于年轻的大学生来说，标题本身非常吸引人，他们试图弄清爱的意义与自己的关系。爱情是大学生活的重要

〔1〕 Grainger, T., Goouch, K., & Lambirth, A., *Creativity and writing: Developing voice and verve in the classroom*, London; New York: Routledge, 2005.

〔2〕 Barrs, M., & Cork, V., *The reader in the writer: The links between the study of literature and writing development at key stage 2*, London: Centre for Language in Primary Education, 2001, p210.

〔3〕 Alvermann, D. E., Moon, J. S., & Hagood, M. C., *Popular culture in the classroom: Teaching and researching critical media literacy*, Newark, DEL: International Reading Association, 1999.

组成部分，但在课堂上，通常是禁忌话题。学生在这个话题上所表现出来的兴奋和热情不难想象。

还有，我们课上要求描述一幅经典名画，学生们坚决主张想要新鲜流行的素材而非古典画，并提出《几米漫画》。我同意将名画换成流行作品，接下来的讨论和写作果不其然变得异常活跃！

从这些经验中，我意识到教师教授的东西并不是学生感兴趣的东西。但是，为了让学生参与进来，激发其写作动机，我们使教学迎合学生的兴趣需要。这也就会引起古典知识和流行文化之间的冲突。这对我来说是比较容易应对的，因为刚刚大学毕业，所以和学生之间有许多共同兴趣。但对于老教师来说，就要难得多。有些老教师认为，无论如何，流行文化不应该在课堂上占据一席之地。

讨论：重新定义二语学生的读写能力

广外教改虽然没有明确提出，但它确实触及了重新定义读写能力和二语写作的问题。现代生活中的社会、经济和技术方面的深刻变化，让我们正迎来一个截然不同的教育时代。在这个时代，人们不可能把读写能力与上述因素分离开来。

例如，2003 年，Kress 曾预测，屏幕将取代书本成为主要表达方式，写作的各个方面也将随之产生深刻变化。新媒体时代使人与符号模式建立起一种全新关系，从而能够使用多种方式来写作。这些变化反过来又将对知识的形式和形态产生深远影响，推动“读写”的含义扩大到包括在这一过程中制作信息所涉及的任何资源。由此出现了对“新文学”的研究，特别是许多研究人员强调“大众读写”而非“学校读写”的重要性。[1] Dyson 认为“大众读写”与“大众文化”有关，在某种程度上与人们的日常兴趣联系在一起。

中国语言教育的官方文件以含蓄间接的方式反映了从学校读写向现实生活读写的转变。例如，教育部多次敦促语言教育从“制度化学习”转变为学习“具有广泛适应性、实用性和综合性的知识”。

---

〔1〕 Kress, G. R., *Literacy in the new media age*, London: Routledge, 2003.

尽管如此，要超越传统的读写观念并不是一件容易的事，在实际教学中实施“新读写”模式更是难上加难。但是在目前教育政策方向上，许多学术标准是为其他时代和目的而设计的。这就像试图“通过频频看后视镜来穿越前方未来的复杂地域”[1]。例如，我们的学生现在生活在一个高度复杂的视觉世界中，他们受到的视觉刺激比以往任何一代人都强烈。年轻人为了自己的目的借用、采用和适应不同写作方式的能力相当强。尽管学生多模态读写能力越来越强，但许多教师仍局限于书面写作。这就不可避免地会引发权力斗争。如果教师没有认识和理解他们所遇到的许多形式的视觉信息，或者没有花时间帮助学生整理这些信息，或更有甚者对大众文化产生强烈的抵触心理，可能会导致学生对读写实践疏远和抵制。因此，如果学校学习仍保持狭隘和静止不变，学生可能会对学校的学习感到失望。[2]

Dyson 认为学校不是适合流行文化传播的场所。由于受过“非流行”教育，教师，尤其是年长的教师，在处理流行文化方面缺乏信心；而对于年轻教师来说，虽然更适应新媒体，在教学上更有创造力，但他们不一定知道如何有效地将各种素材和经验资源转化为知识。

然而，我们不能把流行文化拒之门外。因为无论是否得到老师的认可，在学生玩耍、说话、唱歌、思考、写作和想象的过程中，它都深深植根于学生生活。[3]它不应仅仅被视为“娱乐”或“商业”，也不应仅仅被视为激励或补充知识的工具。流行文化在学校教育和社会认同的产生中扮演了重要角色。离开现实世界被迫接受学校教育的学生就像离开了水的鱼，或者用 Robinson 的话来说，他们“脱离环境后便失去了自我”。因此，在这一领域无论是年轻的教师还是年长的教师都需要专业的培训和支助。

在此，我提议扩大和重塑“读写”的概念。作为教师，我们需要挑战以书面文字为主的传统读写观念，扩大学校的读写课程，以适应上述变化。此

---

〔1〕 Robinson, K., *Out of our minds: Learning to be creative*, Oxford: Capstone; John Wiley, 2001, p16.

〔2〕 Hickman, J., Huck, C. S., Kiefer, B. Z., & Hepler, S. I., *Children's literature in the elementary school* (8th ed.), Boston: McGraw-Hill, 2004.

〔3〕 Dyson, A. H., Foreword. In J. Marsh & E. Millard (Eds.), *Popular literacies, childhood and schooling*, London, New York: Routledge, 2006.

外，引导学生认识读写领域的发展变化能够产生显著效果。为了在写作中保持学生自身声音和写作活力，我们必须认识到目前存在多样化的读写概念，并鼓励学生加以利用。

5.2.4 重塑写作理念

学习一门语言既是进入并维持一个既定语言社区的社会化的过程，同时也是获得个人表达手段以挑战和改变语言传统的过程。所以作家往往有两种声音：社会声音和个人声音。声音是我们写作中的个人印记。这种个人声音是写作的发动机，推动了写作的前进。[1]正如 Grainger 所说：

> 如果作者的声音要充满信念和意义，那么作者自己的个人印记就需要在写作中显露出来。但是书面惯例倾向于使语言标准化，当我们从说话转向写作时，就失去了与听众之间的直接人际接触，面临抹去个性和个人声音的风险。

由于写作具有“语境弱化”的性质，[2]我们很容易在写作中失去个人声音。许多学生，特别是在小学后期，写作时的确没有声音与激情。他们写作能力有限，枯燥乏味，缺乏创意。这一点非常值得关注。我儿子凯尔就是如此。

> 我讨厌郊游，因为我害怕写郊游的作文。
>
> ——凯尔（7 岁）

凯尔在中国时，学校会要求学生在重大活动之后写一篇作文，如郊游、运动会或节假日等。因此，活动兴奋感常常因随之而来的写作任务变成恐惧和担忧。更重要的是，他们并没有足够的自由来表达自己。

例如，凯尔在公园远足后收到了一篇 300 字的写作任务。晚上他来找我寻求帮助时说自己没有写作灵感。我便建议他把远足时的感受写下来，他向

---

〔1〕 Graves, D. H., *Writing: Teachers and children at work*, Exeter, N. H.: Heinemann Educational Books, 1983.

〔2〕 Kramsch, C. J., *Language and culture*, Oxford: Oxford University Press, 1998.

我说道："不可以，必须写些有实际意义的东西，但其实今天下了好大的雨，我玩得一点儿也不尽兴。"我哑口无言，但我还是鼓励他将真实感受写下来，他拒绝了我，去找别人寻求更好的建议。

还有一次，凯尔的写作任务是一个很可爱的话题——春雨。我建议他描写春雨的优点和缺点。但他立即反驳道："我们只能写优点，不然会被老师批评！"这一次我仍然坚持了我的想法，并让他仔细想想自己对春雨的感受。他说："我不喜欢春雨，因为下雨会弄脏我的鞋袜，也没办法去外面玩耍。"听完我添加了几点："春雨让道路变得湿滑，爸爸开车会变得很危险，我购物的心情也变差了。"凯尔写下了春雨的缺点，但在他的强烈要求下还是添加了几点优点，直到我们两个对这篇文章都很满意。

几天后仍没听到关于作文的反馈，我问凯尔："老师看了那篇你对春雨的感受的作文了吗？"他沮丧地回答道："老师看过了，说我的作文不可能成为模范作文。"

很明显，孩子对写作没有任何兴趣。首先，他没什么可写，因为他不能用写作来表达自己的真实感受；其次，当他在表达自己的观点时确实冒了一些风险，且并没有得到老师的回应或鼓励时，写作的激情很快就消失了。因此，当有一天听到凯尔突然说道："我讨厌郊游，因为我害怕写郊游作文"时我并不感到惊讶。

写作的种种限制和规约，剥夺了小凯尔的个人声音，也耗尽了其写作兴趣。凯尔在写作中遇到的困难或失败，导致他缺乏自信，从而认为自己是一个不称职的作者。这种消极态度，若不在早期治愈，很可能会发展成一种长期的写作恐惧。

所以许多大学生觉得写作枯燥无味，是因为有一些人被老师强加给他们的既定期望所束缚。一些学生错误地认为写作是少数幸运儿的领域，是某种不可多得的天赋。这些消极观念在中国大学生中普遍存在。[1]因此，广外的教师提出了通过创设激发语境和提供相关信息，提高学生在写作中表达真实

---

〔1〕 Dong, Y., "Expert's analysis: Four major factors that kill creativity in Chinese", *Journal*, Retrieved from http://news.xinhuanet.com/st/2005-09/22/content_ 3519635_ 2.htm, 2005.

和个性化声音的意识的方法。例如，广外第一个写作阶段“笔随心动”课程就是这样一种积极的尝试。它为学生提供了写任何主题的自主权，以便激发出个人声音和写作激情，否则写作激情可能会被压制。

除自由写作外，广外学生还会尝试不同的文本类型，如记叙文、议论文、说明文等。通过模仿英国本土作家和广外同学的作品范例，为学生提供相应的信息输入，激发学生的创作能力。然而，如果采用不当，这种信息输入可能会造成“清洗作者”的潜在危险——清除个人声音。[1]参与广外项目的老师和学生都对此表示关注。因此，为培养学生的写作表达能力，我们需要提供一种自由和形式的平衡，既支持创新，也支持模仿。

从模仿到创造

> 因此，作品被视为积累和变化的过程，是对突出的思想、技术、文字和图像的存储和重组，直到它们结合在一起，形成一个新的创造性作品。
>
> ——Green[2]

广外的一些老师和学生对借鉴他人观点表示质疑。他们担心此种行为是欺骗和偷窃，借用的思想并非原创的，应加以拒绝。另一种观点认为，从经典文学作品中选取的范文或之前的学生范文能够激发学生的写作创意。对于这些问题，我们可以转到以下关于“互文性”的讨论。

许多研究者已经阐明了复制和创造之间的微妙关系。根据 Eve Bearne 的观点，复制意味着从现有素材中产生某种东西，而创造意味着添加某种新东西。Bakhtin 认为，他人语言使我们产生自己的语言成为可能，从而成为语言创造能力中不可或缺的因素：

> 我们的言语，也就是我们所有的话语（包括创造性的作品），都充满了不同程度的“他人话语”或不同程度的“自己的话语”，不同程度的模仿和创新。

---

〔1〕 Grainger, T., Goouch, K., & Lambirth, A., *Creativity and writing: Developing voice and verve in the classroom*, London; New York: Routledge, 2005, p44.

〔2〕 Green, A., Creative writing: Taking risks with words. In R. Fisher & M. Williams (Eds.), *Unlocking creativity: Teaching across the curriculum*, London: David Fulton, 2004, p37-54.

他人的话语带有他们自己的表达和态度，可以被我们吸收、重组和再次强调。

因此，一方面思想世界在不断自我循环，无法避免不断地使用同一组思想，不断地复述和自我参照。创造力来源于他人的想法、成就和影响。特别是在新媒体时代，互联网可以随时访问任何文本。

但另一方面，“互文性”能够产生创意。创造力来源于基于社会习惯的表达方式，但它能通过个人想象力对现有表达方式进行延展和替换。[1]这些延展和替换将受到学习者所熟悉的无数声音的影响。因此，一个名副其实的“声音之海”有意识和无意识地支持年轻作者成长为成熟的写作者。[2] Grainger 认为：

> 来自文学世界的强有力的声音，诗人、作家、歌手以及电影和电视人物的铿锵之声，与家人和朋友更私人亲密的声音结合在一起，充斥着年轻人的耳朵。他们自己的声音也为周围的话语海洋做出了贡献，他们作为读者、作家、说话人和听话人在这声音之海中徜徉。

正如 Bakhtin 所说，“语言中的词有一半来自别人”。只有当说话者使用这个词，使之符合自己的语义和表达意图时，这个词才会变成“自己的”。所有权和剽窃的概念是一个复杂的跨文化现象。[3]例如，中国的老师和学生可以用和西方人不同的方式来看待援引的文章。他们可能认为，在写作学习的初级阶段，模仿单词、短语甚至段落是一种学习方法，而文本的借用和模仿是有助于新手作家语言和修辞发展的必要步骤。

在广外，我观察到一些写作课程采用了新的教学法，有些则没有。我的总体印象是，这些采用新的教学法的写作课比大多数传统的写作课更吸引人，

---

〔1〕 Cremin, M., “Identifying some imaginative processes in the drama work of primary school children as they use three different kinds of drama structures for learning”, *Research in Drama Education: The Journal of Applied Theatre and Performance*, 3 (2), 1998, p211-224.

〔2〕 Dyson, A. H., “Writing and the sea of voices: Oral language in, around and about writing, In J. R. Squire & R. Indrisano” (Eds.), *Perspectives on writing: Research, theory, and practice*, Newark, Dela: International Reading Association, 2000, p45-65.

〔3〕 Scollon, R., Plagiarism and ideology: Identity in intercultural discourse, *Language in Society*, 1995.

更贴近学生。课程鼓励学生借鉴其他作家的观点，吸收其观点，用于自身写作。作为一种写作练习，他们甚至可以把英文原版故事翻译成中文。当学生们确信模仿可以产生创意时，就会从被指控剽窃的恐惧和疑虑中解脱出来，并自信地在学习过程中发挥能动性。

至于小凯尔呢，有一天他绞尽脑汁地想为过生日的父亲写一首诗，我告诉他完全可以从他读过的诗中借用结构，甚至词语。他松了一口气，转身去看他那堆小小的藏书。那天晚上，他写下了这首诗：

Guess how much I love you?
I love you like my mum,
I love you like when I am playing computer,
I love you like when I go to school.
I love you like when I play soccer.
I love you all the way to Pluto and back,

I love you when I wake up,
I love you when I go to bed,
My love is as much as the night stars,
I love you as high as Yao Ming[1],
I love you as hot as the lava.

I love you daddy.

——七岁的凯尔

写作也是智力的一个方面

正如上文所示，要想增强写作能力，澄清关于写作的错误认识至关重要。除了模仿和创造之间的关系，关于写作另一个普遍存在的误解就是，它不如

〔1〕 姚明是中国著名的篮球运动员，他曾效力于休斯敦火箭队，是 NBA 最高的球员，身高 2.29 米。

科学，因为它不需要科学工作中必不可少的“智慧”。以下是一位学生对“重理轻文”趋势的担忧：

> 我长大后，觉得文科不如理科——重理轻文。因此，文科科目，包括写作，很少被重视，更不用说创意写作了。在课堂上得到最多赞许的学生通常是能很快解决数学或物理问题的孩子。而那些能写出有趣作品的人则被认为是在耍小聪明。因此，在写作中表现出来的创造力是不值得骄傲的，或者根本就不能称之为创造力。
>
> 从我还是个孩子起，我就一直是一个热心的读者和一个充满激情的作家。我收集了大量的读书笔记，珍藏至今。但是和那些擅长数学的人相比，我在课堂上就没有那么自信了。私下里，我为自己热爱阅读和写作而感到羞愧，因为偏科，使我在考试中也无法取得高分。更重要的是，虽然我能写得比别人更有趣，但我仍然不比那些能快速解决数学或物理问题的人聪明。
>
> 和我一样，“重理轻文”的氛围也让许多初出茅庐的作家望而却步，也为那些不愿写作的人提供了借口。因此，越来越多的同学对写作感到恐惧。
>
> 我仍然记得，当无意中听到博闻强记也是智力的标志时，我如释重负。我告诉自己，就算不是天生就高智商，学习还可以开发智力，而且阅读和写作也不应该成为“二流科目”。

“重理轻文”的现象并不少见，文科科目只是理科核心科目的“附加奢侈品”。[1]这种看法贬低了教育中那些难以衡量的方面，如创造力。Gardener 在 1993 年的著作“*Frames of Mind*”中对智力的不同形式进行了分类，其中创造力和想象力是智力的重要组成部分。他认为，人类潜能可以在有利的环境下得到开发，不同智能之间可以相互支持和增强。例如，学习者的写作、读写和智力发展之间存在着确定联系。

中国最伟大的科学家之一，钱学森说过，主要通过艺术发展起来的视觉化思维和想象思维，对科学研究和发明至关重要。Ken Robinson 是国际公认的

---

〔1〕 Burnard, P., & White, J., “Creativity and performativity: Counterpoints in British and Australian education”, *British Educational Research Journal*, 34 (5), 2008, p667-682.

创造力研究的领导者，证实艺术和科学之间联系密切。他注意到，当艺术家从科学思想、发现和先进技术中获得灵感，产生新的艺术表现形式时，科学家往往也会从艺术创作过程和洞见中找到灵感。

艺术和科学的区分，以及对科学和技术的高度重视，根源于特定的历史理性主义传统，这种传统在人类心理学中推动了智力和情感之间的联系，以及整个社会的艺术与科学之间的关联。科学通常与真理、客观性、事实、现实联系在一起；而艺术则被认为与感性、情感和直觉有关。这种观念扭曲了教育中的创造性观念，造成了千百万人的发展不平衡。

Ken Robinson 认为，强调科学的另一个原因来自于经济的需求。人们认为国家需要培养更多的科学家和技术人员，而不是艺术家。因此，学校教育对科学和技术给予了更高的优先地位，艺术和人文学科都对科学和技术教育让路。但是，这是否符合年轻人的最大利益，是否是培养科学家和技术人员的最佳方式，在发达国家是一个很有争议的问题。由于科学与艺术的分工和这些重要能力发展的不平衡，具有较强学术能力的儿童往往无法发现自己的其他能力；那些科研能力较低的人也可能有其他“潜伏”的强大能力，但他们在接受教育时可能永远不知道自己真正的能力是什么。这便导致了对人力和资源的不可估量的浪费。

如果语言专业的学生错误地认为，他们不是理科生，智力水平不高，并且写作与理科学习不同，既不能代表作家的智力，也不能提高作家的智力，那么写作又如何能激发他们的积极性呢？这种思维方式在一定程度上影响了学生的语言学习倾向，包括写作倾向，从而影响了学生智力的全面发展。

语言专业学生智力的培养已经引起许多教育研究者和决策者的关注。例如，由教育部任命的外语专业教育改革启动小组多次强调语言专业学生智力素质的重要性。他们认为，思维能力、创造性、分析问题的能力、形成独立见解的能力等素质都是智力的重要方面，应通过语言教育进行有效提高。

为了推动我们的进步，广外提倡对智力、能力和创造力的本质进行新的理解。学生们开始意识到，人类智力有多种形式，远比某些学科中所能展示的要丰富和复杂。我们都有自身独特的智力取向，如视觉想象力、声音或动作能力、数学或写作能力。不同的人有不同的智力特长，每个人都有能通过系统策略发展起来的创造力。与中国学生普遍持有的错误观念不同，写作是人类智力的重要指标之一，如果系统地加以训练，将可能成为开发人类智力的有力途径。

5.2.5　师生关系

在教学实践中重构权力结构，是批判学者和教师发展写作教学法的首要目标。这一目标可以通过将一些传统上属于教师的权利转移到学生身上，和在写作课堂内外重建师生关系来实现。[1]这种权力的消解和师生关系在写作教学法中的转换，开启了一场学生在写作教育中的赋权运动。在广外，写作教学法成功的一个关键原因是师生关系的转变。换句话说，写作团队的教师已经从传统的“权威”讲师的角色转变为同志、导演和啦啦队长的组合。

2008 年，广外教改团队由十六名教师组成，其中教授四人，副教授两人，讲师五人，助理讲师三人，外籍教师两人。三名教师为博士学位，其他都是硕士。年龄层面涵盖了 20 岁至 50 岁，团队会定期开会、设计写作任务、制定教学计划、准备课程活动、交流教学经验。

在上课前，老师需要开会讨论决定写作任务。他们不遗余力地寻找有趣的话题，以吸引学生并激励他们写作。除了两三位年轻老师，大多数老师和学生都有较大的年龄差异，所以他们必须把自己想象成年轻学生，了解他们的世界，寻找能引起学生兴趣的话题。很多写作任务都是通过这样的努力完成的，比如“生活中的趣事”。老师觉得自身在整个过程中重新焕发了活力，能够和自己的学生一样拥有年轻的心态。

在课堂上，参与这个项目的老师不应再仅是知识的传授者，相反，应该通过讨论和总结来吸引学生，要求学生利用已有的母语和英语写作知识，以及阅读范例，总结写作任务的修辞策略。有时老师是一个导演，分配角色和指导学生发挥；有时老师是一个批评家，评论学生的表现；但大多数时候，老师是观众，在热烈的掌声中用真诚的眼神注视着学生。

---

〔1〕 Hardin, J. M., *Opening spaces: Critical pedagogy and resistance theory in composition*, Albany: State University of New York Press, 2001.

在学生的课堂和课外活动中，写作教师的参与也产生了有效的成果。同时，教师的个性也对师生关系的塑造起着重要作用。在“写长法”的初始阶段，王初明教授亲自进行实验教学，取得了很好的效果。郑超老师认为，其中一个主要原因是王教授是一位优秀的教师和著名研究人员，学生对他非常钦佩。学生认为这是一个能够与王教授一起交流的好机会，所以热切地追随他共同开拓新的写作之路。王教授的坚定信念激励着学生们尽最大努力去实现一个共同目标——对写作课进行改革。

然而，同样的教学方法不一定适用于其他教师。对于缺乏经验的教师，或有较少荣誉光环的教师来说，这种新的教学方法会引起学生质疑。他们可能会抱怨老师没有进行纠错，没有教足够的写作知识，拒绝与老师合作，甚至向老师抗议。

现任英文学院副院长郑老师意识到教师的魅力在写作教学中的重要作用，所以近年来，他特意从高级翻译学院中挑选研究生来做写作教师，因为这些年轻教师的英语口语很棒，性格活泼，他们的个人魅力能把学生吸引到写作课堂上。

富有创造力的写作教师不会忽视语言的形式、功能、规则和惯例，他们试图帮助学生在有意义和引人入胜的语境中探索这些规则和惯例。教师要学习和掌握如何激发和启迪学生写作。如果教师想要“为培养充满创造力、能力和好奇心的学习者做出贡献”，也需要培养和丰富自身的趣味性、开放性和创新性。[1]每一个好老师是创造力的催化剂和解放者，而每一个糟糕的老师都创造了牢笼。而郑超教授就是这样一个催化剂。

> 我是同事们的啦啦队队长，也是和学生们一起并肩作战的战友。
>
> ——郑超

就个人魅力而言，郑超也很出色。2010 年我在广外调研时，郑老师 50 岁出头，相貌并不出众。但是一旦你开始和他交谈，就会惊讶于他的友好、对

---

〔1〕 Grainger, T., Goouch, K., & Lambirth, A., *Creativity and writing: Developing voice and verve in the classroom*, London; New York: Routledge, 2005, p16-17.

教学的热情和对学生的关爱。

郑老师在45岁时开始攻读博士学位，这个年龄很多人都会开始考虑退休事宜，但他坚信如果他全身心投入，就没有什么是做不到的。郑老师在攻读博士学位期间跟着导师王初明教授开始参与写作项目。获得博士学位后，郑老师成为该项目的负责人。2004年被任命为英文学院副院长后，郑老师对教学创新的参与和贡献达到了顶峰，并对学院的写作课程进行了全面改革。

郑老师深知师生合作对改革成功的重要性：[1]

> 很多实际工作都是由学生完成的，如编辑期刊、准备课程活动、做社会调查等。我们写作老师能做的最好的工作就是激发他们的兴趣和热情，与他们并肩工作，为改革写作教育的共同事业努力，你会被他们的想象力和创造力所震撼。

在谈到激发学生写作兴趣的方法时，郑老师说：

> 我的策略是让学生对我们和我们的教学方法有信心，把他们当作同志和队友，刺激他们的写作动力。通过这种方式，你可以挖掘他们的潜力和激情，他们会密切关注你，甚至超过你的预期。

当郑老师回忆起他与学生们一起编杂志、做网站和排戏剧的那些日子，他自豪地感叹道：

> 如果你让学生觉得你是他们的战友，他们会出人意料地独立和富有创造力。在项目开始的时候，我们都是探索者，包括学生和老师，我们谁也不知道会从这种新方法中得到什么。但是在我们充满激情的工作中，无论我们得到什么，满足感和成就感都是不可估量的。那些日子非常难忘，从那以后，我再也没有过这样大的满足感，即便在获得全国知名度和影响力时。

然而，一些教师未能与学生建立这样的关系，导致学生的参与度下降。

---

〔1〕郑超：《大学英语写作通用教程》，科学出版社2010年版。

郑超指出：

遗憾的是，许多老师都把自己当成教书匠，一下课就离开教室。实际上，学生希望得到老师更多的指导，他们渴望证明自己并得到老师的认可。在积极鼓励下，他们将愿意为了某项光荣的事业奋斗和接受挑战。他们的热情是无价的，不可估量的。

“你有没有遭到过学生们的抵制？”我问道。

“当然。但关键是，当学生们意识到你这么做是为他们时，就会尊重你，之后就没有什么困难了。”

除了孜孜不倦的工作精神之外，郑老师还以其丰富的研究和写作成就而闻名，这无疑增加了他在学生心目中的分量。郑老师非常喜欢画画。他给我看了一些他用鼠标在电脑上画的画，是广外一位资深教授的肖像，栩栩如生。“这张照片立刻让教授喜欢上了我”，郑老师没有掩饰自己的骄傲。在浏览《以写促学》课程杂志时，我发现他还是其中一些版块的插图作者和美术编辑。

除了绘画之外，郑老师还是诗歌创作和翻译的爱好者。他的诗歌，以及他的诙谐语言，给学生活动带来了诸多乐趣，赢得了老师和学生的一致好评。

正当我们谈话时，一个女学生走进办公室请假。在填写申请表时，郑老师自豪地向我介绍了这位女孩，她是本市青年高尔夫协会的奖牌获得者之一。他补充道：“我们的学生多才多艺，能力非常强！”他说话的语调和脸上的笑容极富感染力，让人不由自主地被他及他的教学团队和学生所吸引。

5.2.6 跨文化探索

英语写作对社会文化知识的探索

除激发学生写作兴趣和创造力外，广外还通过英语写作努力提高学生的社会文化知识。社会和文化问题的写作主题、“专题写作”课程、为学生搭建互动式网上国际交流平台等都有所体现。

广外许多写作主题都需要社会调查、文献综述和访谈。例如，主题为

“你今天‘宅’了吗？”的作文。“宅”一词最初是“家”的意思，后来被用作当代习惯用语，意指那些整天待在家里上网成瘾者的生活。一名学生对收集写作所需数据的方法解释道：“我利用课余时间采访了一些朋友和老师，并以朋友的表妹为例。调查表明，青少年本身对‘宅’持相当开放的态度，而父母则表示担忧。此外，为进一步调查，我采用了多种方式来获取资源，如报纸和互联网，如《广州日报》、维基百科网站和新华社官方网站。”

在另一篇文章“She is a boy”中，作者对年轻女孩的变装趋势进行描述，写作任务过程如下：

为了更好地进行解释，我要先介绍上学期第12周的写作课。当时，张老师布置的题目为“当今问题青年”，并提供了一些建议，比如吸毒、婚前同居和未成年母亲。但我立即就决定了自己的话题是变装问题，因为这种想法已经由来已久了……

我花了3周时间。第一周进行社会调查，用互联网找到假小子和男同性恋的定义；在图书馆学习关于变装问题的心理学理论；阅读一些朋友关于该话题的评论和留言，将资料都翻译成英语。Sid是我认识的人中最假小子的人，我打电话询问其是否愿意接受采访……

还有一个任务为描写学校农民工。为了了解农民工及其生活，学生集思广益，在工地与其交谈，帮助辅导农民工孩子，甚至提出带他们参观市容的建议。

完成社会调查后，有学生写了一篇文章：《隐形人：广外农民工》。这篇文章描述了农民工艰苦的工作条件，简陋的临时住所，在家庭生活和抚养孩子方面存在的问题等，其中最重要的是，他们对城市发展的贡献并没有得到认可，仿佛他们是“隐形人”。

对大多数学生来说，这次写作任务是一次非常具有变革性的经历。据任课教师欧阳教授介绍，许多学生承认，经历这次写作之后，他们对外来务工人员的态度发生了彻底转变，对他们的工作和贡献表示认可和感谢；还有学生与熟悉的工人继续保持联系，以便在需要时提供必要帮助。

一些学生甚至开始对社会和政治问题表现出兴趣，并开始写信给报社或政府，呼吁重视包括“三无居民”（多指城市流浪人员，没有工作，没有住所，没有身份证）等弱势群体的权利。在学生的呼吁、政府与社会的努力推动下，国家颁布了新的法规。2003 年 8 月 1 日，《城市流浪人员收容遣送办法》被废除，《城市流浪乞讨人员救助条例》出台，以更加人道的支持和救助方式取代强制驱逐城市流浪人员的措施。在这项写作任务中，学生不仅学会了“写作”，而且学会了用写作来“纠正”世界。

跨洋互动写作

“跨洋互动写作”是广外学生与海外笔友之间基于网络的互动写作项目。本项目旨在通过与美国宾夕法尼亚州立大学等海外院校的学生进行网络交流，提高广外学生写作水平。在第一轮交流中，15 名来自广外的本科生将个人或合作作品进行展示，并在网站上提交关于写作过程的报告和相关材料，等待来自美国的 12 名研究生笔友的反馈。通过网络辅助课堂互动、skype、QQ 等进行进一步的自由交流。第二轮交流中，来自广外的 12 名学生就中国播放的美剧进行撰写，并邀请美国的笔友发表评论。该项目旨在促进学生互相了解，提高二语写作意识，并提高他们在不同语言环境下对当代英语风格的认识。

例如，一名学生在一篇名为“开阔视野，敞开心扉”（“Open my eyes，open my mind”）的作文中这样写道：

从初中开始，我就迷上了美剧。每当做完作业，我就会把电视频道换到 TVB Pearl。第一部令我痴迷的美剧是《老友记》，讲的是三对情侣之间的友谊。这些有趣的故事背后，隐藏着家人、朋友和夫妻之间升华的情感。与中国传统的人际关系不同，美国人对待彼此更为直接自然、简单纯粹。谢谢你，你给予了我许多欢乐，使我受益匪浅。

此外这位作者继续大胆地表达了自己对美剧《欲望都市》的好评：

我承认自己思想开放，甚至有点早熟。负疚、坦诚和性，是这部美剧的大众标签。长期以来，堕落成了西方文化的核心。关于性的公开讨论、自由放任和女权主义很难与中国价值观共存。然而，我出生在理应抛弃封建思想和守旧思想的新时代。《欲望都市》以全新的概念闯入我的生活。四个坚强的女人坚持追逐梦想，她们鲜活生动的个性令自身形象熠熠生辉。职业女性可以站起来，女性的社会地位、作用和社会期望发生了重要转变，女性也可以成为世界中心。作为一名女性，我时刻准备着迎接独立和孤独。我们可以在没有限制和歧视的情况下选择自己的生活方式。

这位同学最后评论了人们对西方娱乐的矛盾态度：

在我看来，美剧在中国既不是和平演变，也不是对文化的侵蚀。每当一种西方文化兴起，就会有人对文化侵蚀感到恐惧。但我们应该做的不应只是担心，而应试着去了解、感受，尝试接受其优点。没有绝对正确的事情，也没有绝对错误的事情。俗话说："尺有所短，寸有所长，取长补短，相得益彰。"在发展中国家，应该提倡以开放的心态吸收新思想。人们只是需要一种理性的方式，去更多地了解在大洋彼岸的另一种文明。毫无疑问，美剧热潮将会持续下去，追剧仍然会是我生活的一部分。我会明智地睁开眼睛，理性地敞开心扉。

在谈到美国笔友的评论时，一位学生写道：

这次交流活动令我受益匪浅，它让我有机会了解到英语国家处理文章的方式。我非常感谢宾夕法尼亚州立大学学生的帮助。

需要注意的是，广外的文化探索不仅仅是一种教学方法，而且是帮助学生迎接日益国际化的挑战、寻求跨文化知识的真诚努力。通过这种方式，学生们不只是在学习"语言"或"写作"，也是在学习"观察他人，审视自己"〔1〕。这种文化学习也带来了身份和思想意识的转变。跨文化写作孕育了具有"转变身份和世界观"的作者，通过"向差异和他者敞开心扉"，达到"教育最

〔1〕 Corbett, J., *An intercultural approach to English language teaching*, Clevedon, Buffalo, Toronto, Sydney: Multilingual Matters, 2003.

深层次的目的"[1]。

5.3 为写作教师赋能

改革参与者常常会因为压力太大而陷入进退两难的境地，他们需要理解改革的内容和目标，承受改革带来的改变和冲击，因此会感到焦虑和无助。[2]广外正是如此。在为期十余年的项目中，教师不仅要经历写作思想的痛苦转变，吸收新知识和信息以跟上该领域的最新发展，而且还要在项目的期望和现实的实际制约之间挣扎，同时还要协调好教师和研究人员的角色，家庭需求和社会经济的挑战。所以很多时候，教师和学生一样需要被赋能。本节将要讨论如何对教师进行赋能，以及如何为他们创造一个具有创造性和灵活性的环境，使其成为创新写作者的催化剂。

5.3.1 教师作为作者

一些二语写作研究者认为，作为作者，教师的写作经验越多，就越有可能清楚认识到二语写作中的问题，并与学生产生共鸣。这可以从王教授的亲身经历中得到说明：

大学时，我并没有从写作老师那里学到多少东西，因为他们知道这门课程很难，不值得去尝试。就我个人而言，写英文日记也主要是为了情绪低落时发泄情绪。大学毕业后，我被分配到一所中学教书，1978 年申请了研究生学习。令我惊喜的是，我发现自己的写作经验产生了巨大帮助，有幸成为 185 名申请者中被录取的 5 名学生之一。在硕士和博士学习期间，我写了很多很长的文章（作为"写长法"练习），极大地提高了自身写作能力。所以我认为，大量写作和大量阅读是学习英语的主要方法，可以创造以英语为母语的

---

〔1〕 Lo Bianco, J., Culture: Visible, invisible and multiple. In J. Lo Bianco & C. Crozet (Eds.), *Teaching invisible culture: Classroom practice and theory*, Melbourne: Language Australia, 2003a, p34.

〔2〕 Rizvi, F., & Kemmis, S., *Dilemmas of reform: an overview of issues and achievements of the Participation and Equity Program in Victorian schools 1984–1986*. Geelong, Vic.: Deakin Institute for Studies in Education, Deakin University, 1987.

生活语境。总之，数量和长度发挥了重大作用。

对于教师来说，重要的文化经历、难忘时刻和影响他们作为作家的自我意识的人，写作中的挣扎、突破和乐趣，都有助于他们形成一个教师作者的身份。郑超的经历也说明了这一点：

我爱写作。我从小学开始就发表汉语文章；十三四岁时，我开始编辑校报。之后，我担任村宣传队的队长，为队里撰写剧本以供表演。从那时起，我学会了用生动的语言进行写作。

尽管教师作为作者的经验能发挥重要作用，但日常课堂教学中诸多限制因素仍会产生不良影响。如果教师不断受到强制性课程、高风险评估和规约性文化的影响，很有可能会停滞在传统教学方法的安全地带，较少使用创造性和创新性的教学方法。这样的教师更像技术员，而非艺术家。尽管他们自己擅长写作，教学上却不敢大胆尝试和改革。优秀的教师应该敢于承担风险，尤其是在充满信任的环境中。

什么样的条件能够促进这种信任和冒险的教学？在下一节中，我们将针对写作教师所面临的挑战，以及如何为其赋能和营造积极教学环境进行讨论。

5.3.2 关于写作教师的刻板印象

“为什么教写作？因为你不会教其他科目。”作为第一批使用“写长法”的老师之一，李老师（化名）对她所扮演的写作教师的角色持有非常负面的看法。她解释道：

人们对写作老师有一种刻板印象：如果你不能教其他科目，那就只能教写作，因为学生最不需要的就是写作老师。

对写作教师的负面刻板印象在中国学校并不少见。在我曾经任教的大学里，写作课程通常会留到最后还没有老师愿意选。写作教师通常由新教师、外籍教师或研究生担任，因为他们是教师队伍中相对“弱势”的群体，因此他们的发言权和选择机会相对较少。郑超教授在担任广外英文学院副院长后，决定改变这种情况。

首先郑超邀请有经验的老师加入写作团队。然后，他鼓励现有教师继续深造，提高自身学术水平。他甚至采取了一些极端的措施，如为写作团队“长脸”：

> 我现在特意挑选高翻学院的应届毕业生来我们系教授写作。首先，他们良好的英语发音可以引起学生的兴趣和钦慕；其次，广外的传统便是年轻教师更受学生欢迎。

至于先前提到的李老师（化名），她在获得博士学位后，上课变得更加自信：

> 我的主要挑战在于如何引起学生兴趣。学生热衷于学习，所以对老师有很高的期望。因此，我们面临着很大压力。早在2001年刚上这门课时，我觉得学生们都很优秀，我甚至都不敢开口。但在获得博士学位后，我的自信增加了。有意无意地，我会向学生展示我的学识。同时，在写完一篇很长的博士论文后，我对写作中出现的问题也变得更加熟悉了。

那么如何给这些教师赋能，采取创新教学方法呢？Robinson认为创造力不仅仅是个人表现，而是一个文化过程。创造力在有系统措施和结构支持的条件下最活跃；创造力作为文化过程的观点强调了全校投入建立“创新环境”的重要性——这是培养创新教学法的有利条件。

5.3.3 创造性环境为教师赋能

创造性的环境意味着提供选择和鼓励冒险。[1]这种环境既具有支持性，也具有挑战性。尽管它需要安全性和支持性，但也需要拥有不同专业知识的人之间的思想交流，鼓励冒险、试验和批判，而非扼杀、压制。这一环境可能会受到外部因素的影响，如社会经济背景，导师、负责教师和学校管理者

〔1〕 Grainger, T., Goouch, K., & Lambirth, A., *Creativity and writing: Developing voice and verve in the classroom*, London; New York: Routledge, 2005.

的影响。也可能涉及无形的内部因素，如教师的思想和信仰、教育背景、个性和认知风格、素养以及可以影响教学决策和态度的创新和变化。[1]

与其他院校相比，广外具有更为灵活的教师环境，但也存在着诸多的制约因素，这一点不容忽视。在旁听老师的写作团队会议时，可以真正感受到思想和观点在紧密团结的群体中自由交流。广外项目的领导权已经移交给了年轻一代。20 多岁的年轻男教师卢老师被任命为该项目的“领头羊”，一群年轻教师承担着该项目的主要教学工作。这些教师凭借各自的学术造诣，创造性地将写作教学法推向新的发展方向。

5.3.4 教育和理论为教师赋能

王初明教授曾获得应用语言学硕士学位和语言学博士学位。他的主要兴趣为心理语言学和第二语言习得。早在 1990 年，他就出版了专著《应用心理语言学：外语学习心理研究》。1991 年，他在中国著名的学术期刊《外语界》上发表了文章《外语学习中的认知和情感需要》。在随后的几年中，王教授在这一领域发表了一系列文章。他的教育背景，加上他的研究兴趣和经验，使得他在 20 世纪 90 年代末开始关注英语学习教学法。

王教授的“写长法”主要基于 Swain 的输出假设理论（Swain's Output Hypothesis）[2]，即可理解的输出（如口语和写作）可以有效地增加二语学习的投入。另一个理论基础是情感过滤假说（Affective Filter Hypothesis）[3]，该假说认为二语学习的成就在很大程度上取决于自我概念、自信、焦虑、态度和动机等情感因素。

“写长法”推出后，王教授还发表了一系列关于创新教学法的文章。他还在第二语言习得方面继续进行研究，特别是在心理语言学领域，包括母语对二语学习的束缚、外语学习的情感因素、发音和自我形象之间的关系、外语

---

〔1〕 Casanave, C. P., *Controversies in second language writing: Dilemmas and decisions in research and instruction*, Ann Arbor: University of Michigan Press, 2004.

〔2〕 Swain, M., Communicative competence: Some roles of comprehensible input and comprehensible input and comprehensible output in its development. In S. M. Gass & C. G.

〔3〕 Krashen, S. D., *Principles and practice in second language acquisition* (1st ed.), Oxford; New York: Pergamon, 1982.

学习过程、上下文的外语学习、英语学习中的补缺假说理论、语言学习中的交互等。

郑超老师是一位语言学博士，在第二语言习得研究专业委员会担任主任，并对语言学、第二语言习得和翻译方面有浓厚的学术兴趣和学习背景。20 世纪 90 年代初，郑超在利物浦大学期间受功能语言学家 Geoff Thompson 影响，编写了一本《前沿英语》高级阅读教程，这本教科书在 1995 年荣获了国家二等奖。另一本著作《当代语言学导论》被纳入国家“十一五”计划的教科书计划。

郑超教授有深厚的语言学背景，他认为“写长法”应该辅以一些语言元素，比如“小笔吧”，来向学生教授语法和写作知识。与王教授批改很少的长作文方式不同，郑老师在课程中增加了短文写作，并要求老师对学生的作文进行“适当”批改。除其他因素外，王教授与郑教授在理论取向上的差异也导致了他们在写作教学法上的不同。

教师的学术背景对其教学实践的强烈影响也可以从年轻一代教师对“写长法”的反应中得以说明。在课堂观察的过程中，我对他们独特的教学风格印象深刻。

一位顾姓的年轻男老师毕业于高级翻译学院，他在开始上课前一周总结学生作文时，非常注重英语的“习惯用法”。他引用了一些学生作品中的例子，如“I fully believe”或“obtain knowledge”等。为了避免这些非习惯用语，顾老师建议学生应该多读英语报纸。他还说可以通过翻译所读文章，提高对这些差异的敏感度。

另有一位获得英国文学硕士学位的年轻教师何老师，与顾老师相比，他对待学生的语言缺陷时要轻松得多。与顾老师相反，他花了大量时间带领学生对范例作品进行文学鉴赏，鼓励学生找出文章的文学特色，写出优美的句子，并在课堂上进行朗读。尽管他和顾老师面对的是同样的写作任务，但教学方法却大相径庭。

刚刚获得批判性话语分析博士学位的钟老师则采取了另一种方式。在教授学生如何准备求职简历时，她向学生介绍批判性话语方法，并要求学生欣赏关于同一主题的不同写作，不同时期的不同作者的不同写作，以及从原文翻译而来的不同作品之间的细微差别。我不知道学生们能理解多少，但钟老师似乎非常投入。

其他教师也根据自己的理论偏好调整教学实践。例如，欧阳老师是一位颇受学生欢迎的老师，因为他在人类学和民族志研究方面的专业知识非常出名，所以他会指导学生进行大量的社会调查写作。像顾老师和卢老师这样的年轻教师则会结合自身在翻译和口译方面的优势，将流行文化融入课程内容中。

教师的理论背景在很大程度上是通过他们的高等教育和研究生教育形成的，尽管它可能会通过教师对文献的持续研究、参加会议和撰写论文，以及导师和同事的影响和在整个职业生涯中的体验式学习而不断建立和发展。除现有教学知识外，教师教育迫切需要为二语教师提供必要工具——母语和目的语的语言和文化知识、与教学相关的写作惯例和创新、甚至是二语写作领域的问题和争议，以保持其思考、研究、学习和反思。

简而言之，广外的创作语境是让原有的“写长法”演变成不同的方法，以适应各自的教师和课堂的需要，因此它不是一种停滞不前的教学法，而是为了自我完善而不断流动和发展的教学法。故而一位高级教师这样评论道：“广外的好处在于，在这样一个金钱至上的城市和时代，仍有一群兢兢业业的学者致力于教学和研究，令人赞叹不已。”

有一个安全性的环境并不意味着教师之间只存在共识。一直以来，广外教改的发展都伴随着阻力和不确定性。

5.3.5　模糊性和不确定性

信任意味着能够感受到某种安全感，但很明显，创新在充满风险和不安全感的环境中最能茁壮成长。这似乎是一个悖论。本节的基本主题之一是模糊性和不确定性的专业价值。每当教师开始一个课程开发项目时，就会有一种不可避免的不安全感，有时甚至会有坚持既定的“确定性”的冲动。其中一些可能值得坚持，但诀窍是认识到哪些是值得保留的，哪些可以丢弃。郑超教授说：

到目前为止，我们遇到了来自各个方面的挑战。一些学者对我们的写作方法提出质疑，认为它不是一种恰当的写作教学法。来自学生的挑战是我们需要不断寻找新的刺激来吸引学生。我们的教学团队内部也有争议。但幸运的是，广外是一个非常好的群体，大多数老师关心学生的利益多于对自身利益的关注。因此，当他们意识到“写长法”是有益于学生的，而非逃避教师的责任或忽视教学原则的教学法时，就会放弃反对意见，投身其中。

广东部分教师对新教材的使用表示质疑：

当一种教学法完成并系统化，它就会变得固定，失去灵活性和创造性。因此，我认为新教材更适合其他学校的教师，或自学的学生。我建议写作教师把一些评论资料单独放在教师用书里，以免影响学生和老师的创造力。此外，新的素材，例如最新的作业和写作范例，也需要补充到课本当中。

除了质疑和模糊性之外，不同年龄和职位的教师之间的权利分配也存在问题。在我们私下谈话中，广外的一位老师说道：

位置决定创造力。如果你有时间做研究，而不是把所有时间都花在教学上，如果你能获得所有资源，如果你有机会参加不同的会议，了解最新的发展，如果你能与权威人士和著名学者接触并从中得到启发，你也能产生创造力。

权威的声音可以成为开放、灵活和变革的有力倡导者。[1]强烈而有说服力的声音，会让老师们相信，应该重视语法，应把长度作为写作的关键，应该鼓励学生在写作中表达个人声音。王教授的例子和“写长法”的成功就证明了这一点：

一开始，“写长法”遇到了巨大的阻力。然而，即便我是这一教学法的创始人，也很少有人与我对抗，因为当年我是广外少数拿到博士学位的教师之一。

但我的博士生郑超就没有那么幸运了。他在试图传播“写长法”时遇到了巨大阻碍。当我去美国学习半年后，情况越发严重，以至于郑超曾提出想

〔1〕 Casanave, C. P., *Controversies in second language writing: Dilemmas and decisions in research and instruction*, Ann Arbor: University of Michigan Press, 2004.

要退出。有些学生甚至张贴出“打倒写长法”的海报！在我们的教学法获得国家奖后，障碍才开始慢慢消退。

相比之下，我先前的硕士唐老师却成功地实施了这项教学改革，因为他是广外国际商务英语学院的副院长。现在唐老师正在美国攻读博士学位，并在自己的孩子身上试验“写长法”。不久前，他兴奋地告诉我，他的女儿在美国一项重大写作比赛中获得优胜。“写长法”因此在他的美国同学中引起了热烈讨论，它与美国一些新的教学理论产生了共鸣，比如 SCT（社会文化理论）。

对于中青年教师来说，一方面他们不得不为建立家庭和事业而奋斗，为完成教学任务而不得不加班加点。这使得他们几乎没有时间和精力进行基础研究，更不用说进行创造性的教学实验了。另一方面，如果他们确实想出一些有创意的想法，也不太可能会被注意到，因为他们还是“学徒”，期刊编辑更倾向于尊重有名望的学者而非新手研究人员。

与权力问题相关的是创造力的角色分配。在一个创意群体中，不同的成员会被分配不同角色，作为一个团队在创意议程上进行合作。例如在广外教改中，“写长法”的发起者王教授提出创新想法；郑超老师将其思想发展为全面的课程改革，并将创新的影响推向全国；团队中较年轻的教师，如陆、顾、梁则根据自己的需要和特长，对教学法进行创造性应用。

在广外考察时，我意识到权力问题所带来的微妙冲突，使得创新教学更加复杂。没有一个完美的教学法能够满足每个学生的需要，并适合所有教师的风格。正是通过不断的协商，教学法才得以存在。创新教学法，尤其是在跨文化方面的教学法，则需要更多协商。

然而，在二语写作语境中，有助于教师培训和教师教育的资源少之又少。写作教师在很大程度上只能靠自己去探索有效的教学策略，他们自身的创新能力没有得到充分挖掘。

本章的研究结果表明，中国英语写作教师能够创造出有效的本土教学法，他们的教学创新会受到中国社会政治语境和教师的意识形态、身份、经验、理论以及师生关系等因素的影响。通过认识到教师是教学法形成的中心，迫切需要围绕教师自身的关注和需求以及创造更大的教学灵活性为专业发展腾出空间。

然而，除上述方面外，许多复杂因素也可能促成教师对教学方法的革新，例如结构性限制（班级规模、课堂管理）、强加的课程和评估、教师的社会经济条件、学生的身份和经验、学校目标等。

5.3.6 结 论

增强学生写作能力的途径之一是通过挑战传统的写作语境，塑造一个关注情境、互动、互文和文化层面的新语境。广外的语境重塑主要体现在“写长法”中，它将作家从传统语境中解放出来，如文章长度、反馈和评价。随后的综合课程改革通过建立新的、创造性的写作环境增强学生作家的能力，其重点是弥合学生的学校文化素养与实际生活兴趣之间的差距，改变对写作和创造力的错误观念，培养合作和互动的师生关系，以及在写作中进行文化探索。这些尝试不仅使广外学生受益，也为二语写作教学法的创新开辟了新的可能。

作为广外教学改革的倡导者和参与者，我受到项目中许多方法的启发。首先，它改变了我以前对写作和写作教学的一些观念，例如我意识到获得写作能力的唯一途径是大量练习。同样的道理也适用于听、读、说以及任何我们想要获得的技能。“熟能生巧”在广外对其二语写作教学的可行性中得到了有力验证。其次，一群敬业的老师大胆地挑战现有的写作教育传统，让我充满了希望和勇气。至少我知道，在中国有一些志趣相投的人，同样肩负着解放和赋予英语作者权利的使命。这促使我与其他研究人员和教育工作者一起，利用现有研究和实践的成果，制定出一种创新教学法，将我国写作教育提升到更高水平。

以下，笔者将对“以写促学”的教学理论进行进一步总结和提炼。

5.4 “以写促学”教学法的理论解读

“以写促学”的理论依据有很多，是原创者王初明教授和后来以郑超教授为首的推广者的理论与经验的综合，其中包括心理语言学中关于情感、动机及自我意识等理论，Raimes 的输出理论，互动协同理论，动态系统理论，语境理论及文化、社会批判理论等。可以说“以写促学”综合了所有参与者的理论灵感，但是至今为止，这一教学法没有建立一个系统的理论体系，这既招致了一些人的怀疑和异议，也影响了它的进一步提升和推广。以下笔者将对“以写促学”的理论基础进行探讨、整理和归纳，以期解决这一教学法理论体系缺失的不足。笔者认为，“以写促学”理论框架的主干是后现代批判思想和语境的突破与重塑。

后现代批判教育观认为教育不是中立的，它时刻受到意识形态的制约，不仅如此，教育的目的就是改变社会。语言学习的过程既是学会和使用该语言进行群体交际并沿袭原有语言传统的过程，又是学会表达个人思想，进而挑战和颠覆这个语言传统的过程。[1]究竟应该承袭社会沿革还是表达个性声音，应该屈从目的语语言文化还是保护母语文化，一直是外语界争论不休的问题。外语学习中母语与目的语力量的不平等既导致了“无助”和“压迫”，也催生了“力量”与“解放”。[2]批判教学法（critical pedagogy）的基本观点是所有学生应该认识到外语言学习中目的语与母语之间的力量不平等关系；教师应该肩负起赋予学生力量的社会责任，帮助他们认识到语言的社会、文化和政治功能，从而质疑、反抗和挑战现有的语言传统。[3]在外语写作教学中，教师要引导学生发现写作沿革背后隐含的价值观，拒绝不加批判地接受这些传统，探索新的写作方式，以满足写作者个人和文化表达的需求。批判思想的三大基本概念是“解放”（emancipation）、“赋能”（empowerment）和“平等”（equality）。

语境与写作的关系似乎是不言自明的：任何语言的使用都发生在语境中，因此教语言就必须同时教语境。Halliday 将语境定义为“文本展开的环境”[4]，并进一步把语境分为五个层次：语言本体语境（linguistic context）、情境语境

[1] Kramsch, C. J., *Context and culture in language teaching*, Oxford: Oxford University Press, 1993.

[2] Kramsch, C. J., *Language and culture*, Oxford: Oxford University Press, 1998, p77.

[3] Benesch, S., *Critical English for academic purposes: Theory, politics, and practice*, Mahwah, N. J.: Lawrence Erlbaum Associates, 2001a.

[4] Halliday, M. A. K., *Language as social semiotic: The social interpretation of language and meaning*, London: Edward Arnold, 1978.

(situational context)、互动语境(interactional context)、互文本语境(intertextual context)和文化语境(cultural context)。语言本体语境指影响文本连贯流畅的语言形式的选择。情境语境是文本之外的交际环境，Hymes(1977年)把它细分为八个方面，即环境、参与者、结局、过程、要点、工具、规则和文体，其中任何一个因素的变化都可导致情境语境的变化。互动语境是交际者之间互动产生的语境，包括他们的信仰和成见等。文本的产生还受两种更大范围的语境的制约：互文本语境强调文本和其他文本、思想产品之间的联系；而文化语境是一个语言群体所有知识、信仰和观念的总和，它往往让不属于这个群体的人产生交际障碍。

以上五个层面的语境不是静止不变的，它们与文本的关系是辩证和动态的，并且因参与者之间的互动和对话而不断得到改变和重塑。换句话说，写作语境是由所有语境层面和次级语境因素组成的一个动态系统，[1]改变其中任何一个部分都可以造成语境的改变，从而影响文本的产生过程和效果。在写作教学中，如果能有目的、有意识地改变和控制这些语境因素，则可能突破传统语境，创造出无穷无尽的新的语境组合，为学生写作提供一个崭新的环境。笔者认为这正是广外"以写促学"教改的主要理论思路。

"以写促学"教学法首先通过"突破"传统语境，比如作文长度、错误修改和评估体系等，把学习者从束缚中解脱出来，释放他们的写作激情和创造力，培养他们的学习兴趣和自信心；然后通过创造性地"重塑"新的写作语境，使其符合学习者的认知规律，满足学习者的情感需求，从写作观念、目的意义、任务设计、训练方法和师生关系等诸多方面塑造全新的语言环境，给学习者以"力量"，从而实现写作教学的重大变革。具体来说，广外"以写促学"教学法的理念和教改实践可以从对语境五个层面的"突破"与"重塑"加以分析。

[1] De Bot (Kees De, Wander, & Marjolijn, 2007) 等人运用 Dynamic Systems Theory 解释二语现象，按照这一理论，语境的动态系统也可视为社会系统中的动态子系统，包含大量相互作用的属下动态子系统，这些不同层面的动态系统相互交互，形成人的认知生态系统。

5.4.1　语言本体语境（Linguistic Context）

首先，“以写促学”教学法彻底打破了传统教学法对语言本体语境的限制，从教学步骤、作文长度、改错方法和评估体系等方面将学习者彻底解放出来，在新的语境中释放写作激情和潜能。传统教学法大多遵从“词句—段落—篇章”的分阶段教学法，“以写促学”强调从整体语篇的写作入手，让学习者一开始就尝试写作文甚至是长作文，通过构思和修改作文的过程进行思考和探索。“写长”是“以写促学”教学法的核心理念，它彻底打破了作文长度的限制，给学生充足的时间，鼓励学生课后“常写”和“写长”，当然这并不代表鼓励学生写冗长重复的文章。相反，“以写促学”教学法将“写长”视为“手段”而不是“目的”，在教学初期通过“笔随心动”等环节让学生放开手写，从而激发他们的写作兴趣，释放他们的写作潜力，为后阶段“由长到精”的教学环节奠定基础。为此“以写促学”教学法在后期的评分体系中特别增加了“精炼”这一项。“以写促学”教学法提倡教师不改或少改错误，对学生的作文反馈以积极鼓励为主，辅以对常见语法错误的分析和讲解。这样一来，不仅可以将教师从繁重的“改错”任务中解放出来，将注意力和精力投向更加有效的工作中，[1]例如设计写作任务、搜集写作范文和组织写作活动等；二来学生写作时可以将大量注意力从语言层面转移到思想和观点的探讨上。“以写促学”教学法的评估体系也完全不同于传统体系，把作文“长度”放在“准确性”等其他指标之前，并以“开放式”课后作文为主要衡量标准。总的来说“以写促学”对作文长度、改错和评估等传统语境的“突破”主要基于以下理念：

（1）作文的构思和写作需要充分的时间，写作者需要通过交流、阅读、想象、思考来酝酿作文，并通过写草稿和反复修改来完善作文，[2]这在传统

---

〔1〕关于教师给学生作文改错的有效性业界仍然存在争论，至今为止改错的有效性仍未得到有力的证明。

〔2〕Raimes, A., What unskilled ESL students do as they write: A classroom study of composing. In T. J. Silva & P. K. Matsuda (Eds.), *Landmark essays on ESL writing*, Mahwah, N. J.: Hermagoras Press, 1985, p37-62.

语境中是不太可能实现的。大多数情况下学生被作文时间和长度所限制，作文流于应付和肤浅。长此以往，势必影响学生的写作兴趣和学习效果。

（2）反思和修改是写作过程中必不可少的一部分。学生应该通过讨论分享、合作创作和自评互评等活动体会写作全过程，而不应被僵化的时间和程序所束缚。

（3）传统作文评分集中于可观察到的和可测量的因素，诸如结构是否清晰、是否使用了适量的副词和形容词、标点和连词是否准确或是否使用了复杂句和复合句等，而写作者的写作兴趣、意图、个人风格和个性化思想则完全不在测评的范围内。这使得学习者屈从于狭隘的传统写作模式，逐渐丧失写作中的创造力和乐趣。

广外“以写促学”教学法给学生以更多的时间和空间，让他们找到适合自己的写作方法，让个人的需求、兴趣和个性在其中得到满足和表现。“以写促学”教学法的根本目的是帮助学生成长为具有创新精神和社会意识的写作者，而不仅仅是机械被动的应试者。这些思想借鉴了许多国外写作和语言教学流派的理念，比如“自由写作法”对个性的抒发和表达，“过程写作法”的多稿法和合作写作，以及“流利领先”原则中“先求流利，再求清晰，然后才是准确性”等观点。不过，“以写促学”教学法也受到了这些外国写作法曾受到过的质疑，即关于“流利与准确性”“过程与产品”“该不该改错”“写作个性化还是社会化”的争论等。为了应对这些质疑，“以写促学”教学法在突破传统语境的同时也保留了一些传统元素，比如语法讲解；但是这些知识以更加生动有趣的形式穿插在写作教学中，比如教材《以写促学：英语写作通用教程》中特设了“防火墙”和“小笔吧”的栏目，列出了作文中常见的语法错误，供学生对照和自查。课堂中语法知识也主要以“归纳错误”的方式提醒学生注意，再加上同学之间的互评互改，一些“低级错误”能够慢慢消失，但是较高层面上的语言错误（如冠词的使用等）则只能靠大量的输入和长期的写作练习来逐渐避免。

5.4.2 情境语境（Situational Context）

情境语境主要指文本之外的写作环境，包括写作者的心理状况和认知环境，写作规则的设定等。“以写促学”教学法特别注重从以下三方面营造激发学生写作热情和潜力的情境语境：

首先，该方法特别关注学生的情感需求。以写作为突破口学习外语符合中国人学外语的特点：读写机会多，听说机会少；写长作文易于让学生增强自信心，获得成就感，尤其是对口语较差的学生，是打开外语学习情感通道的良方；不改或少改错误能保护学生自尊心，让他们把注意力放到思想和语篇的层面来；教师和学生的角色转换让学生对老师产生情感认同，减少了师生之间的沟通障碍；课外写作活动也培养了学生的团队合作精神及独立精神。

其次，“以写促学”教学法符合学生认知规律。“以写促学”写作四个阶段的设计集中反映了这一理念。第一阶段“笔随心动”让学生放手写长，不受任何写作规范的约束，从而让他们“爱上”写作，欲罢不能。第二阶段“立论谋篇”让教师开始引导学生通过阅读和实践总结一些写作规律，用于指导自己的写作，这一环节中“精炼”也成为评分的一个标准。通过前两个阶段，学生对写作有了初步认识，产生了更多的输入需求。第三阶段“品味创作”让教师鼓励学生模仿优秀的作品进行文学创作，一方面拓宽了写作学习的视野，同时也激发了学生的创造力和求知欲。第四阶段“走进报刊”使学生开始关注写作的社会意义，通过社会调查进行专题特写，并尝试为报刊投稿。总而言之，“以写促学”的四个教学阶段密切联系学生的情感和认知需求，环环相扣，形成了一个完整的教学体系，从某种意义上来说，综合了西方“自由写作”“过程写作”和“学术写作”等教学法的精华并弥补了它们的某些不足。

最后，建立学校知识和学生生活知识的联系也是“以写促学”教学法营造情境语境的重要手段。后现代批判思想认为传统的学校教育割裂了学校知识（school literacy）和学生生活知识（real life literacy）的联系，片面强调书本知识的重要性，不理会日新月异的社会发展给学生带来的冲击和影响，在制定教学大纲和教学计划时没有听取学生的声音，使得他们缺乏学习动机，达不到理想的学习效果。这样的教育无异于“往前开车两眼却只盯着后视镜”。“以写促学”教学法在设计写作任务时，教师们经常开会讨论，“绞尽脑汁”寻找学生感兴趣的话题，如“我的第一次约会或游泳或吸烟…”“校园里能不能勾肩搭背”等。这些话题有利于将学生的生活体验和学校学习紧密联系起来，从而激发他们的写作兴趣。同时这些话题也能引导学生对他们所处的社会进行反思，从而实现后现代批判教育变革社会的目的。

通俗文化进入课堂是“以写促学”激发学生写作兴趣的另一关键举措。Bakhtin 认为通俗文化是激发写作创造力的主要源泉，但是长久以来却不为教育者所重视。“以写促学”教学法认为学生耳濡目染的通俗文化，比如电视节目、音乐、广告、杂志、电影等让他们突破有限的生活环境，开阔眼界，对写作有积极影响，应该得到足够的重视。例如“读后续写”和“观后续写”中教师让学生给自己喜欢的人物和故事写对白或情节；此外教师还鼓励学生利用各种现代多媒体手段进行写作，将文本变成舞台剧、电视短片或其他音像产品，在广外一年一度的作文朗诵会和戏剧演出上可以看到很多这样的成功作品。

5.4.3 互文语境（Intertextual Context）

许多教师和学生对借鉴别人的观点和模仿别人的写作手法心怀戒备，认为这是抄袭的行为，应该避免。另有一些人认为照搬佳作范文是学习写作的捷径，鼓吹大量背诵例句和模板的价值。这两种倾向在某种程度上都束缚了学生，导致学生对模仿或创造感到畏缩。为了理顺写作中模仿和创造的关系，“以写促学”教学法特别关注互文语境的营造。

营造互文语境对写作教学有重要意义。Bakhtin〔1〕认为所有的话语都是互相影响和模仿的，语言的创造力在于对他人声音的吸收、加工和再生。整个语言系统是循环使用的，每个人的话语都不可避免地源自这个语料库，并成为其中的一部分。因此，写作应该是一个不断吸收和转化的过程，是不断储存、重组别人的思想、技巧、词汇与意象，直到它们融合成为新的作品的过程。〔2〕正因为语言的互文本质，“以写促学”教学团队鼓励学生借鉴他人的

〔1〕 Bakhtin, M. M., *Speech genres and other late essays* (V. W. McGee, Trans.), Austin: University of Texas Press, 1986.

〔2〕 Green, A., Creative writing: Taking risks with words. In R. Fisher & M. Williams (Eds.), *Unlocking creativity: Teaching across the curriculum*, London: David Fulton, 2004, p37-54.

观点，模仿优秀范文或经典名篇的风格和写作方法，甚至可以通过改写或翻译来增加写作素材。当学生明白创造力可以来自于模仿和发挥，他们的顾虑打消了，能够更加自信地学习和吸收他人的精华用于自己的创作当中。

与互文性密切相关的是语言的协同和启动机理。王初明教授对二语习得中的交互现象进行研究，并引入动态系统理论、交互协同模式和构式语法等理论来认识语言学习变量之间的交互关系。他认为正确和大量的输入对外语学习至关重要，因为一方面人们倾向于使输出与输入匹配，另一方面话语双方为了交流顺畅，倾向于在语言的多个层面协同起来。这种词语的重复使用也可称为结构启动。[1]进一步研究发现第二语言产出中的结构启动效应受语言水平和任务类型的显著影响。[2]正因为语言互文性和协同启动等机理的作用，“以写促学”强调把输入作为写作教学中必不可少的一部分。

广外的“以写促学”教学法主要从输入内容和输出方式上为学生创造了新的互文环境。除了第一阶段“笔随心动”中鼓励学生放手去写，其他写作任务基本都有范文以供参考和模仿。这些范文主要分两大类，经典名作和历届广外学生的优秀作品。前者着重为学生开拓思路并提供语言的熏陶，后者则更容易被学生接受和模仿，更容易产生协同效应。此外，学生被要求大量阅读和收听小说、报刊和视听节目等英文材料，通过交互协同作用提高语感，为输出做准备。“以写促学”教学法采用的输出方式包括“读后续写”“说后续写”和“观后续写”等，即通过读、听、看等输入方式让学生产生结构启动。王初明教授曾将这些方法称为“读长”“说长”和“听长”法，认为它们和“写长法”有同样的机理，并应成为“写长法”教学必不可少的一部分。

5.4.4　互动语境（Interactional Context）

本书中互动语境主要指写作者之间、教师之间和学生与教师之间的人际互动。后现代批判教学法的基本观点之一便是教育中权利的重新分配，即把

〔1〕 Pickering, M. J., & Garrod, S., “Toward a mechanistic psychology of dialogue”, *Behavioral & Brain Sciences*, 27 (2), 2004, p169-226.

〔2〕 王敏：“语言水平及任务类型对第二语言产出中结构启动的影响”，载《现代外语》2009年第3期。

传统中教师的权利部分转移到学生中来，这要求改变原有教师和学生的关系和定位。[1]这种力量的转移和再分配是批判教学法赋予学生力量的重要渠道。“以写促学”教学法之所以取得成功，其教师和学生关系的根本变化是至关重要的因素。简言之，“以写促学”教学团队的教师不再是传统意义上的“权威”或“知识传授者”，而是学生的“伙伴”“导演”和“啦啦队长”。

“以写促学”教学团队包括各种年龄和资历的教师，从20多岁的青年教师到50多岁的教授博导，教学中他们都力争走近学生，成为他们的朋友。这对年龄较大的老师尤其不容易，为此他们需要有意识地通过阅读、收听和观看年轻人喜爱的书籍、网站和节目，经常和学生交流来了解他们的世界，创造与学生平等对话和沟通的条件。课堂上老师把“主角”的位置让给学生，让他们有充分的机会展现自己的作品，探讨思想和分享观点。教师的主要任务是引导学生在现有写作知识的基础上，综合有关的输入材料，总结出适合自己的写作方法。在某种意义上，教师就像一个“导演”，给学生分配角色和任务，引导他们摸索并完成该项任务；有时，教师也是“评论者”，对学生的表现提出意见和建议；但更多的时候，教师只是“观众”，用关注和鼓励支持学生探索写作之路。

课堂外“以写促学”教学团队的教师是学生写作活动的“啦啦队员”。广外围绕写作教学组织的活动有“读书会”“作文朗诵会”和一年一度的“英文戏剧演出”等，这些活动主要由学生组织和筹办。以“戏剧表演”为例，筹款、编剧、舞台布置、道具、表演和主持等工作全部由学生负责，教师只提供指导、鼓励和作为嘉宾观看。除了以上活动，广外学生还承办了《以写促学》杂志（包括电子版）和网站。通过这些课外活动，学生不仅拉近了和老师的关系，而且从根本上改变了对教师的依附性和与教师之间的依赖关系，锻炼了自主能力，极大地发挥了他们的积极性和创造性；同时这些活动也拓宽了写作教学的功能，反过来刺激了学生的学习动机和输入需求。

---

〔1〕 Hardin, J. M., *Opening spaces: Critical pedagogy and resistance theory in composition*, Albany: State University of New York Press, 2001.

5.4.5　文化语境（Cultural Context）

除了激发学生写作积极性和创造力、提高写作能力外，“以写促学”教学法非常注重培养学生的跨文化交际意识，为学生写作创造了丰富的文化语境。这主要表现在写作任务中对文化话题的重视、“报刊特写”阶段对社会问题的关注和与国外学生建立“跨洋互动”写作平台等方面。

“以写促学”进行的文化探讨可分为两方面。一是对中外文化差异的比较，借此增加学生对跨文化交际意识的敏感性，这样的写作题材包括对国外文化、影视、文学的评论和续写等。二是对我国内部不同文化之间的了解和沟通。这些由地域、历史和社会经济状况导致的国内文化的多样性不同于跨越国界的文化差异，笔者将其称为“内文化差异”〔1〕。加强国内不同文化传统和群体之间的相互沟通和理解是建造“和谐社会”的必由之路。“以写促学”团队在探索“内文化”写作题材方面可谓煞费苦心。首先，教师鼓励学生描写自己身边的人和事。例如“我们家的第一件电器”“我们村的新鲜事”等，通过交流写作和交流各自的生活背景，增进了解，拓宽视野。文化传统也是写作的重要素材，比如“泡菜”“茶道”“端午节”等，通过写作让学生对自己的文化进行思考，一方面增强民族认同感，一方面学会反思自己认为理所当然的文化传统和价值观。

“报刊特写”这一写作阶段常常要求学生走出教室，进行社会调查，通过采访、问卷调查等方式收集资料，并利用互联网、图书馆等多种渠道阅读相关文献，对某些社会问题进行深刻思考和阐述，例如“北漂人群”“蚁族英雄”〔2〕等社会问题。访谈中学生给我讲述了一个生动的例子：他们写过一篇主题为“校园里的农民工”的特写。在此之前大多数学生对校园里的农民工基本是视而不见，仿佛他们是“隐形人”，更不用说关注他们的生活和工作。通过这次写作任务，学生走进农民工的生活，了解了他们的喜怒哀乐，认识到他们对广外发展的贡献。许多学生表示这次写作对他们有很大触动，很多同学开始

〔1〕叶洪：“跨文化外语教学中的‘内文化交际’研究与实践”，载《外国语文》2012年第3期。

〔2〕“蚁族”在这里指“80后”大学毕业生低收入聚居群体，他们是蚂蚁般的弱小者。

对自己原有的世界观和价值观进行反思，有些同学还和农民工交上了朋友，还有一些同学开始关注社会、政治问题，对“三无”人员等社会弱势群体表示同情和关心。

除了从写作题材和方法角度创造文化语境，“以写促学”教学法还创建了“跨洋互动”的写作平台，让广外学生通过网络、skype 和 QQ 等互联网技术和国外大学生进行写作交流和互动，目的是增进中外大学生的相互了解，提高跨文化交际意识和英语写作技巧。这样的写作任务包含对一些中外流行文化的评论，例如广外学生撰写对美国电视剧《欲望都市》的观后感，同时附上写作、思考过程和参考资料，让美国笔友评论和反馈意见。这些活动丰富了学生的跨文化知识，有助于学生形成世界视角，适应目前日益加快的全球化趋势。这样的写作活动不仅仅是学习写作的手段，而且是学生“认识自己和认识世界的工具”，[1]能够帮助学生建立科学的世界观和自我意识，从而达到教育最深刻的目的——育人。

5.4.6 小 结

21 世纪的世界市场需要具有出色的外语写作能力、创造力和跨文化交际能力的毕业生，[2]日益强大的中国将发展文化软实力作为国家发展和社会和谐的重要战略，发挥语言教学的社会和文化功能，因此，培养学生的创造力将不可避免地成为外语教学的发展方向。“以写促学”教学法对传统写作语境的突破和重塑正是朝这个方向努力的一种尝试。毋庸置疑，这一教学法还存在诸多不足，为其建立的理论框架也不一定能涵盖其丰富的思想内涵，但是它对写作教学的目的、写作的社会文化功能、写作的互文本质、师生关系等进行的思考和突破是很值得研究和借鉴的。

---

〔1〕 Corbett, J. , *An intercultural approach to English language teaching*, Clevedon, Buffalo, Toronto, Sydney: Multilingual Matters, 2003, p18.

〔2〕 Lee, I. , *Issues and challenges in teaching and learning EFL writing: The case of Hong Kong* , Second Language Writing, 2008.

第六章

跨越桥梁：跨文化写作教学法

显然，全球化对英语教育的影响，对外语文化的教学和学习提出了更高的要求。与此同时，具有较高写作能力和创造力的学生是当前市场的宠儿。面对这些挑战，迫切需要能够提高学生写作能力、创新能力和跨文化交际能力的创新写作教学法。受广东外语外贸大学教改的启发，结合自己的写作和教学经历，以及相关文献和研究，我提出了一种新的写作教学法——跨文化写作教学法。这种方法意味着什么？为什么我们在语言教学中需要这种方法？在中国这样的第二语言环境下，如何在英语课堂上使用？这种新方法的含义和挑战是什么？在这一章中，我们将讨论这些问题。

6.1 新教学法的界定

6.1.1 什么是“跨文化写作教学法”？

新的写作方法主要包括两个教学层面：一是通过在写作中创造跨文化接触，提高学生的跨文化能力；二是通过重塑语境要素，如反馈与评价、师生关系、声音、视角、叙事选择等，增强第二语言作者的写作能力。这两个层面绝不是相互独立的，相反，它们是内在地相互联系和彼此嵌入的。例如，在写作中创造跨文化的接触，在某种程度上，就是创造一个真实的或想象的新环境，这可以帮助作家在写作中改变他们的文化身份，改变他们的声音和观点。不仅如此，二语作家的语境变化往往是为了给学习者创造跨文化交际的机会。在这里需要重视语境塑造的跨文化方面，因为它在当代教育中具有特殊的意义。

跨文化语言教学支撑跨文化意识和跨文化能力的发展。文化意识既能促进语言能力的发展又是语言能力发展的结果。跨文化语言教学推动了真正跨文化的语言和文化第三空间的创造，这可以通过文化探索来实现。所谓文化探索就是指寻找文化之间的接触点，将文化障碍转化为文化桥梁。“文化或跨文化”一词通常指“两种文化或两种语言跨越民族国家政治边界的相遇”，也可指“来自不同民族、社会、性别文化的人在同一民族语言边界内的交流”[1]。因此，对于第二语言学习者来说，跨文化语言学习既包括文化间的接触，也包括文化内部的接触，有时作者在面对陌生的文化主题和情景时需要创造力和想象力。Hay and White 认为，只要它能激发写作并促进文化学习，它就能引导我们“超越真实”获得真正的学习机会，进入跨文化的探索和理解。简言之，在跨文化研究中，“语言就是文化”。语言渗透到人类生活的各个方面，文化也渗透到人类生活的各个方面。因此，语言教学应该是一种“文化渗透”的活动。[2]这些理论和需求支撑着该教学法的跨文化层面。

在语境这一方面，既定语境在写作过程中可以被操纵和重塑，以帮助学生更深入和更广泛地探索意义。与广东外语外贸大学一样，这可以通过打破传统的写作语境，并创造一种新的创作语境（例如建立新的思想认识、新的评分和评估制度），在写作和学生的实际读写能力之间建立联系，将流行文化纳入课程，以及改变师生关系等方式来实现。例如，在微观层面上，Hymes[3]的八个情境语境中的每一个都可以被改变，从而产生不同媒介、体裁、叙事结构、受众和指称世界以及各种不同声音和视角的文本。

写作中的跨文化和语境维度的结合，使我们能够有意识地操纵现有的写作语境，挖掘其教学潜力。这不仅为写作提供了丰富的资源，而且可以激发

---

〔1〕 Kramsch, C. J., *Context and culture in language teaching*, Oxford: Oxford University Press, 1993, p81.

〔2〕 Lo Bianco, J., Preface, In J. Lo Bianco & C. Crozet (Eds.), *Teaching invisible culture: Classroom practice and theory*, Melbourne: Language Australia, 2003b, p4.

〔3〕 Hymes, D., *Foundations in sociolinguistics: An ethnographic approach*, London: Tavistock Publications, 1977.

学生的创造力和写作兴趣。最重要的是，它可能有助于提高学习者的母语和第二语言文化以及跨文化意识。这是当代教育家、政治家和中国英语学习者所共同追求的教育目标。但是，我们为什么要在语言教学中采用跨文化教学法呢？为了回答这个问题，让我们从我在跨文化交际中所遇到的一个难题开始。这个难题关系到我的名字。

6.1.2　为什么采用跨文化教学法？

此故事写于2010年我在澳大利亚读博士期间。

我叫叶洪，是一名38岁的中国女性，五年前来到澳大利亚。此前在中国的一所重点大学做了10多年的英语老师，现在跟两位澳大利亚导师Trevor和Julie攻读博士学位，研究主题是“批判性和跨文化写作教学法”。

我自己在跨文化交流中的“纠结”始于我的名字。我个人认为我有一个很漂亮的名字。叶，我的中文姓氏，意思是“叶子”，而名字“洪”，听起来像“红色”，所以我的整个名字便描绘了一个风景如画的秋天，漫山遍野被红叶覆盖的优美场景。尤其当中国著名诗人杜牧在其著名诗行“霜叶红于二月花”中应用了这两个字，“叶洪”这个名字便显得更美了。

然而，当我到达澳大利亚时，我像大多数中国人一样立刻为自己取了一个英文名Ally。我理所当然地认为应该“入乡随俗”，所以毫不犹豫地放弃了自己可爱的中文名。有一两次，我的导师Trevor和Julie都问到我为什么不用自己的原名，而我只把它当作了一个礼貌的提议，没有放在心上。

然而随着时间的推移，我对自己的英文名“Ally”越来越不满意，因为从各种意义上来讲，这个名字无法代表我，无法展示我的个性。实际上，更多时候我会将它与美剧中的女孩Ally McBeal联系在一起。但我能做什么呢？我担心如果换回中文名字，大多数的澳大利亚人可能不会说我的名字，那我不就面临失去名字的危险吗！

与此同时，我很羡慕一些来自印度、泰国或日本的朋友，他们有勇气保持自己的原名，其中一些只是简单地把他们的名字变成相近的英语字母，然后教人们发音。那我为什么不能呢？

为了恢复我原来的名字，我向导师 Trevor 寻求帮助。长谈之后我们总结出以下几个选择：

(1) 如果像西方人一样把姓放在名字后面，叫“Hong Ye”听起来很漂亮，但名字颠倒过来在中国就显得很滑稽；

(2) 如果我用自己原本的中文名“Ye Hong”，国外的朋友可能不知道哪个是姓哪个是名；

(3) 如果让别人单叫名字“Hong”也会显得很尴尬，因为在中国，如果一个人的名字只有一个单字，除了最亲近的家人，一般人都不会直呼这个单名。所以叫我“Hong”似乎也不合适。

正当我们感到棘手气馁时，突然想到了一个好主意。为什么不把名和姓放在一起组成一个复合名“YeHong”呢？这样一来，不仅和汉语发音相同，人们也可以从拼写来判断它的发音。此外，单词内部的大写字母赋予了它独特的时尚气息，就像在网络语言或电视广告中那样。最重要的是，它是我，代表着我的身份，我的文化和我的个性！

我松了一口气，向导师道了谢，走出了他的办公室。自从来到澳大利亚以后，我从未像现在这样自在过。我作为一个中国女人站在这里，我的名字意味着金秋灿烂的红叶，象征着美丽和成功。我意识到这个名字对我如此重要，它给了我一个全新的身份。与此同时，我不禁想知道为什么中国的老师从来没有和我们讨论过这个命名难题。我也为自己感到羞愧。作为多年的英语老师，我也从来没有和自己的学生们讨论过这个重要的话题。我想知道我的学生们如何在没有足够的跨文化交流知识的情况下独自面对这个问题。我想知道他们中有多少人像我一样幸运，在导师的帮助下，成功地找到了文化的“第三空间”，使自己的文化和外国文化的习俗都得到了沿袭、尊重和满足。

“跨文化名字”的成功协商经验使我明白了很多道理。首先，我们不需要在进入西方文化时自动遵循他们的习俗，因为这既不能保证顺利的跨文化交流，也不能满足来自两种文化的对话者的需求。其次，“第三空间”确实存在，能够使我们既保持自己的身份，又可以遵守西方的习俗，来自两种文化的人都可以在其中感到舒适。最后，舒适区只有通过不断地跨文化探索和协商才能实现，其中创造性、灵感、文化知识和技巧同等重要。

在更大的背景下，随着加速的国际化，社会必须获得更多的文化能力，以应对日益增加的跨文化交流的需要；现代市场还需要全球文化间的融合，以促进日益一体化的经济统一；或许最重要的是，我们需要跨文化意识和敏感性，以便在多元和有争议的世界中共存，实现跨文化和谐。

但是在传统的语言教学中很难做到这一点。正如我们所知道的，语言是由具有不同权力和地位的人使用的，这就导致了语言交流中的不平等权力地位。“第三空间”中不同群体的人是平等的，这在传统语言教学中几乎不可能实现，传统语言教师对此也无能为力。对中国语言教育的历史考察表明，在世界文化影响下，偏向民族中心主义或偏向同化主义的不平衡教育取向对我国一个半世纪以来的发展造成了不利影响。因此，外语教学迫切需要引起“明确、系统和审慎的关注”[1]。

尽管在语言教学中，越来越多的人呼吁将文化从边缘转移到中心，也有将文化融入课程等新的尝试，然而，令人遗憾的是，目前的英语写作教学方法仍然忽视了语言与文化之间的紧密联系，或未能均衡地融合国内外文化。他们中的许多人倾向于关注英语规范或“中华文明的辉煌成就”，而不是支撑这些规范的文化意识形态和实践。所以在两种写作文化之间协商一个跨文化空间像是天方夜谭。郎咸平是中国最著名的经济学家之一，他指出了不利于中国经济发展的几大因素。其中之一是，中国人对西方世界了解不够。他表示，对外国文化漠不关心的态度导致清王朝的衰落和倾覆，若不加以改变，将使我们的经济前景毁于一旦。

与对西方文化漠不关心的态度相反，另一种趋势是中国英语教育中的同化主义。为了获得交际能力，有一种倾向是试图消除母语和母语文化的影响，使语言学习者沉浸在目标语言文化中。例如，许多语言专业的学生在开始学习时，会立即放弃中文姓名，改起英文名字。[2]他们中的大多数人开始单纯

---

〔1〕 Lo Bianco, J., A 'syntax of peace'? In J. Lo Bianco, A. Liddicoat & C. Crozet (Eds.), *Striving for the third place: Intercultural competence through language education*, Melbourne: Language Australia, 1999, p62.

〔2〕 Tian, G., & Zheng, Y., The use of English names by college students in China. In Y. Gao (Ed.), *The social psychology of English learning by Chinese college students: Motivation and learners' self identities*, Beijing: Foreign Language Teaching and Research Press, 2003, p168-189.

关注英语语言和文学，会有意识或无意识地脱离自己的母语和母语文化。这种对语言学习者来说“不均衡的饮食”可能会导致母语和母语文化的严重“营养不良”[1]；更严重的是，它可能会导致其中的文化认同感和自我价值的弱化甚至消失。一方面，这种语言教学方式是适得其反的，因为所有人都有权利表达自己的民族身份。[2]另一方面，“模仿别人”的能力不能保证一个人更容易被目标语言文化群体接受，也不能保证产生相互理解。此外，它切断了母语和第二语言文化之间的联系，限制二语写作的资源，损害了学习者的信心和跨文化身份的建立，从而抑制了写作。如果将文化成分排除在外，写作教学和课程的创新就会达到“瓶颈期”，学生的写作能力、创造力和跨文化能力都会被限制在一个有限的水平上。

因此，我认为在语言教育中，应该充分重视学习者的母语和第二语言文化，探索“跨文化的第三空间”。为此，我们应该鼓励学生把自己的知识作为跨文化探索的起点，从跨文化的角度进行创造性的写作，用跨文化的敏感性来写作。例如，我们可以鼓励学生将中国的传说改写成适合英语观众观看的剧本，让他们注意到来自不同文化观众的不同视角和期望。或者我们可以让学生写关于西方的电视节目或电影的观后感，并在主题、价值和习俗等方面与中国的节目进行对比。我们可以引导学生讨论如何在不同的情况下使用合适的修辞策略，应该避免哪些文化禁忌等。这些活动可以帮助学生识别一个民族内部或国家之间的文化异同，从而在跨文化交际中为自己探索一个舒适的跨文化空间。

6.1.3　如何使用跨文化写作法?

在英语写作课堂中把文化与语言联系起来是一项复杂的任务。它包括对跨文化知识和技能的界定、教学和测试，以跨文化交际能力为语言教育的最终目的。它使教师在塑造 21 世纪的写作教学法过程中发挥突出和重要的作

〔1〕 Belcher, D. D., & Connor, U., Editors' introduction. In D. D. Belcher & U. Connor (Eds.), *Reflections on multiliterate lives*, Clevedon, Buffalo, Toronto, Sydney: Multilingual Matters, 2001, p1-19.

〔2〕 Rizvi, F., *Multiculturalism as an educational policy*, [Waurn Ponds], Vic.: Deakin University: distributed by Deakin University Press, 1985.

用，但同时也要求写作教师重新思考其主题的内容，其中还包括新的实践指南和新的教学材料。

王永阳[1]主张在对外汉语教学中，采用“跨文化主题法”来选择中国文学。这一实践的目的是通过探讨某些跨文化主题来培养学生的跨文化能力。这些主题指的是在跨文化交流中具有重要意义的任何文化要素。例如，“女性”这一主题使对外汉语读者能够通过阅读各种文学文本来理解动态的、当代的中国女性形象。

Arrue[2]也采用了类似的方法，为在西班牙学习的美国学生开设了一门跨文化交际课程。该课程的目的是使学生更加了解他们所带来的文化包袱，以及文化对他们在当前跨文化的理解和反应中所发挥的作用。课程的十个主题包括“刻板印象与以偏概全”“主流价值观”“非语言沟通”“群体与流动性”“正式与非正式教育”“关系与生活方式”“性别与性”“身份多样性与社会地位”“伦理道德与宗教”“跨文化冲击与阶段”。本课程虽然处于“留学”的背景下，但对中国英语学习者写作主题的发展提供了一些实用的指导。

对于旨在提高跨文化意识和能力的教学方法，Kramsch 提出了非常有见地的建议。特别是，她强调学习者需要通过探索和改变文本创作中的叙事方式，如“媒介和体裁、叙事结构（例如视角和文本时间）、听众、故事的指称世界以及文本中的各种声音和沉默”，来塑造话语的语境。Hay 也提出了类似的方法，以识别和试验对讲故事至关重要的话语要素。Corbett 提出了在会话课堂中实施跨文化方法的框架，我对其进行了修改，以适应写作课堂的需要：

（1）参与者角色。参与者之间的关系是什么？他们在主题或活动中的地位是平等的还是不同的？

（2）写作重点。目前正在练习的是哪项或哪些写作技能？还是仅仅是有比较笼统的写作目标？

---

〔1〕 Wang, Y., & Hay, T., “Reading Chinese literature or reading China? — On an intercultural thematic approach to the reading of Chinese literature in the TCFL (Teaching Chinese as a foreign language) curriculum”, *Journal of Guizhou University (Social Sciences)*, 29 (2), 2008, p107-112.

〔2〕 Arrue, C., The eye of the beholder: Study abroad in Spain viewed through multi-cultural lenses. In V. Savicki (Ed.), *Developing intercultural competence and transformation: Theory, research, and application in international education (1st ed.)*, Sterling, Virginia: Stylus, 2008, p236-258.

(3) 文化目标。这里的文化活动有什么意义?是为了揭示文化差异性和相似性,还是为了协商个体的地位,或是为了确定共同的民族规范,又或者是为了探索跨文化空间?

(4) 程序。如何完成任务?活动中需要采取哪些步骤?有切实的结果吗?

(5) 语言负载。参与者是否有足够的语言能力和资源来完成任务?

(6) 反思的机会。可以进行哪些后期写作活动,以引起对所审查的文化问题的讨论和反思?如果作者的角色被改变,是否有不同的方法来处理同一主题?

王永阳的“跨文化主题法”和 Hay 及 Kramsch 的语境和话语法,以及 Corbett 和 Arrue 提出的实践框架,都给了我很大的启发。根据这项研究,以及我们对跨文化写作中跨文化写作方法的讨论,我将提出一些写作活动来说明如何在英语写作课堂中尝试跨文化写作教学法。这些活动旨在通过创造性地让学生参与有关跨文化主题的写作,特别是那些能够激发学生对本土文化和目标文化的理解和比较的主题写作,从而提高学生的跨文化意识。对于这些写作活动,我的目标对象是中国大学英语专业的学生,尽管这些话题可以在其他的环境中使用,但是要适当调整。

主题一:姓名和身份

写作任务:写一篇关于你的中文名字来源的故事;为自己提出一个“国际名字”,供自己在跨文化交流中使用,并解释你为什么选择这个名字。

文化目的:关于姓名的故事可提供对语言、文化、身份和权力问题的见解,因此具有特殊的教学重要性。[1]首先,这个活动让同学们注意到自己的中文名字所蕴含的文化意义——一个人的名字和其家庭背景之间可能的联系、出生时的历史情况、当地文化和习俗的影响等。其次,这个活动让学生思考跨文化交流的复杂性,鼓励他们探索一种自己认为合适的跨文化身份。

反思:进行写后活动,对姓名的文化问题进行讨论和反思;通过分享故

---

〔1〕 Kiang, P. N. -c., Voicing names and naming voices: Pedagogy and persistence in an Asian American studies classroom. In V. Zamel & R. Spack (Eds.), *Crossing the curriculum: Multilingual learners in college classrooms*, Mahwah, N. J.: L. Erlbaum Associates, 2004, p207-220.

事，学生可以了解不同地区的命名习俗和注意事项。

主题二：中国功夫精神

写作任务：想象你是一位好莱坞导演，想把一个典型的中国故事改编成一部适合西方观众的英语电影。将一个典型的中国故事（民间故事、历史传说、古典小说、电影、肥皂剧等）改写成英文的剧本或故事，要特别注意随着语言、视角和观众的变化进行风格、精神和效果的调整。

文化目的：通过从一个局内人到一个局外人的视角转变，引导学生以一种不同的方式思考自己的文化。

程序：看电影《功夫熊猫》（Kong Fu Panda）[1]，并讨论电影中所披露的西方对中国功夫的看法。学生们认为中国功夫的精髓是什么？这些观点之间有什么不同呢？鼓励学生参考其他资源，如迪士尼动画片《木兰从军》（1998 年）和香港喜剧《功夫》（2004 年）等，其编剧技巧及样本同样可供学生参考，英语戏剧、舞台剧等表演可作为写后活动。

主题三：东西方的时尚

写作任务：想象你是一名时装模特、时装设计师或时装评论员等；向外国人介绍一件民族服装，或者写下你认为西方和中国对于时尚、美丽的原则和标准。

文化目的：揭示中西方在服饰和时尚方面的文化异同。对一些话题进行讨论，比如西方的着装规范。

程序：鼓励学生收集关于时尚和着装的照片、图片、视频剪辑，撰写关于时尚的故事、评论和建议等。写后讨论可以包括如何在西方和中国的不同场合得体着装，比如在教堂、婚礼、工作、晚宴和葬礼上的着装；什么历史和社会因素形成了这种穿衣习惯？在中国和西方，穿着如何影响一个人的外貌和身份？

语言负载：学生可能需要查阅资源，并为他们的写作开发一个时尚词汇

〔1〕《功夫熊猫》是一部由 Mark Osborne 和 John Stevenson 执导，梦工厂动画公司于 2008 年制作的奥斯卡提名影片。故事以中国古代为背景，讲述了一只笨手笨脚的熊猫立志成为一名功夫大师的故事。

表。不同文体（个人故事、评论、描述等）的不同写作风格也需要进行讨论。

主题四：公开演讲

写作任务：为想象中的听众写一篇关于你最关心的问题的演讲，比如中国在全球环境保护中的角色，或者中国商业或文化产品的推广。运用多元文化的知识和视角，以及适当的修辞手段，加强论证和演讲效果。

程序：收听一些著名的演讲，包括马丁·路德·金（Martin Luther King）、奥巴马（Obama）、林肯（Lincoln）在美国的演讲，以及傅莹〔1〕、李阳〔2〕等人的著名演讲，还有易中天〔3〕、于丹〔4〕、中国前总理朱镕基和温家宝等用中文发表的演讲。识别并比较这些演讲中使用的话语策略，包括语言风格、语音语调、肢体语言、面部表情、眼神交流、与观众互动、礼仪等。这些策略在不同的环境中以何种方式变化？为什么他们可以达到预期的政治、文化、经济、个人目的和影响？如何让演讲适合以下不同人群：学术人群、普通人群、学生、老年人、儿童，受过教育的和文化水平较低的观众？

主题五：写信

写作任务：给一个想象中的人写一封信，比如给你的爱人写一封情书，给学校食堂写一封抱怨信，或者给海外大学写一封申请信。根据语境和目标，读者使用适当的策略和文化知识。

文化目的：写信是一种特定的文化活动，它包含许多文化规范，如问候、请求和赞美等；〔5〕帮助学生认识到这些规范的异同，特别是如何表达爱、愤

---

〔1〕 傅莹是中国第一位少数民族女性外交部副部长。她以善于利用公开写作和演讲来解决政治和外交危机而闻名。

〔2〕 李阳是“疯狂英语”（Crazy English）的创作者，这是一种流行的非正统英语教学方法。他做了许多鼓舞人心的演讲来宣传他的英语学习方法。

〔3〕 易中天是中国历史学家、作家、学者、电视名人。2005 年，他在中央电视台成功举办了一系列有关中国历史的讲座，从此家喻户晓。

〔4〕 于丹拥有中国古代文学硕士学位和影视研究博士学位。《于丹论语》系列讲座在中央电视台播出，受到观众的热烈欢迎。

〔5〕 Crozet, C. , & Maurer, L. , Teaching French culture in language use. In J. Lo Bianco & C. Crozet (Eds.), *Teaching invisible culture: Classroom practice and theory*, Melbourne: Language Australia, 2003, p119-145.

怒、真诚等情感，如何在不同的语境中表达家庭、工作、伦理等情感和价值观；学习使用适当的文化和修辞策略，在不同的情况下促进跨文化交流。

程序：阅读西方和中国的书信、诗歌或散文，包括莎士比亚、亚伯拉罕·林肯、罗伯特·伯恩斯、徐志摩[1]等，以及你所喜欢的现代作家的作品。讨论不同国家、不同历史时期、不同社会文化或个人背景下的不同或者相似的写作技巧、风格和措辞。根据你的读者调整你的修辞策略。朗诵会可以作为写后的活动，优胜者的作品可以被挑选出来发表。

在这一节中，我们讨论了跨文化教学法在英语写作教育中的应用，包括为什么应该使用以及如何使用。作者提出了一些写作主题和活动，以说明在实际教学中使用该方法的可能性。主题选择的基本原则是能够有效比较学习者的母语文化和目标语文化，与学习者的生活兴趣和关注密切相关。例如，时尚和爱情（主题三和五）是大学生最喜欢的话题，尤其是对于英语专业的学生，多是来自中国城市富裕家庭的年轻女孩。这些话题很可能会激发她们学习语言的兴趣和动机，并将她们的兴趣带入课程学习中，从而弥补学校文化与现实文化之间的差距。除了关联原则外，跨文化方法的一个关键点是我们应该强调以学习者自身的知识作为跨文化探索的起点。以上主题以学生现有的文化习俗知识为基础，鼓励他们探索中西语言文化的异同。

同时，中国不同地区、不同历史时期的不同修辞手法和文化特征（如上文所述）也值得老师和同学们关注。这些文化多样性和内部文化差异在跨文化语言教育中发挥着重要作用，因为学生对自己文化的知识、技能和态度，使他们能够反思自己的文化假设，这是进一步提高其跨文化交际能力的基础。[2]

然而，令人遗憾的是，在外语教学中，由于外语及其文化的教学是最重要的，而母语和母语文化的教学主要被视为中学语文教师的任务，因此，内文化能力在很大程度上被排除在外。这种心态导致了中国大学生尤其是语言

---

〔1〕 徐志摩是20世纪初的浪漫主义诗人，一生追求爱情、自由和美丽。他留下了四部诗集，包括许多爱情诗和情书。

〔2〕 Sercu, L., & Bandura, E., *Foreign language teachers and intercultural competence: An international investigation*, Clevedon, Buffalo, Toronto: Multilingual Matters Ltd., 2005.

专业学生的语言文化能力的下降。此外，母语文化的“淡化”阻碍了学生比较文化和探索跨文化能力。在下一节中，我们将讨论这个问题，并深入探讨文化教育的“内文化”组成部分。

6.2 “内文化”交际能力

任何改革，如果不能激发人民发展的动力，不能得到革命的某种内在动力的支持，就难以产生深刻的民族意识，就难以在国际环境中有效地表现自己。

——Ding G.〔1〕

值得注意的是，到目前为止，关于“跨文化方法”的讨论主要涉及不同民族国家之间的文化意识教育。然而，在这一节中，我想把这个概念推到一个更加“微观”和“深层”的层面，包括一个国家内不同群体之间的文化多样性，以及一个国家历史发展过程中文化传统与现代性之间的联系。为此，我创造了“内文化”（*intracultural*）这个术语，以区别于我们一直在讨论的“跨文化”方法。此外，我还区分了两种形式的“内文化”知识：“横向交际”与“纵向交际”。Lo Bianco 提出了这样一个问题：中国人希望如何对待自己的传统，以及中国的独特性将使重新崛起的中国在全球中扮演什么样的角色？我的观点是，在教育中，内文化意识的教与学（横向和纵向交际）与跨文化意识同样重要，因此在课堂中应该给予足够的重视。

6.2.1 横向交际

每个民族国家都有不同的文化群体，人们有不同的地理环境、社会、经济背景和传统。这通常是人们价值观和世界观形成的关键。例如，中国是一个人口众多的民族大国。北京的小男生应该和云南的白族大爷或者西藏的僧侣有很大的不同。提高不同文化群体的文化敏感性，可以使人们更加尊重彼

〔1〕 Ding, G., Nationalization and internationalization: Two turning points in China's education in the twentieth century. In R. Hayhoe, G. Peterson & Y. Lu (Eds.), *Education, culture, and identity in twentieth-century China*, Ann Arbor: University of Michigan Press, 2001, p183.

此的文化差异和需求，减少文化冲突，从而有助于实现中国构建更加和谐的社会的国家目标。

近年来，政府将“构建科学和谐社会”作为国家工作的目标。Samovar 认为，实现国家目标的希望在于教育，在于如何在学校里教育我们的儿童。但是如何在语言教学中，尤其是在英语写作教学中，提高内文化能力呢？

正如 Dyson 所观察到的，语言课堂的社会文化差异具有丰富的多样性，其基础是不同文化风格以及家庭、经济和性别的差异。这种多样性为课堂提供了不同的视角、不同的声音和丰富的可能性。遗憾的是，这些差异很少被视为资源。因此，Kress 强烈主张，应该认识到学生的社会文化差异，并将其视为积极因素而非问题，以便在课堂上激发有意义的互动。换言之，应该抓住这种体现内在文化差异的机会，在其自身经验所提供的有限资源的基础上，超越和改变学生的价值观和思想意识。一方面，在写作课堂上，我们应该对学生的文化多样性和民族多样性保持敏感，这可以成为创造力的丰富来源。特别是，我们可以鼓励学生写一些故事来认识和庆祝他们的文化历史和特性。这一点很重要，因为它将学习与社会、情感和文化联系起来。另一方面，我们可以鼓励我们的学生走出教室，接触不同文化的群体。通过了解他们，描述他们，丰富学生的生活经验，反过来超越其原有世界观。

6.2.2　纵向交际

在特定的历史时期，一个民族国家内部的地理、民族、社会和经济的多样性除了造成“内文化”差异中的“横向交际”之外，历史还产生了另一种形式的文化多样性，即传统与现代之间的“纵向交际”。以基督教为例，它在其历史发展的过程中发生了重大的变化，现在已经分为许多亚群，每个亚群都有自己的信仰和教义。中国的知识传统也是如此。例如，儒家在不同的历史时期有不同的思想流派，以及不同的哲学和政治取向。

以儒学和理学为代表的中国传统文化历来被认为是僵化的、缺乏创造性的，重记忆、重模仿、轻创新，阻碍了中国的创新和改革之路。我认为，这种观念部分源于对儒家思想的刻板印象和不完整理解。以（新）儒家思想为特征的书面语文化，在历史上经历了巨大变革。古典学术的社会和文化声望受到一系列运动的致命破坏；取而代之的是对大众教育的巨大需求，这在某种程度上可以从中国大众传媒和学校中“汉学复兴”的最新趋势中体现出来。鉴于这些变化，对中国文化的全盘否定或者盲目崇拜都“抹杀了文化差异”，[1]是对丰富而复杂的中国知识传统的简化看法。

可以提供许多证据来反驳这种对儒家思想的指责。这里我想举两个反例。首先，儒家教育非常重视批判性和独立思考，这也是创造性的一个重要方面。孔子本人也曾指出:“学而不思则罔”，即“学习若不思考便会一无所获”。在所有的儒家著作中，《诗经》是大约2500年前最早的诗集，被认为是孔子编订的。这本书充满了对当时人们生活的富有想象力和创造性的描绘。而且这些诗可以用优美的音乐演唱出来。例如这本书第一行的第一句：“关关雎鸠，在河之洲，窈窕淑女，君子好逑。”这首诗描述了一个年轻农村男孩对他的爱人的思念之情。它使用了大量的修辞策略，如赋、比、兴。诗中所传达的形象，苗条的少女、渴望的男孩、求爱的鸟儿，如此鲜活生动，至今仍流行于现代汉语语言中。除了这些意象，像赋、比、兴这样的书写手法，虽然被贴上了不同的名字，但在中国人的书写中仍然被广泛使用。

那么，在我们的写作传统中存在创造力的源泉吗？答案似乎是肯定的。但我们需要以一种更具情境化的视角来看待中国的知识传统，而不是将其过于简化或泛化。

汉语和中国古代文化的成就与英语的教与学有怎样的联系，这是一个值得思考的问题。因为“中国的命运、历史、威望和荣誉，尤其是其语言和古典文学典籍，都牵涉在英语的教学中，并受其影响”。[2]那么，如何挖掘中国知识传统的丰富资源，并将其作为批判性和创造性写作教学法的源泉呢？就我看来，它们至少可以有两种用途，即丰富写作内容和拓展英语修辞策略。

---

〔1〕 Peterson, G., & Hayhoe, R., Introduction. In R. Hayhoe, G. Peterson & Y. Lu (Eds.), *Education, culture, and identity in twentieth-century China*, Ann Arbor: University of Michigan Press, 2001, p5.

〔2〕 Lo Bianco, J., Being Chinese, speaking English. In J. Lo Bianco, J. Orton & Y. Gao (Eds.), *China and English: Globalization and the dilemmas of identity*, Bristol, Buffalo, Toronto: Multilingual Matters, 2009, p307.

写作内容

大量的中国文学和历史可以为英语学习者提供丰富的写作主题和内容资源。这样一来，英语写作不仅能够成为教学的目的，也能成为一种重新审视学习者自身文化的手段，从而在帮助语言学习者批判性地吸收和阐述其文化精髓和遗产方面发挥重要作用。

此外，由于学生对中国传统故事和历史比较熟悉，经过多年的语文、历史等课程的学习，其中一些人对这些故事和历史有着极大的热情，利用这些资源可以缩短他们现有知识与目标学习之间的心理距离，从而大大减少英语写作中的恐惧和焦虑。

我仍然记得初中的时候，当我发现我可以用英语给同学们讲“寺院里的和尚”（The Monk in the Temple）时，我有多么的惊讶和兴奋。我还记得我的学生们是如何热情地将中国古典小说《西游记》改写成一部现代英语喜剧，并将它搬上舞台，吸引了成千上万的观众。还有一次，我们让学生扮演《红楼梦》中的贾宝玉、薛宝钗、林黛玉等人，让他们接受其他同学的采访，以揭示这部伟大小说中三个主要人物之间的微妙关系。在随后的写作任务中，许多学生表现出了极大的兴趣，在写作中展示出少有的个性和洞察力。

然而，我们目前的教学，似乎在英语写作中忽视了这些丰富而易得的资源，在我们的英语教学中，也显然忽视了优秀的文学和文化遗产。当然，把这些资源运用到英语写作中并不意味着我们应该忽视英语写作的其他写作任务。例如，写与学生生活和他们生活的世界直接相关的话题。此外，富有想象力地描写世界其他地方的人和生活也是提高学生创造力和跨文化敏感性的重要途径。在此，我建议，在为英语写作学习者设计写作话题时，我们可以考虑另一个资源——中国文学和文化的丰富遗产，因为建立在学生现有知识基础上的写作任务可以减少他们对英语写作的恐惧，激发他们的兴趣和创造力，并加强母语文化认同感，而这种认同感在语言学生中一般较弱。

写作技巧

除了借用中国文化遗产中的主题和内容外，我们还可以适当运用传统的修辞策略，以达到现代使用的目的。游晓晔认为中国的修辞传统极其丰富，具有西方修辞学的特征，如思想的清晰排列，归纳推理和演绎推理的线性结构。此外，在中国古典诗歌和散文中还具有对仗等独特的修辞策略。由于历史的发展和中西修辞传统的融合，在现代写作中这些特征并不是很突出。但如果使用得当，它们可能会为学生的英语写作创造力提供额外的动力。对中国学生来说，汉语修辞传统可以成为英语写作的盟友，而不是应该彻底铲除的死敌，这让他们有了利用现有知识探索跨文化舒适区的许可和信心。

在英语写作中是否或如何引入汉语修辞传统，是一个非常复杂和有争议的话题。由于时间和空间的限制，无法在本书中进行详细的讨论。本人认为，中国文学传统中丰富的修辞策略可以激励中国学生将自己的写作知识融入汉语和英语中，在寻求一个舒适的跨文化空间时，不应该把这些传统视为二语写作中的害虫或稗草；相反，如果使用得当，它们可以成为创造力和文化学习的源泉。如果日本的俳句可以用在英语写作上，我们为什么不能用中国的古典诗歌或词来探索新的英语写作方式呢?

为了说明这一点，我借用《诗经》中的一些修辞策略，包括赋、比、兴，在我丈夫 33 岁生日的时候给他写了一首诗。这绝不是一篇好的诗作，但它锻炼了我想象力的肌肉，至少满足了我以更艺术和创造性的方式表达自己情感的需要。

To Husband's 33 birthday

Dear me! The boy is thirty-three.
Can you believe it? How can he be?

Like yesterday, he first met she,
Can you dance with me, he asked, I am almost eighteen.
Then you need to wait, she answered, let's just go and see.

They walked, hand in hand, tight but free,
until she has a ring, and two become three.

He is growing, branching out in green,
She is climbing, up and around the tree.

The vine says to her companion,
Thank you, my darling,
for the shade and for the cling,
also for your lovely young seedling.

The tree is sighing,
I'd rather hold you to my skin,
than to let you go and swing.

Fifteen years pass in a spree,
Now they are separated by the sea.
So life is the most dramatic movie,
What can be a better love story?

宝藏还是垃圾?

在英语写作课堂中，学生的表现取决于他们所能获得的“文化工具包”以及教师和环境所提供的许可、支持和空间大小。“文化工具包”既包括一个国家由于地域、民族差别带来的多种多样的文化资源，也包括这个国家历史传承下来的丰富文化遗产。采用这种方法进行语言教育，不仅可以提高学生对目的语和目的语文化的认识，而且也为学生提供机会重新思考自己的文化，以一种全新的视角看待语言与文化之间的联系，从而为自己争取一个跨文化的空间。正如 Bruner 所主张的那样，教育的大部分过程就是通过反思自己的知识，学会用一种理性的客观的视角来看待已知的世界。

总之，“内文化”知识是“跨文化”能力不可或缺的一部分，在英语写作教学中需要进行充分考虑。由于语言文化的维持与国家的经济和政治实力有关，而世界正在经历“汉语的崛起”和当前的“再中国化”趋势，[1]因此，即使是在英语写作课上，剥夺学生加强母语文化机会的行为都是不明智的，甚至是严重错误的。因此，我们应该鼓励中国的英语学习者不仅要“接触”写作资源，还要“接触”自己的文化，通过英语写作来丰富他们的内文化知识，从而使他们能够以一种多元文化的思维，而不是一个被割裂的头脑来创造性地进行英语写作。

此外，跨文化教学法在英语写作课堂的实施与英语写作和教学方式的变化密切相关，而这种变化又与读写和写作观念的变化密切相关。在下一节中，我们将讨论这些变化是如何影响包括写作任务、资源和产品在内的写作过程的。

6.3　多媒体创作面临的挑战

虽然全球化要求跨地域和跨学科的多语言写作研究，新的信息和通信技术已将多模态写作深深地融入写作实践中来，给写作方式带来了深刻的变化，拓展了潜在的写作资源（输入）、写作作品（输出）、写作任务和提示设计。

大量的资源可用于生成写作主题和提供写作输入，例如图片、书籍、视频剪辑、声音、电影、电视节目和网页等。写作产品的形式也变得越来越多种多样。一些学生在混合模式写作中表现出了兴趣和热情，他们创造性地将声音、视觉形象与书面文本结合在一起，并发展了自己的艺术风格。

同时，对多元文化的研究促使我们理解和认识与日常生活、大众媒体和互联网交织在一起的“非官方”、多语言和多模态写作实践。例如，学生经常访问的“My Space”和“Facebook”等社交网站上出现了大量的表达方式，包括文本、图像和照片、音乐和歌曲、视频和电视，以及flash制作的内容等。通过设计、管理和在自己的网站账户上书写，用户能够得到更多尝试多模式的写作和交流的机会。

这些变化给外语写作的跨文化教育带来了机遇，也带来了挑战。一方面，教师作为知识传授者甚至是发起者的角色受到了威胁，因为不同来源的信息

〔1〕 Joseph Lo Bianco、刘国强：“澳大利亚的语言政策与中文教学生态环境”，载《世界汉语教学》2007年第3期。

远远超出了教师对知识的掌握。另一方面，文化学习和比较所需要的信息是广泛开放的，学生能够通过不同的渠道轻松获取。例如，互联网给英语学生带来了一个全新的学习环境，特别是它支持和挑战学习者的创造性想象力，参与和动机。[1]在跨文化主题的写作中，教师不应该也不可能提供文化比较所需要的全部信息和知识，所以教师可以鼓励学生通过互联网、文学和流行文化去探索答案。同时，由于这种学习的效果很大程度上取决于学习者的自主性、时间和方法，所以教师应该在整个过程中对学生进行系统的指导。

以上一节的写作活动“西方的时尚”为例。任务是通过一个虚构的角色，如模特、时装设计师或评论员，来写一篇故事、描述或评论了解中西方时装的异同。为了完成这个任务，时尚杂志、视频剪辑、红毯明星的照片、教堂礼拜、晚宴以及婚礼和葬礼都可以成为写作的素材。学生可以上网查找这些参考资料，而不是一味地依赖老师的输入；或者，他们可以自由分配任务，以团队的形式来收集信息。至于写作作品，我们不需要将写作拘泥于打印形式上，而是鼓励学生将文章与多种表达模式混合。例如，他们可以把文字转换成电子形式，用音乐、图像甚至视频来补充；或者他们可以举办一场时装秀，或者举办一个多元文化日，来展示由于地理、历史、宗教和社会文化的多样性而产生的多元时尚。

总之，多模态写作通过让学生探索反映21世纪符号学世界的混合交际模式，将跨文化写作变成了培养创造力的一部分。跨文化写作法不仅可以发挥学生的聪明才智，用文字和图像创作三维作品；还可以把自己的“认知”与“学校学习”联系起来，反思校外发生的变化以及多模态交流的真实世界。

6.4 跨文化写作的“第三空间”

新兴的现代语言教育方法——跨文化语言教学法已经将语言学习的目标从目的语交际转移到寻求两种文化之间的“第三空间”，这是一个通过跨文化

〔1〕 Loveless, A., & Wegerif, R., Unlocking creativity with ICT. In R. Fisher & M. Williams (Eds.), *Unlocking creativity: Teaching across the curriculum*, London: David Fulton, 2004, p92-102.

接触和对话获得文化洞察力的地带。在通过对话寻求彼此理解的过程中，“每个人都试图在不失去自我的前提下通过对方的眼睛看世界”。

鲁迅有一句名言，只有民族的，才是世界的。这句话似乎有些矛盾，但不正是跨文化的本质吗?

最好的例证便是2008年北京奥运会的开幕式。它是中国古代艺术和文化(如巨大的卷轴和鼓点等）的一个丰富集合与现代西方文化和技术元素的完美融合，如火炬传递和现代舞表演。现代与传统、中国文化与世界文化的融合壮观而迷人，被观众和国际媒体称赞为是一个空前的巨大成功。

正如习总书记在2014年文艺工作座谈会上所强调的：传承中华文化，绝不是简单复古，也不是盲目排外，而是古为今用、洋为中用，辩证取舍、推陈出新……实现中华文化的创新性转化和创新性发展。

“跨文化”似乎已经渗透到了现代生活的方方面面，从体育史上的一个值得纪念的事件，到造型师的服装和美味的快餐，创造了许多奇迹。那么，如何才能在英语写作中找到“第三空间”呢?

我认为可以从写作主题、表达方式、语言特征等方面进行探讨。在创作内容上，许多作家描写了自己在西方和中国的流居生活，探讨了影响跨文化交际的各种文化主题。林语堂便是一个经典的例子，他写下了许多介绍中西文化异同的佳作。在艺术形式上，有中国故事与西方歌剧或芭蕾的融合，比如“文革”中的样板戏，[1]以及最近将《牡丹亭》改编成当代歌剧、舞台剧和供海外观众欣赏的电影，都是文艺创作中“第三空间”的例子。在语言特征方面，郭小橹（2007年）的小说《情人间简明汉英词典》（A Concise Chinese-English Dictionary for Lovers）也不失为一个好例子。她故意使用“糟糕的英语”(或中式英语)，给我们展示了理解中国语言和中国思维模式的另一种方式。她巧妙地运用英汉两种语言在形态学、句法和语义上的差异，不仅表现出“滑稽的中式英语”，还表现出一种“跨文化对话”的形式。[2]换句话说，英语的非

---

〔1〕 Hay, T., China's proletarian myth: *The revolutionary narrative and model theatre of the Cultural Revolution*, La Vergne, US; Milton Keynes, GB: Lambert, 2008.

〔2〕 Hay, T., & Wang, Y., On speaking terms with elder brother, *Creative Approaches to Research*, 2(2), 2009, p58-71.

标准使用有时可以作为一种积极的形式来凸显文化和思想意识的微妙之处。[1]

中国作家通过跨文化主题的创造性写作、中西艺术形式的融合以及英汉语言的语言差异，创造了大量的“第三空间”，这些实例为我们的英语写作教学开辟了新的可能性。

我提出的新的写作教学法是“建构主义”和“以学习者为中心”，学习者的背景和传统，或其内文化知识是跨文化探索的关键和积极因素。从学习者自身的文化和身份入手，创造性地撰写关于跨文化和内部文化主题的文章，运用英汉两种语言不同的表达方式和语言模式可能是积极探索英语写作中“第三空间”的有效方法。我们不能将英语放在首位，慢慢地把学生推向“被动式双语教育”。[2]此外，让学生参与富有想象力的文化主题的写作，可以提高学生的创造力和写作能力，鼓励他们以不同的方式写作，突破自己的原有风格，进入新的语言境界。

总而言之，“第三空间”不是“对立的平衡，也不是意见的折中，而是一种矛盾的、必然的对抗，人在探寻它的过程中可能会发生变化”。它不是一个目的地，而是一段旅程。在这一过程中，学习者形成了对自己、他人和世界的概念，这些概念是灵活开放的，可以根据观点而变化。这是一个个性和知识成熟的“增值”过程。没有人知道别人的“第三空间”在哪里，因为每个学生的起点不同，在成长过程中，他们到达的境界也不尽相同。但学习和教学的经验和情感支持将为学生创造安全的环境，让他们尝试改变自己。沿途获得的文化洞察力虽然在当时可能无法察觉，但是会出现在不同阶段的理解中，出现在个人探索和反思的不同时刻。

同时，文化探索本身也可以是一种教育目标，因为即使学习者没有达到一定的语言能力水平，或者停止学习这门语言，他们通过这种教学法获得的跨文化能力对其未来的发展也是非常有价值的。即使写作课不太可能，或者不能教给学生成功的写作交流所需要的所有技能，对学生文化“宝藏”的认

---

〔1〕 Canagarajah, A. S., The place of world Englishes in composition: Pluralization continued, *College Composition and Communication*, 57 (4), 206, p586-619.

〔2〕 Ng, B. C., & Wigglesworth, G., *Bilingualism: An advanced resource book*, London; New York: Routledge, 2007, p253.

可和积累也可能会增加他们的动机、知识保留和满意度。[1]在某种程度上，这种文化知识可以比作保单的退保价值，这是一种值得庆贺的收获，应在语言教育中加以重视。

最后让我们回到第二章提出的天平的比喻上，天平两端分别是学习者的母语文化和目标语文化。历史证明，在跨文化交际中，学习者要么以自己的文化为中心，要么完全屈从于目标文化，因此，跨文化交际的天平一直在向一端或另一端倾斜。能使两端保持平衡，给予两端同样重要性的“第三空间”很难到达，即使到达了也很难保持。为了争取到达第三空间，我们需要努力、策略和智慧。我认为，内文化和跨文化写作教学法就是这样一种努力。

〔1〕 Leki, I., *Undergraduates in a second language: Challenges and complexities of academic literacy development*, New York: Lawrence Erlbaum Associates, 2007.

第七章

跨文化写作的应用

本章首先从国家文化安全的视角，提出我国外语教育的战略地位、所面临的隐患及改革的新方向——跨文化外语教育；然后从个人和机构两个维度举例说明了跨文化写作教学法的应用方法。

7.1 文化安全、外语教育与公民文化传播

中共中央办公厅、国务院办公厅印发的《关于实施中华优秀传统文化传承发展工程的意见》，提出到2025年，基本形成中华优秀传统文化传承发展体系，协同推进研究阐发、教育普及和传播交流等，显著提升中华文化的国际影响力。作为文化交流的重要工具和前沿阵地的外语教育，在中华文化复兴这一国家战略中，应该扮演怎样的角色呢?

7.1.1 外语教育中的文化安全隐患及原因

外语教育处于不同文化交往的前沿，既是文化碰撞和激烈交锋的疆场，也是捍卫本国文化安全、塑造社会核心价值观的重要领地。文化安全指一国观念形态的文化（如民族精神、政治价值理念、信仰追求等）生存和发展不受威胁的客观状态。朱阳明将文化安全定义为一国在文化、精神生活方面不受外来文化的干扰、控制或同化，从而保持本民族的价值观念、生活方式的民族性以及本国意识形态的自主性。文化安全是国家安全的重要组成部分，随着文化在综合国力竞争中地位和作用的日益凸显，维护国家文化安全已成

为各国的共识。

国际上日益激烈的文化竞争和日益显著的文化与经济加速融合发展的趋势，要求教育必须培养民族文化的自豪感、危机感和使命感，以抗拒西方的文化霸权主义。探索新的外语教育发展战略，实现外语学习者本国文化和外国语言文化的共同发展，积极利用外语传播本土文化，提高国家文化软实力，这不仅是一个学术问题，也是关乎我国政治、经济、文化发展前途的重大现实问题。

英语的广泛传播和政治、经济、教育的全球化使得世界非英语国家的民族文化和国家认同遭到前所未有的威胁。以亚洲的日本、韩国、越南、印度等国为例，高等教育的国际化和过度、片面提倡英语学习的教育政策削弱了这些国家的本国文化认同，导致某些“唯英语论”的思维方式和不平等的国际关系。在全球化思潮兴起、国际化意识增强和我国教育面临变革的时代境遇下，外语教育在享受时代赋予的学科繁荣的同时，也要对潜藏于其背后的文化安全保持清醒的认识。

从2000年南京大学的从丛教授在《光明日报》撰文呼吁外语教学要加强中国文化的英语表达开始，该问题引起了外语界的普遍关注，之后出现了数千篇相关文献。这些研究发现：中国外语学习者的中国文化知识普遍掌握得不够理想，且民族文化意识薄弱，价值观取向不明，严重威胁到我国的文化安全。外语教育中要时刻警惕文化教育安全方面的隐患，而作为外语政策制定和执行主体的政府部门和教育界，特别是外语学术界，应该积极应对课程教育过程中的“文化进化论”“西方中心主义”等现象，防止外语教育成为新一轮“文化帝国主义”或“文化殖民主义”的工具，特别要克服外语传授和习得过程中的“自我殖民主义”。

我国外语教育中出现的“中国文化失语”现象有诸多原因，其中最主要的原因是外语教学理论的误导。传统外语教学观过多强调母语的“负迁移”作用，认为学习者会无意识地将母语的语音、词汇、语言结构、思维方式和文化内涵等移植到外语学习中，不利于习得“地道”的外语。这一理论引导下的外语教学鼓励“浸泡式”的外语学习，要求外语学习者将母语语言文化排除在外语学习之外，以减少对外语学习的干扰。在这种思想导向下的外语专业一般不开设中文课程，教学中很少涉及母语文化知识，唯恐会“干扰”地道的外语表达。长此以往，必然导致母语文化“失语”。因此，急需对外语教育理论进行创新，从注重外语听说技能的“交际教学法”向母语、目的语并重的“跨文化交际教学法”转变。

7.1.2　外语教育的新方向：跨文化外语教育

20 世纪末以来，在英美澳德等西方主要国家，跨文化交际教学法研究正日益受到各国教育界的重视。跨文化教学法突破了传统的单向度外语培养模式（即要求学习者掌握目的语的知识体系和行为规范，以便与该语言群体进行有效交流），要求学习者通过外语学习，实现本族语言文化和目的语语言文化的共同发展，能根据不同文化情境选用准确、恰当的方式进行交流。该教学法强调发挥母语在外语教育中的“正迁移”效应，认为母语文化不仅不会阻碍外语学习，而且能成为外语学习的丰富资源和有力工具。在跨文化外语教育理念的指导下，外语教育的目的不再仅仅是习得外国的语言和文化，更重要的是在学习外语的过程中通过文化比较，加深对本国文化的了解，增强对本国文化的认同感和自信心。

跨文化外语教学研究在中国尽管只有 20 多年的历史，却取得了显著成果，在如何树立文化认同、改变教育理念、修订教育政策、设计文化教材、提高教师素质、丰富教学方法、设立评估机制等方面皆有著述。具体来说，跨文化外语教学可总结为学习文化、比较文化和探索文化三个步骤。（1）学习本国和外国语言文化。本国文化不再被排除在外语教育之外，而是成为外语学习的重要内容和工具。有些文化形式，比如思想和价值观，看不见摸不着，文化教学可把这些笼统的文化分解为多个主题，比如“婚姻家庭观”“教育体制”“宗教、道德、伦理观”“非语言交际手段”等，这对教材的内容和设计都提出了新的要求。（2）比较本国文化与外国文化。学习者通过比较外国和本国文化，可以了解语言文化形成的原因，从而有机会重新审视自己认为“理所当然”的文化习惯和思想，加深对本国文化的理解。进行文化比较的题材很多，例如，将中国传统文化精髓和当代通俗流行文化相比较，或与同样经典和鲜活的外国文化进行对比，发掘其共同性和不同之处，探讨其背后的历史、经济、政治和哲学根源，从而加深对不同文化的理解，不断拓宽价值观和世界观。(3) 进行文化探索和创新。借助语言优势，学习和借鉴各民族优秀文化成果，从而发展创新本民族文化。由此可见，跨文化外语教育把本国文化安全放在首位，把本国文化传承与传播作为外语学习者的最终使命，让每位外语学习者都成为本国文化传播者。

7.1.3 外语教育的终极目标：提升公民文化传播能力

要实现中华民族伟大复兴，让中国文化走出去这一战略目标，仅仅依靠政府推动的渠道是不够的；随着互联网的普及和国际交往的增加，公民个人的参与已日益成为对外文化传播的重要途径。个人文化传播主体不再局限于外交官或对外汉语教师等从事对外交流的人员，也包括生活在国内的普通公民，通过外语学习，他们也可以成为中国文化的传播者，成为“不出国门的外交官”。习近平总书记早在 2013 年中共中央政治局集体学习会议中就提出，“让 13 亿人的每一分子都成为传播中华美德、中华文化的主体”。可见提高公民的文化传播能力是推动中华文化走向世界的重要途径。

为了维护我国文化安全，实现公民文化传播这一目标，必须改变我国外语教育战略，改变教育理念、修订教育政策、创新外语教材、提高教师素质、丰富教学方法、改善评估机制等。目前，对于外语教育中应该教授怎样的中国文化，怎么教，如何在外语教育中实现文化传承与创新等问题，还缺乏深入细致的研究、界定和探讨。再者，目前研究大多针对高校学生以及高校教育，随着外语教育在各个年龄段的不断普及，分析对象应扩展到中小学，甚至超越校园关注到各社会群体。此外，由于对外语教育现状分析缺少实例证明和国际比较，对文化的多元背景带来的价值观冲突的具体表现也缺乏深度认识，这些问题都有待外语教育家和学者进一步研究。

7.2 探索跨文化传播的“第三空间”

跨文化交际的重要目标之一便是探索跨文化的“第三空间”。1993 年，“第三空间”(The third place) 的概念由美国加州大学伯克利分校的 Kramsch

教授首次提出，之后得到澳大利亚著名语言教育专家 Lo Bianco 教授等的系统阐述和推广。“第三空间”指通过跨文化的探索和协商，创造性地摸索出本族语言文化和外来语言文化之间的一个中间地带；在这里母语和外来文化都会得到加强和深化，融合成一种新的文化，让来自不同语言文化背景的交际者能成功自如地交流。“第三空间”不是折中的文化拼盘和杂烩，而是一种文化创新，在这里本国语言文化和外国语言文化实现真正的平等和对话，使交际者形成跨文化的复合人格，以适应当今世界不断增加的政治、经济、文化交流的需要。

7.2.1　“第三空间”的跨文化传播

跨文化传播，指不同文化背景的人们之间的信息传播和文化交往活动。与同质传播不同，跨文化传播促使人们把目光转向处于不同文化背景的个体之间的异质传播；有效的传播是将异质的个体间的误解降到最低水平，在各自保持自我文化特征的前提下取得相互的理解。[1]跨文化传播总是从对冲突的特别关注中寻找文化间理解的途径。跨文化传播的目的不在建立个人的文化主体性，而是形成从他者出发的相互理解的文化主体间性。跨文化传播的特定问题是在矛盾、冲突、差异、多元、焦虑等文化交往语境中如何建构和谐的传播。[2]自从 20 世纪 50 年代在美国兴起以来，跨文化传播研究主要在三个层面展开。

跨文化传播的“第三空间”源自文化语境的弹性或流动性（contextual flexibility or fluidity），这种弹性或流动性给互动者构建了一个具有文化间性（interculturality）的第三文化空间。在这里，互动者可以相互协商与调整，建立一种互惠互补共生共赢的跨文化关系。

跨文化身份：文化接触可能产生整合、同化、分离和边缘化这几种文化适应策略。处于新文化环境中的个体在保持传统文化身份和被主流文化所同化的矛盾中挣扎，容易出现单一文化视野，排斥其他文化的价值观的倾向，

〔1〕单波、薛晓峰：“西方跨文化传播研究中的和谐理念”，载《国外社会科学》2008 年第 6 期。
〔2〕单波、薛晓峰：“西方跨文化传播研究中的和谐理念”，载《国外社会科学》2008 年第 6 期。

其原因是对文化主体身份的过度看重；必须回到文化的主体间性上来建构文化身份，建构第三向度的文化身份。即个体将跨文化传播中所扮演的多样化角色融合成一种新的文化身份，这样在跨文化交流中就超越单一模式和心理规律，随着文化传播的活动和文化多样性不断重构文化身份。这是一个动态过程，由新的文化实践不断重建，永远处于过程之中。

文化接口："第三空间"的跨文化传播是对传统静态文化观的挑战。它认为文化边际并非是静止不变的，而是可以通过互动双方的沟通，实现有效的彼此渗透、彼此融合，甚至彼此转化。[1]陈国明认为跨文化传播是一种边际博弈（boundary game）的过程。在整体的互动环境下，双方经由协商重新定义彼此之间的边际线，然后将狭窄的边际线逐渐扩展为边际区，提升彼此之间的跨文化理解度。为了持续扩大跨文化传播的共同中心领域，互动双方需要边际智慧（boundary wisdom）：互动双方以开放之心，开发与积累边际博弈的知识与技巧，通过自我收缩的过程而达到一种和谐的相互渗透状态。边际智慧包括敏觉力与创造力两个要素。敏觉力能区分和识别互动和语境的多样性，协助互动者建立彼此间可共同分享的沟通符号。而创造力则是实现融合的有力手段，能突破主客体之间的壁障和误解，凭借同理心（empathy）伸入对方的思想和情感领域。[2]

第三种视角：文化具有民族中心主义（ethnocentrism）倾向，即每一种文化都试图用自己的文化价值去观察和评价他者，特别是在文化冲突发生的时候，每一种文化都习惯于抬高自己的文化价值，以凝聚文化群体的信念，取得对他者文化的支配。[3]与此相反，跨文化传播理念指引着一条更冷静的和谐之路：交流的挑战不是忠实于我们的地盘，而是对别人持有原谅的态度，理解他们不可能像我们看待自己一样来看待我们，因为我们不可能完全相同。

要培养第三种或跨文化的"陌生人"视角，即在对某种符号形式作出识别时，不是立即将其与特殊的含义联系起来，而是理解其在不同文化语境下

---

〔1〕 陈国明、安然：《跨文化传播学关键术语解读》，中国社会科学出版社 2010 年版。

〔2〕 Chen. G.（陈国明），Moving beyond the dichotomy of communication studies：Boundary wisdom as the key. In G. Wang (Ed), *De-westernizing communication research*：*Altering questions and changing frameworks*, New York：Routledge, 2011, p157-171.

〔3〕 单波、薛晓峰："西方跨文化传播研究中的和谐理念"，载《国外社会科学》2008 年第 6 期。

可能具有的不同含义。我们必须要从他者的视角来考虑跨文化传播，而不是从自我出发，要缓和主体性视野的内在紧张关系，从各种角度观察文化，并在相互合作、相互保护的基础上获得各自的权利。

7.2.2　“第三空间”的跨文化传播典例

“第三空间”理念下的跨文化传播要求传播者打破单一的文化认同和思维模式，树立跨文化人格，在跨文化“第三种”视角的指引下寻找文化接口，进行平等、冷静、和谐的跨文化交流。“第三空间”的跨文化传播理念在不同情境中可能有不同的应用，笔者用三个典例，分析跨文化传播创新“第三空间”的应用策略。

构建复合文化身份的“危机大使”傅莹

傅莹是我国首位少数民族女大使，曾任中国驻菲律宾、澳大利亚、英国等国大使，以善于跨文化沟通著称，享有“危机大使”的美誉。傅莹尤其善于利用媒体的公关职能化解外交危机。在西方出现对中国的不利报道时，她主动撰文并投书英文报刊，借助媒体畅通的信息传播渠道，实现与西方媒体和公众的双向沟通、良性互动，得到公众的理解。不仅如此，傅莹善于化危机为契机，利用西方媒体，发出中国声音，传播中国文化。构建复合文化身份是傅莹成功进行跨文化传播的前提和基础。她一改“不苟言笑、铁板一块”的传统中国外交官形象，塑造了一个集中西方文化身份于一体，集普通女性、母亲和政治家、外交官身份于一身的复合文化身份，用让人难以抗拒的柔性表达方式，以个性化、人性化的话语体系，展示了中国新一代外交官的人格魅力。这一点可以从傅莹巧妙化解中国驻伦敦使馆和周围民众发生的一次冲突中，得到淋漓尽致的体现。

2009 年 11 月，英国《太阳报》刊登了一条很有意思的新闻，说《X 元素》（X Factor）这档电视选秀节目的选手，就住在中国大使馆的旁边，“粉丝”们没日没夜的守候与喧哗打扰了大使馆的日常工作，与使馆人员发生了冲突。

傅莹马上在《太阳报》撰文做出回应，请看她幽默的开场：“这真是太逗了，当读到关于我们大使馆卷入‘外交纠纷’的报道之后，我发现自己竟然也陷入了《X 元素》的热潮之中。”

傅莹爆料说，其实大使本人也是《X 元素》的“粉丝”。而且傅莹点评起选手来不吝赞美之辞：“他们十分有天赋，他们能拥有如此众多的粉丝，一点也不奇怪!”

接着，傅莹化“危”为“机”——向英国民众介绍中国的流行文化“超女”“快男”等选秀节目，趁机让他们了解，地球另一端的中国年轻人也有着同样的娱乐与时尚。

最后，傅莹提出建设性意见，“但是在中国，制片方可不会让选手住到居民区里去，否则成千上万的‘粉丝’一来，还不得把居民区淹没了吗”，坦然承认大使馆已经不堪忍受“粉丝”的骚扰了。

不得不承认，傅莹的沟通技巧实在高明，不仅把误会澄清了，还让英国人看到了大使可爱的一面，甚至了解了当今中国年轻人的时尚生活。她站在中西文化的中间，不断进行身份转换，一边“讲故事”，一边“讲道理”，既阐明了自己的立场和观点，又潜移默化地达到了说服效果，引发了人们对该事件的重新认识和思考。这种温婉亲切的态度消除了一些西方媒体和读者的敌对情绪，激发了他们内心柔软的同理心，让他们愿意用善意、平和的心态来倾听这位中国女性的心声。

由此可见，成功的跨文化传播，需要传播者改变原有的单一的文化身份，根据文化传播实践的需要扮演多样化角色，并将这些角色融合成一种新的文化身份，找到中西文化的和谐交汇点——“第三空间”。试想如果我们能培养出更多傅莹这样的文化交流大使，世界将减少多少冲突与危机。

寻找文化接口的“哈佛先生”戈鲲化

戈鲲化（1838-1882）是哈佛大学中文教育创始人。1879 年他应哈佛大学邀请，带领全家远渡重洋来到美国，成为中国在西方大学任教的第一人。虽然他在两年多后便因病客死他乡，但是在大清帝国腐朽没落、饱受西方列强欺凌的背景下，戈鲲化却以跨文化传播的自觉和令人赞叹的交流智慧与技巧，成功地向美国精英文化阶层传播了中华文化，成了中美文化交流史上里程碑式的人物。戈鲲化是如何在中国文化处于绝对弱势和“西学东渐”的逆差中进行“中学西传”的呢？笔者认为，寻找文化接口是他的重要策略之一：即在建立文化复合身份的基础上，找到中外文化之间的接口或交集，并以此为突破口，进行中国文化的传播。

戈鲲化独具匠心的跨文化传播行为，突出表现在他对文化交流载体的选择上。他把中国文化的精髓——诗歌，作为文化传播的主要工具。在中国传统文化中，诗歌具有无可取代的地位，从形式到内容，经过千载百代的锤炼已达到了极高的境界。而在欧美文化中，诗歌同样为精英阶层所钟爱，用以抒情言志。选择这种双方文化共有的载体，不仅体现了戈鲲化对母语文化的深刻认识、强烈的自豪感和责任感，更体现了他自觉的交流智慧。在各种场合，他几乎都会赋诗、吟诗或讲解诗，致力于把诗的精神带到美国。他还专门编纂了中文教材《华质英文》（Chinese Verse and Prose），这是最早的一本由中国人用英文编写的、介绍中国诗歌和文化的教材。这本书中收录了戈鲲化自己的 15 首诗作，包括中文原诗、英文译文，以及对于诗中词句、用典的英文解释，甚至还标出了平仄，尽量展示中国诗歌原汁原味的魅力。

在展示诗歌语言之美的同时，戈鲲化通过诗歌向西方传播中国文化理念。在《华质英文》中，他选入的第一首诗就是《先慈奉旨入祀节烈祠》。戈鲲化的母亲在咸丰十年（1860 年）太平天国军队攻陷常州时自尽殉节，受到皇帝的褒奖，入祀节烈祠。这首诗传达的是对以身殉节的传统美德的赞誉和自豪。据当地报纸的报道和友人的回忆，戈鲲化和他介绍的诗给当时的美国精英文化圈留下了深刻的印象；戈鲲化的言行，让他们真切地感受到两种文明的碰撞与相互吸引。

一百多年前，面对当时强势的西方文化，戈鲲化试图将其精华与国学精粹融会贯通。他意识到：利用“文化接口”进行跨文化传播，将传播者和受众置于同一文化环境中，可以促进文化传播的进行，提高受众对传播内容的认知和接受程度。戈鲲化在激烈的文化冲突中找到文化共通点——诗歌，在发现人类认知共性的基础上，寻找跨文化传播中的共识。他在共同话语的基础上建立了一个和谐自然的交流平台，让人们看到了文化的多元与交流的平等，看到了文化共存及其互补的重要性，认可了一种异质文化的存在，并承认其存在的合理性与相互间学习的可能性。

选择“第三种”视角的专家贝淡宁

贝淡宁（Daniel A. Bell，又译为丹尼尔·贝尔），1964年出生于加拿大，1991年获牛津大学政治哲学博士学位，现为清华大学伦理学和政治哲学教授。贝淡宁曾先后在新加坡、美国等国家和地区从事教学与研究工作，著有《中国新儒家：变革社会中的政治和日常生活》《超越自由主义》《东方遭遇西方》等著作，被英国《金融时报》誉为“中国模式”专家（The China Model）。贝淡宁不仅本人谙熟和热爱中国语言文化，而且擅长用中西合璧的视角审视中西政治体制和文化价值，传播“中国模式”。

以政治体制为例，中国官员的选拔模式一直受到西方所谓民主选举制度的诟病和抨击。贝淡宁跳出这两种对立的政治观，倡导民主政治和贤能政治的结合。[1]他认为选民政治可能存在选民利益狭隘、官员能力平庸等诸多问题，如果能与中国基于“尚贤”举荐的选拔制度结合，可能会产生一种更科学合理的政治制度。他指出自由主义民主不一定是普世的理想，西方强权不应该把人权与民主强加于亚洲国家之上。他借鉴西方从柏拉图到19世纪自由精英派的政治观点，结合中国儒家治国思想，提出儒家民主之路可能为世界政治提供富有启示的贡献。

贝淡宁自称为儒家学者，主张用新的视角来看待西方眼中“老迈、严肃和保守”的儒家思想。[2]随着文明的进一步发展，在面对不同文化和价值观如何赋予现代性建制以不同启示这个重大命题时，贝淡宁援用哲学分析和广泛的经验知识，审视儒家思想及其与民主、人权和资本主义的关系。随着世界多元文化格局的形成，他意识到，中国文化也是全球现代化中的一种重要力量，也可以为人类和平、社会发展做出贡献。当跨中西文化交流过程中出现文化分歧时，他擅长转换文化视角，填补信息真空，最大限度地消除西方对中国的误解和对立。他和其他有识之士提出的以东方文化救西方文化之弊

---

〔1〕 D. A. Bell, *The China model: Political meritocracy and the limits of democracy*, Princeton University Press, 2015.

〔2〕 D. A. Bell, *China's new Confucianism: Politics and everyday life in a changing society*, Princeton University Press, 2010.

的主张，在某种程度上影响了西方读者，使得对东方文化的学习和研究在西方发展得更为迅速。

综上所析，跨文化传播中有“主位”和“客位”两种视角，即从“自家人”（insider）或“旁观者”（outsider）的视角去理解某种文化。“第三空间”的跨文化传播要求将这两种视角有机结合起来，或者灵活进行转换，以形成“第三种”视角。贝淡宁跳出主客对立的二元立场，在人权与民主的各种极端性国际争论中寻找中道，采用“第三种”视角进行灵活的跨文化传播。他用生动的语言和西方易于接受的方式，将绵延千年的中国文明及其价值带到西方，给正在高速发展的资本主义文明提供了另一种价值参照，使人们看到文化共存及其互补的重要性。

7.2.3　小　结

整个跨文化传播的实践就是一个话语的战场，是一种力量的博弈。[1]要取得国际话语权，提高中国在世界话语体系中的地位，必须建立新的跨文化传播理念。“第三空间”理论引导我们重新审视原有的文化身份，根据传播需要建构新的跨文化复合身份；在此基础上，要善于寻找世界文化的共核——文化接口，并以此为突破口进行文化传播；传播过程中还要善于转换视角，打破主客二元立场，用客观、公正的“第三种”视角分析和解决问题。在公共外交的新时代，这些文化传播理念不仅适用于国际新闻传播人才的培养，也能为更广泛的跨文化传播人才培养提供参考。

7.3　中南大学英语专业写作教改

7.3.1　批判教学法概述

批判性教学法是一种教学取向或教学方式，它力图帮助学生质疑、挑战

〔1〕 姜飞：“试析当前跨文化传播中力量的博弈”，载《中国社会科学院研究生院学报》2007年第5期。

传统信念与规约，是一种帮助学生发展“批判意识”的理论与实践。批判教育观认为教育和知识都不是中立的，而是和权力紧密关联。教育既可巩固原有的权力模式，也可以挑战这种模式。[1] Paulo Freire 是批判教学法的创始人和代表人物，他认为学生应该对自己的受教育状况进行批判性思考，找到个人经历和问题与社会大环境之间的关系，从“觉悟”走向“行动”。Joe Kincheloe 把 Freire 的批判教育思想发展为全球范围内的去殖民化教育理念，主张倾听和吸收弱势的、被边缘化的人群的声音，强调解放个性、消解中心、解构权威。

在外语教学领域，批判教学法赋予外语教师和学生社会责任，让外语学习者超越自身的历史和文化束缚，获得个人自由与解放。外语教师应该引导学生认识到语言的社会、文化、政治属性，从而质疑、抗拒和挑战不平等的社会现象。对于写作而言，批判教学法认为写作既是学会融入和维持现有语言群体的过程，也是获得自我表达手段从而挑战和改变传统习俗的过程。写作教学应该帮助学生发现语言和权力之间的关系，然后通过批判性写作改变周围的世界，即“Write to right the world”[2]。在二语和外语写作教学界，人们逐渐认识到过去所依赖的传统理论和各种典型的写作教学方法都不再可靠，需要寻找适合学生文化身份、权力关系和社会需求等的新途径。批判性二语和外语写作教学法强调写作不是目的和产品，而是行动和手段；学习者通过外语写作，反思自己的身份、意识和价值观，从本族语言文化中获取力量，不断与二语和外语写作规约及其隐藏的思想意识进行“协商”，发出自己的声音从而“构建”一个更民主的全球社区。[3]

国内对批判教学法的研究迄今为止尚不多见，有关批判理论的研究主要集中在批判性思维的意义和培养方式，以及批判性语篇分析等方面；有学者

---

〔1〕 Rizvi, F., Speaking truth to power: Edward Said and the work of the intellectual. In J. Satterthwaite, M. Watts & H. Piper (Eds.), *Talking truth, confronting power*, 2008, p113-126.

〔2〕 Wilson, L., *Writing to live: How to Teach Writing for Today's World*, Portsmouth, NH: Heinemann, 2006.

〔3〕 Canagarahah, A. S., Understanding critical writing. In P. K. Matsuda, M. Cox, J. Jordan & C. Ortmeier-Hooper (Eds.) *Second Language Writing in the Composition Classroom: A Critical Sourcebook*, Boston, New York: Bedford/St. Martin's, 2011.

对批判理论进行了概括性介绍，有个别学者探讨了批判教学法在音乐教学、高中语文教学[1]和英语阅读教学[2]中的应用，但在二语和外语语境中的批判性写作教学法研究还十分罕见，亟待加深认识和构建能付诸实践的理论体系。

7.3.2　二语和外语写作教学法的实用性与批判性之争

二语和外语写作教学史上一直存在实用性与批判性之间的较量。其主要争议之一是教师的角色。写作教师的主要任务是教授学生实用的写作技能，还是引导他们探索写作的社会政治功能，从而通过写作来改变世界？批判教学法认为，教师要引导学生发现写作沿革背后隐含的价值观和学习中的力量不平等关系，拒绝不加批判地接受这些传统，从而探索新的写作方式，以满足写作者的个人和文化表达的需求。通过培养学生的批判性写作、阅读和思维能力，写作课堂可以成为重构社会组织和程序的重要场所。

二语和外语写作教学史上的另一个争议是写作者个人和社会声音表达之间的矛盾。历史上出现的各种二语写作流派，比如自由表达派（the expressionist approach）、控制作文（controlled composition）、现实传统修辞派（current-traditional rhetoric）、过程写作（the process approach）和学术写作（writing for academic purposes）等，即反映了对写作者个人与社会功能的重视的不同程度。近年来，教育的个人发展功能正不断得到加强。批判教学法认为，这种个人功能不仅是表达个人情感，更重要的是“从学生的个人兴趣出发，引导学生探索自己的历史和文化定位，从而意识到语言和语篇的局限性和可能性”。

第三个主要争议是二语写作者母语和目的语语言文化及身份的冲突问题。外语学习中母语与目的语，学生与教师之间的力量是不均衡的，这种不平等既导致了“无助”和“压迫”，也催生了“斗争”与“解放”。中国外语教学史上的体用之争正是这种矛盾的体现：这种“本国中心主义”或“崇洋媚

---

〔1〕张秋玲、闫苹：“后殖民批判教学法视野中的教师角色分析——以高中语文选修课教师为个案”，载《教师教育研究》2009年第6期。

〔2〕原雪：“二语和外语语境下的批判性阅读理论构建研究”，上海外国语大学2010年博士学位论文。

外”的极端思想给中国近代发展造成了深重的灾难。全球化要求教育打破“非此即彼”的二元思想，引领和谐共存。因此，急需通过批判教学法创造性地赋予学生力量，打破文化桎梏，造就世界公民。

英语在教育中位置的凸显和中国融入世界经济一体化进程的不断加快为中国英语教学带来了前所未有的机遇和挑战。具有创新思维能力和跨文化交际能力的外语人才日益成为人才市场的宠儿。遗憾的是，我国的英语教学仍面临“投入多，产出少”的困境；[1]尤其是英语写作教学，也许受到20世纪80年代以来“听说领先”的交际教学法思潮的影响，写作课没有得到足够重视，以应试为目的的写作教学常常用模式化训练代替正常教学，导致学生写作水平低、厌恶写作、害怕写作、公式化写作和抄袭盛行，损害了他们对外语学习的兴趣和信心，不利于学生思维能力和创造力的培养。

以中国大学英语专业的写作教学为例，许多大学在四年学制中可能开设2-3年的英语写作课程。这些课程较多以“讲授”为主，采用从英语语句、语段到语篇的教学过程，注重传授写作技巧，培养学生语法正确、符合规范的英语表达能力。英语专业学生需要参加国家统一的英语专业水平考试（四级和八级）。这些考试中都有写作任务，要求学生在几十分钟内完成一篇到两篇英语短文，题目和字数一般都已限定。因为这类考试是衡量学生英语水平和教师教学效果的主要手段，许多大学的写作教学在很大程度上围绕这类作文题展开。有的教师为了让学生获得高分，甚至鼓励学生走“捷径”，借助所谓的“快速作文法”达到“事半功倍”的效果。笔者认为，这种以应试为目的的写作教学主要有如下弊端：

（1）教学过度强调语法等语言技术问题，采用模式化的控制写作以及总结性评估方式压抑了学生写作的乐趣和个性化表达，甚至会引发对写作的恐惧和焦虑感。更严重的是，由于写作教学脱离学生生活实际，使得学生缺乏写作动机和兴趣，长此以往影响他们的整体学习动机和学习能力。

---

[1]《入世与外语专业教育》课题组：“关于高校外语专业教育体制与教学模式改革的几点思考——写在中国加入WTO之际（一）”，载《外语界》2001年第5期。《入世与外语专业教育》课题组：“关于高校外语专业教育体制与教学模式改革的几点思考——写在中国加入WTO之际（二）”，载《外语界》2001年第6期。

（2）教学以脱离语境的机械模仿和程式化训练为主要手段，容易滋生抄袭、剽窃等不良倾向，造成“高分低能”现象，导致学生写作范围狭窄、内容空泛、写作形式单一等问题，不利于创造力和批判思维能力的培养。

（3）教学中忽视对学生本国语言文化资源的开发和利用，阻碍了学生跨文化交际意识的形成，容易造成外语类学生本国文化知识薄弱、文化身份缺失等现象，不利于培养具有世界视野和跨文化复合人格的外语人才。

以上问题在全球化背景下的当代中国变得尤其尖锐和复杂，因此迫切需要具有批判意识的学者和教育家合力应对。当然，中国写作界也出现了许多锐意改革的教育家，解决了外语学习的一些迫切问题。笔者结合在墨尔本大学博士学习期间对批判教学法的研究成果[1]和国内写作教改经验，于2011年9月至2012年6月在中南大学二年级英语专业学生中进行了写作教改实验。以下结合该教改实验对批判教学法在中国英语写作教学中的应用进行探讨。

7.3.3 批判教学法在中国英语写作教学中的应用

笔者主持的中南大学教改团队结合《英语写作通用教程》的教学思路，将大学专业二年级的英语写作教学分为四个阶段：第一阶段（第一学期1-8周）以自由写作为主，旨在激发学生写作热情，培养自信心和创造力；第二阶段（9~16周）主要关注议论文的写作，注重布局谋篇，发展批判思维；第三阶段（第二学期1~8周）鼓励学生进行文学创作，尝试包括剧本、诗歌等文体的写作，开发学生的写作潜能；第四阶段（9~16周）引导学生关注社会，进行社会调查，撰写调查报告。四个环节遵循学生的心理和认知规律，始终贯穿跨文化知识的教学和批判意识的培养。考核以形成性评估为主，包括作品集、作品展示，“限时”与“非限时”相结合的考核方式。教学过程中特别注重写作者写作兴趣、意图、个人风格和个性化思想的形成和发展，培养写作者的自主学习能力，其根本目的是帮助学生主动完成对外部知识的建构，成长为具有创新精神和社会意识的写作者。

---

〔1〕 叶洪：“后现代批判视域下跨文化外语教学与研究的新理路——澳大利亚国家级课题组对跨文化‘第三空间’的探索与启示”，载《外语教学与研究》2012年第1期。

具体来说，中南大学英语专业的写作教改可以从以下三方面进行阐释：重新构建写作理念、突破原有写作语境、改变教师角色和师生关系。

重塑写作理念

批判教学法认为学生面临的最大障碍之一是心理和理念的障碍。作为教师，必须让学生意识到他们有希望、有潜力改变被“压迫”的现状。一旦他们认识到自己的潜能，便能成为真正的、具有自我意识的人。[1]重塑学生和教师的理念是实现“自我意识”的重要方法之一。教改中笔者和所属的团队首先澄清了一些关于写作的模糊或错误认识，包括模仿与创新的关系，是否存在“标准英语”等问题，然后从批判教学法的视角重新界定了“写作”概念，从思想上为写作改革做好了准备。

许多学生对写作中模仿与创新的关系感到困惑，教改尝试用互文性理论来帮助学生认识两者的关系。所有话语都是互相影响和模仿的，语言的创造力在于对他人声音的吸收、加工和再生。[2]因此，写作应该是一个不断吸收和转化的过程，是不断储存、重组别人的思想、技巧、词汇与意象，直到它们融合成为新作品的过程。教改强调输入是写作教学中必不可少的一部分，鼓励学生大量阅读和收听英文材料，通过创造性地模仿提高技能。当学生意识到模仿是再创造的必由之路时，便可以放下包袱，主动、自信地掌握自己的求知过程和机会，从模仿走向创新。

教改对“标准英语”概念进行了解构，认为不应用单一和静止的视角看待全球化语境下的“英语”，鼓励学生将中国语言文化作为英语写作的丰富资源，积极主动地“协商”写作中的语法和语义表达，探索新的话语方式，更好地表达个人的兴趣、文化及价值观。这样不仅实现了母语和外来语言文化的共同发展，而且从一定程度上消除了学生“害怕犯错”的焦虑心理，激发了他们的创造力，能够将大量注意力从语言层面转移到深层次的思想和观点

---

〔1〕 Freire, P., *Pedagogy of the Oppressed* (30th anniversary edition ed.), New York: Continuum, 2000.

〔2〕 Bakhtin, M. M., *Speech genres and other late essays* (V. W. McGee, Trans.), Austin: University of Texas Press, 1986.

的探讨上来。

教改在进行过程中逐渐引导学生改变对传统“写作”的认识，转向“立体多维”写作方式。“立体”写作指从传统以书面为主的写作过渡到可包括音频、视频等多媒体手段的立体写作；“多维”写作将写作与演讲、戏剧、访谈、辩论、社会调查等多种形式的学习活动结合起来，以写作带动各项语言技能的全面提高。比如学生把各种题材的写作作品用“演讲”“访谈”“辩论”“综艺”等形式展示出来，完成书面的社会调查后可以拍摄专题片，或者把自创的“微剧本”拍成“微电影”等。通过“立体多维”写作，学生有机会使用他们在现实生活中获得的多模态知识（multimodal literacy）[1]，为写作学习提供资源和动力。

通过对上述理念的重新认识，学生意识到包括“写作”在内的“读写能力”（literacy）等概念并不是一成不变的，而是具有鲜明的历史、社会和意识形态内涵。新技术、新媒体时代的到来必然挑战传统的写作模式，随之改变传统的“知识”和“教育”等概念。作为学生，他们有权利、有责任探索新的写作方式，在课程改革中注入自己的声音和力量。

重构写作语境

批判教学法的核心就是为师生创设一个适宜的教学情境及对话空间。中南大学的教改首先通过“突破”传统写作语境，把学习者从束缚中“解放”出来，释放他们的写作激情和创造力，培养他们的学习兴趣和自信心；然后通过创造性地“重塑”新的写作语境，使其符合学习者的认知规律，满足学习者的情感需求，从教学环节、作文评改、话题设计等方面塑造全新的语言环境，给学习者以“力量”，从而实现写作教学“改变世界”的社会功能。

首先，教改一改传统英语写作教学从句到段到语篇、限定作文时间和长度、考试为目的的倾向，始终重视自然写作能力的培养。学生从整体语篇的构思与展开入手，不受篇幅和时间的限制，放手尝试各种写作方式和题材，

---

〔1〕 Kress, G. R., *Literacy in the new media age*, London: Routledge, 2003.

在表达真情实感的过程中加快外语知识的内化和向运用能力的转化。

其次，教改一改教师评改为主的纠错模式，对学生的作文反馈采用自主修正、组内互评，高低年级互评和教师点评相结合的方式。这样可以激发学生学习的主动性，在同伴互评中共同成长；而且可以将教师从繁重的“改错”任务中解放出来，将注意力和精力投向更加有效的工作；[1]同时还可以消除学生的恐惧焦虑心理，增强学习兴趣。

教改的重要举措之一是精选和设计激发学生写作欲望的话题，将学生的生活体验（real life literacy）和学校知识（school literacy）紧密联系起来，从而激发他们的学习动机。以议论文写作为例，教师可以引导学生总结近两年的网络流行语及其形成原因，并预测2012年的最热网络流行语。因为社会流行语（比如“神马都是浮云”“我爸是李刚”“伤不起”“hold住”“淡定”“给力”“亲”等）是在中国特有的国情下形成的，一定程度上反映了社会的价值观念与文化特征，这种写作过程既能激发学生的社会责任感和使命感，也是引导学生自我反思批判的过程，以达到“生长性外语学习”的目的。[2]

重建师生关系

批判教学法的基本观点之一便是教育中权力的重新分配，即把传统教师的权力部分转移到学生中来从而赋予学生力量；这要求改变原有教师和学生的关系与定位。[3]传统的写作课堂由教师讲解、布置和灌输写作技巧和方法，这种以教师为中心的教学是“压迫”学生的工具，影响了学生的求知欲、创造力和对话。“去中心化”的写作课堂中教师从“威严之师”的角色转为学生实现知识内化的中介；这种中介作用绝非向学生提供单向指导，而是在与

---

〔1〕 Truscott, J., “Arguments and appearances: A response to Chandler”, *Journal of Second Language Writing*, 18 (1), 2009.

〔2〕 高一虹：“外语学习社会心理的结构化理论视角”，载《外国语言文学研究》2005年第2期。

〔3〕 Hardin, J. M., *Opening spaces: Critical pedagogy and resistance theory in composition*, Albany: State University of New York Press, 2001.

学生的互动中起到“支架作用”（scaffolding）[1]，让学生自由探索和自主学习。师生共同对写作学习负责，并在学习过程中共同成长。

教改中学生以小组为学习单位，每组 6-7 人，由学生轮流选举并担任组长和主编。教学中充分发挥“小组自治”原则，组员分工合作，共同承担写作任务，互评互改，合作发表作品集，集体表演和展示作品等。比如，在第一环节“自由写作”和第三环节“品味创作”结束后组员互相评改，选出写作精品，汇编成小组作品集，由组员分别担任责编、美编等工作。第二环节结束后的辩论大赛中组员轮流担任一辩、二辩、自由辩手和总结辩手等角色；而在第四环节“社会特写”中组员则通力合作，自编、自导、自演、自摄、自制电视专题片对社会问题进行深度报道。在这个过程中，单纯的学生和教师身份已经不复存在，取而代之的是一种新型关系：教师学生和学生教师。在一个友爱、对话、充满想象力的空间，师生自由进行思想碰撞，充分探索自身和周围的世界。

经过一年的写作教学改革，中南大学英语系 2010 级学生得到了普遍受益。学生人均年写作量达到 30 000 单词以上，大多数同学克服了怵写心理，变得爱好写作，对学习的动机显著增强。学生创造力得到了较大提高，在第一学期的作品风采展示中，同年级的任课老师和班导师普遍反映“看到了学生充满创意的另一面，令人震撼”。学生了解社会、思考社会、服务社会的意识明显增强，在第二学期末的“社会特写”中对部分热点问题（比如大学生心理疾病、校园食品健康问题、大学课程设置弊病等）进行了深度调查和报道，形成了一定的社会积极影响。当然，批判写作教改只是刚刚开始，还有许多亟待完善的地方，比如需要对参与教师进行培训，让教师自己成长为具有批判精神的写作者，并承受“反传统”所带来的不确定性和压迫。此外，需要创造一个充满安全感和信任感的教改环境，让师生敢于穿越传统教学法的界限，进行大胆创新与探索。

---

〔1〕 Vygotski, L. S., & Kozulin, A., *Thought and language* (Translation newly rev. and edited ed.), Cambridge, Mass.: MIT Press, 1986.

小结

在以英语为重要交流工具的今天，探索英语写作的社会文化功能，通过批判教学法授予学生批判性资源和能力去甄别和破解隐藏于外语写作背后的权力运作，使学生通过写作学习认识自身及周围的世界，在一定程度上“发现人性、发展人性和完善人性”[1]，应该成为外语教育者的使命之一。这样学校便可能成为“充满希望、奋争和民主的场所”。但是，由于这一研究在中国教育界还刚刚起步，对于批判性写作教学的相关概念和理论有待进一步厘清和构建，本节旨在抛砖引玉，提请写作教师和学生从新的角度认识外语教学的本质、目标和内容，创造性地使用批判教学法来实现教育变革社会的目的。

---

〔1〕 李洪儒：“中国语言哲学的发展之路——语言哲学理论建构之一”，载《外语学刊》2011 年第 6 期。

第八章

结　论

结束本书之前，让我们来重新审视回顾一下本书所研究的问题，再一次梳理可能的答案和启示，接受质疑、迎接挑战。因为我很明白，这不是结束，而是一个新的开始。

近年来，尽管在中国教育中对创造性和跨文化意识的要求有所提高，但目前的英语教学方法仍面临着“投入多，产出少”的困境。在英语写作中，对作者个人声音和文化声音的忽视，导致了学生对写作的恐惧，写作水平低，抑制了他们的创造性，同时还丧失了民族和跨文化身份。这些问题在当代中国已经变得越来越严重和复杂，因此迫切需要创造性的方法来激发学生写作，以此发展他们的创造力，提升母语和目的语语言文化水平。我的研究从以下三个方面解决了这个问题：

首先，通过对广东外语外贸大学民族志项目研究，我发现，尽管在国际上人们普遍认为儒家传统知识在教育体系中是“死胡同”，但事实上，中国的大学完全有能力发明创造性的写作教学法，在认知、情感和文化成长以及提高创造力方面，这些学习者已经被赋予了权力，并从“生产性双语教育”中受益。这一点主要是通过打破传统写作语境，建立新的写作语境来实现的。建立新的写作语境的方法包括更新外语写作理念，在学生的写作和真实生活文化之间建立联系，在文化探索中重塑师生关系。

其次，作者从一个胆小拘谨的英语学习者和写作者变成了一个无所畏惧、充满激情的作者，这一转变得益于她的跨文化交流和写作经历，特别是通过电子邮件与博士生导师进行的“跨文化对话”。通过创造一个真实的、互动式的学习环境，笔者和导师创造性地利用中英两种语言、文化发现写作题材、提高写作技能和跨文化敏感性。

最后，跨文化语言教学与交流促进文化学习，推动创造跨文化的“第三空间”，使学生的母语和目的语文化同时得到强化。在此基础上，本人结合对广东外语外贸大学教改的研究和自己的写作经历，提出了一种新的外语写作教学理论——跨文化批判写作教学法。该教学法的目的是通过在写作中创造跨文化接触，并充分利用各种语境可能性，如声音和视角，以及写作语境的各种相互作用和互文影响，赋予学生力量。这种新的写作方式从学习者自身的文化和身份出发，通过创造性地设计跨文化、内文化主题，运用英汉两种语言的表达方式和修辞手段，鼓励学生在跨文化交际中构建“复合作家身份”。

本书的总体目标是激发教师进行写作教改试验，并对实践进行反思，特别是通过批判性和跨文化的方法，创造性地理解和表达文化，从而改善中国的写作教育。本书主要适用于语言教学，尤其是中国的外语写作教学；同时，我希望本书所讨论的内容对文化研究、比较研究、批判教育学和文学研究的教师也能产生积极影响。

这项研究的意义是多方面的。对决策者来说，跨文化能力和内文化能力是在国际化世界中生存和发展的重要工具，应在教学大纲和课程中予以强调。在英语写作教育中，提高学生的创造力和跨文化意识的必要性与语言能力同等重要。因此，应系统地设计和实施教材、内文化项目，制定评价标准和设置教师培训课程。

作为英语写作教师，我们需要重新审视教学和学习的本质、目标和内容。这就要求我们真正认识语言教学的跨文化本质，重新审视文化、写作、创造力和读写能力等常识概念。要想通过创造性写作提高学生的跨文化能力，教师需要先获得并表现出高度的跨文化态度和技能，努力成为创造性的作者，同时还需要探索教学方法和技巧，创造性地将英语写作教育“跨文化化”，抓住每一个机会，让学习者为他们所生活的跨文化世界做好准备。

对于英语学习者来说，这种新的英语写作方法有助于将创造力与写作能力和跨文化能力联系起来，通过满足他们的认知和情感需求，将其现实生活兴趣与学校写作实践联系起来。最重要的是，通过创造性地运用不同的视角（跨文化视角和内文化视角）进行写作，写作者可以获得取之不尽的写作题材和写作技巧，同时还能够发挥自己的创造力和想象力，摆脱对写作的恐惧。

对于二语写作研究者来说，创造性写作与跨文化写作的融合不仅为二语写作研究提供了新的方向，也可能会提出更多的问题，例如：我们如何为跨文化写作教学法培养教师？哪些教材能更好地将跨文化知识与写作发展结合起来？写作、创造力和跨文化能力的概念是如何随着全球政治、经济和文化的发展而演变的？写作、文学、文化和身份之间复杂的相互关系是什么？这些问题都需在今后的研究中深入探讨。

推广外语写作的跨文化批判教学法不会是一条坦途。我们不能以一种“整齐划一”的方式来实施，而应考虑到不同教学环境的社会文化特殊性，因地制宜、坚守教师职业道德。我不希望将跨文化教学法固化下来，相反，我希望其接受质疑、试验和修正。只有经历这个漫长而痛苦的过程，新思想才能发展并确立，进而成为新的教育理念的一部分。

现在，让我们以我在2010年博士答辩前夕写给导师Trevor和Julie的信来结束本书：

亲爱的Trevor和Julie：

你们好吗？

这些天我在写论文的结论部分，我一直在想，“写作是一种研究方法”这句话是多么得正确。对于像我这样的二语学习者，我想说“跨文化写作是一种改变人生的方法”。

开始写这篇论文的时候，我并不清楚成品将会是什么样子。过去五年中我一直在阅读、思考和研究，这些都被写作过程紧密联系在了一起。更重要的是，写作带来了很多灵感、新的思维方式、新的学习需求。如果不是这篇论文，我不敢想象自己将会错过多少优秀的作家和著作。开始写论文之前，几乎一半的参考文献并未出现在我的阅读清单上。如果不是为了这篇论文，我也不会想到用与Trevor的邮件通讯作为一个章节来阐述自己的观点；当然，如果我们当初没有写下这么多丰富有趣的邮件，这个想法也没法实现。

一言以蔽之，正是写作，尤其是我们之间多年的跨文化写作，帮助我重新发现自己的创造力，重新找回了自己的文化身份，重新设计研究方案，最重要的是，重新点燃了我几乎熄灭的写作之火。

谢谢你们带着我走上“跨越文化的桥梁”。

让我们为这一刻欢呼！

叶 洪

致　谢

仿佛昨夜，在墨尔本亚拉河边的住宅里，我正聚精会神地写博士论文，6岁的儿子Kyle踮着脚凑到我桌边，轻声说："嘘！妈妈，我不是来捣蛋的，我会自己上床睡觉的。不过——"他指着电脑屏幕上我正在写作的一个标题问："妈妈，'acknowledgement'是什么意思呀？"今晨，窗外蝉声正浓，我在北京紫竹院公园旁的家中，写下本书的最后一节"致谢"。已在UCLA读大三的儿子打来电话，"嘿，老妈！你的书稿写得不错，auto-ethnography（自我民族志）还挺有趣！"15年一晃而过，许多画面和瞬间在眼前闪现，让我感动和感恩，却无法言表。

出现在我脑海中的第一个画面是2005年秋天的一个午后，Trevor Hay——我的大胡子导师，在墨尔本大学办公室的转椅里转过身，惊讶而亲切地和我打招呼，好奇地问："你为什么要申请英语写作方向的博士？""因为我想帮助自己和我的学生战胜对写作的恐惧。"我小声但坚定地回答。他微笑着点了点头，这便是我生命中最神奇的学术生活的开端，同时也是一段深厚而美丽的友谊的开始。

副导师Julie White是我的另一位伯乐。还记得我们见面的第一天，她手里挥舞着几张表格，兴致勃勃地说："我看了你的简历，你用'Research fruits'这个词实在是太有创意了！"Julie是我想象力的催化剂，在我低落或停滞不前时，是她给了我不竭的鼓励和动力。

2003年广东外语外贸大学英文学院，悬挂在展室里的学生作文令我眼花缭乱，第一次接触"写长法"，就让我对这个团队教师与学生的激情和创造力印象深刻，后来他们成为我研究的伙伴和对象。王初明先生，一位视名利为粪土、视工作为生命的真正学者，每每和我谈起他的研究便会忘记时间。在他身边，我总会充满力量、灵感和崇敬。郑超教授是我探索写作教改的老师和战友，2017 年夏天我们通话时，他兴奋地说："我身体好多了，又可以工作了！"不想一个多月后，他便猝然离世。他用毕生的精力和智慧推动英语写作改革，直至生命的最后一息。我很想把这本书献给他，但不知他会不会满意。无论如何，我会在他的注目下，继续前行。

三年前，李立院长领我走进中国政法大学外国语学院，我们一起创立了"法大写作中心"，一同参加学术论文写作教学培训，举办中国政法大学学术论文报告会。自此，我有了一个新的平台，刘雅笛、段敏两位研究生的加盟让我们的团队不断壮大。中国政法大学出版社的张琮军老师和牛洁颖老师，感谢你们热情的支持和审慎把关，你们的辛勤付出，最终促成了这本书的出版。

这短短的致谢不足以表达我所有的感激之情。最深沉和最伟大的爱往往是无形的，无法用语言来形容。所以，我想在此鞠躬感谢所有在过去和现在，在生活和学术上帮助我成长的人们。遇到你们我感到非常幸运，我希望将来能够以同样的关爱来报答你们！

叶洪于北京紫竹院

2019 年 7 月